LEADING-EDGE PSYCHOLOGICAL TESTS AND TESTING RESEARCH

LEADING-EDGE PSYCHOLOGICAL TESTS AND TESTING RESEARCH

MARTA A. LANGE
EDITOR

Nova Science Publishers, Inc.
New York

For permission to use material from this book please contact us:
Telephone 631-231-7269; Fax 631-231-8175
Web Site: http://www.novapublishers.com

NOTICE TO THE READER

The Publisher has taken reasonable care in the preparation of this book, but makes no expressed or implied warranty of any kind and assumes no responsibility for any errors or omissions. No liability is assumed for incidental or consequential damages in connection with or arising out of information contained in this book. The Publisher shall not be liable for any special, consequential, or exemplary damages resulting, in whole or in part, from the readers' use of, or reliance upon, this material.

Independent verification should be sought for any data, advice or recommendations contained in this book. In addition, no responsibility is assumed by the publisher for any injury and/or damage to persons or property arising from any methods, products, instructions, ideas or otherwise contained in this publication.

This publication is designed to provide accurate and authoritative information with regard to the subject matter covered herein. It is sold with the clear understanding that the Publisher is not engaged in rendering legal or any other professional services. If legal or any other expert assistance is required, the services of a competent person should be sought. FROM A DECLARATION OF PARTICIPANTS JOINTLY ADOPTED BY A COMMITTEE OF THE AMERICAN BAR ASSOCIATION AND A COMMITTEE OF PUBLISHERS.

LIBRARY OF CONGRESS CATALOGING-IN-PUBLICATION DATA
Leading-edge psychological tests and testing research/Marta A. Lange, editor.
    p. cm.
  Includes index.
  ISBN-13: 978-1-60021-571-1 (hardcover)
  ISBN-10: 1-60021-571-8 (hardcover)
  1. Psychological tests. 2. Psychology—Research. L. Lange, Marta A.
BF176.L43 2006
150.28'7—dc22
            2006102903

Published by Nova Science Publishers, Inc. ✦ *New York*

CONTENTS

PREFACE

Psychological testing has grown exponentially as techological advances have permitted it to and societal complexities have necessitated it's growth. Psychological testing or Psychological assessment is a field characterized by the use of samples of behavior in order to infer generalizations about a given individual. By samples of behavior, one means observations over time of an individual performing tasks that have usually been prescribed beforehand. These responses are often compiled into statistical tables that allow the evaluator to compare the behavior of the individual being tested to the responses of a norm group. The broad catagories of psychological evaluation tests include: Norm-referenced, IQ/achievement tests, Neuropsychological tests, Personality tests, Objective tests (Rating scale), Direct observation tests, Psychological evaluations using data mining. New and important research is presented in this book.

Chapter 1 - *Introduction.* A neurological foundation of both cognitive and emotional phenomena has not yet been conclusively defined. However, nobody denies the interactive functioning of cognition and emotion. Understanding this interaction involves the understanding of behavior on a neurological basis. Both cognition and emotion, internal processes, can be assessed by means of external behavioral expression. Since 1994, we have counted on the PASS theory of intelligence, and since the 1980s we have known part of the painful emotional-feeling processing. From a holistic perspective, the authors have integrated both concepts to explain, at least partially, the reason of human behavior in both a normal condition and dysfunctional condition.

Method. Since 1994, they have conducted a line of research based on this framework, using both quantitative and qualitative method.

Results. The results have to do with normal and non-normal subjects. They have translated and factor-analysis validated the DN:CAS battery for assessing PASS processing (*P*lanning, *A*ttention, *S*imultaneous, *S*uccessive). In general, they concluded that mixed processing deficits are more frequently found than single ones. We have defined characteristic DN:CAS profiles in dyslexia, attention deficit hyperactive disorder, and childhood benign epilepsy. Likewise, the profile of vulnerable gifted children. Of particular relevance is the finding of a DN:CAS profile related to dysfunctional emotional behavior. Furthermore, we have established the relationship between planning and emotional processing, using functional magnetic resonance image methodology. A significant success rate in dysfunctional emotional behaviors that includes conduct disorder, among others, oppositional defiant disorder, asocial – aggressive behavior, bullying, teasing, and intimidation, drug abuse, but also somatization and other behavioral dysfunctions have been accomplished by using a procedure based on the cognitive-emotional concept mentioned.

Discussion and conclusions. Neurobiologically speaking, behavior must be considered as any body expression, whether verbal or non-verbal. In this sense, any behavior fulfills the PASS processing principle that says input, neurological central processing, and output or behavior itself must be differentiated. So, behavior is what we can directly observe, but the neurological central processing, non-directly observable, is what we must diagnose and treat. Beyond any concrete behavior, which we can call it, gifted child, dyslexic, ADHD, epileptic, dissocial behavior and so on, there is always a neurological central mechanism based on both cognitive and painful emotional-feeling processing, that is, both the cognitive component and the feeling-sensitive component of personal beliefs memorized throughout. The PASS mental operations, put in action to process any information entering central nervous system, account for the personal beliefs. The main conclusion is that this conception has proved to be useful to diagnose and treat any dysfunctional behavior.

Chapter 2 - *Background:* Epidemiological evidence suggests that anxiety and depressive disorders are the most common mental disorders. A common way to assess anxiety and depressive symptoms is through self-reports. Relevant to the aims of the present study is the fact that content validity of self-reports can vary across different cultures. As a consequence, validity should be established when the instrument is used with cultural groups on which it has not been standardized. Therefore, the purpose of this study was to present data on the Italian versions of the Beck Anxiety Inventory (BAI) and Beck Depression Inventory-II (BDI-II), probably among the most common self-reports that measure the severity of anxiety and depressive symptoms.

Method: the Italian version of the BAI was administered to a sample of 831 individuals belonging to the general population and to a sample of 122 patients with either anxiety or depressive disorders. The Italian version of the BDI-II was administered to a sample of 723 college students and to a sample of 72 depressed patients. Alpha and test-retest reliabilities were computed along with associations with age and education. The BAI and BDI-II were also subjected to a Confirmative Factor Analysis and a second-order factor analysis. Convergent validity was ascertained by computing the product-moment correlations with other conceptually-related self-report measures. Lastly, to ascertain the discriminative power of the BAI and BDI-II, normal and clinical samples were compared by means of ROC analysis.

Results: Overall, demographic variables did not influence the scores of the BAI and the BDI-II. Confirmative factor analysis for both measures showed the best fit for a multi-factor solution; however, a second-order factor analysis showed strong support for a higher order unidimensional structure of the BAI and BDI-II. Validity was confirmed by the significant association with other measures of anxiety or depression. Lastly, ROC curves indicate excellent discriminative power of the BAI and BDI-II for distinguishing patients from non clinical individuals.

Conclusions: The BAI and BDI-II proved a reliable and valid measure of anxiety and depressive symptoms in the Italian context. The present study confirmed the excellent psychometric properties of the BAI and BDI-II on Italian individuals and supported its use in both normal and clinical individuals.

Chapter 3 – Many psychological constructs cannot be directly observed. The first challenge for the psychological researcher, then, is to develop ways to measure unobservable traits in convincing ways. One builds evidence for the validity of one's measurement by showing that a measure relates to measures of other psychological constructs in theoretically predictable, consistent ways. Thus, to argue for the validity of a measure is to show that the measure conforms to a theory, of which the target construct is a part. Since the validity of each measure is similarly dependent on theory and on empirical relations with other imperfect measures, there is no single, final test establishing the validity of a measure. Instead, validation is an ongoing process. The authors provide a concrete example of this process, using a theory of their own: they first consider the evidence supporting the theory, and then they criticize their own work to explore the uncertain, provisional nature of validity evidence. They emphasize that appreciating the nature of this ongoing, critical process contributes to scientific advancement.

Chapter 4 - In the past 20 years, health related quality of life (HRQL) has gained increasing recognition as a health outcome measure. Although no consensus exists about the precise definition of HRQL, a plethora of instruments have been developed to assess it. However, measurement standards and approaches to development may also differ between instruments, which can make choosing an appropriate instrument complex for would be users. The aim of this chapter is to reduce this barrier to HRQL application by providing a guide to the psychometrics of HRQL measurement. The chapter begins with a general overview of the current approaches to measuring HRQL, with the emphasis on quantitative methods. The psychometric approach is then compared to other approaches (e.g. the clinimetric method) and the advantages and disadvantages of each considered. Psychometrically based methods of instrument development are discussed and the main psychometric properties of a good HRQL instrument are outlined. Finally, some of the specific measurement problems of HRQL assessment (e.g. the need for and use of proxy reports) are also discussed. Points are illustrated through out with examples of instrument development.

Chapter 5- The study examined the validity and reliability of the Standardized Asthma Quality of Life Questionnaire-AQLQ(S) (Juniper, 1999a) in Greece. The AQLQ(S) incorporates 32 items, presented in a 7 point Likert scale, with four factors: 'Activity Limitations', 'Symptoms', 'Emotional Function' and 'Exposure to Environmental Stimuli'. Following translation validity evidence, 60 Greek adults were examined. The participants were divided to 30 patients and 30 non patients, from Athens, Greece. The group of asthmatics was tested during their visits at private clinics. The non asthmatic group was recruited from the general population and assimilated the asthmatic group according to age, gender and socioeconomic status. Construct validity was tested through the following comparisons: a) patients vs non patients with asthma, b) atopic vs non atopic patients, c) younger vs older patients with asthma and d) patients with mild, moderate and severe asthma. Statistical analyses, based on multivariate and univariate tests, supported our research hypotheses. Specifically, non patients scored significantly higher than patients in AQLQ(S), indicating, therefore, higher Quality of Life (QoL). Further, atopics scored higher than non atopics, younger scored higher than older patients and finally, patients with mild and moderate asthma scored higher than patients with severe asthma. Reliability was tested with the test retest method: a) for the total sample and b) for the asthmatic group. For the total sample, r was .911 for the total AQLQ(S) score, and ranged from .834 to .946 for the four AQLQ(S) factors. For the asthmatic group, overal r was .957, while test retest correlation coefficients, for the four separate factors, ranged from .915 to .966. At this point, the first validity and reliability evidence of the Greek AQLQ(S) are reported. The construct validity of the Greek AQLQ(S) must be re examined in the near future, through exploratory and confirmatory factor analysis, to strengthen the present findings. Further, Cronbach alpha reliability coefficients will provide internal consistency evidence for the four separate AQLQ(S) factors.

Chapter 6 - This article describes the steps of construction, standardization and validation of two tests for measuring moral development (MD) in Spanish-speaking children and adults. Both tests were developed on the basis of a moral development notion that includes moral feelings and several differentiated aspects of moral reasoning. The test for adults was standardized with 623 subjects, employees or candidates for employments in various companies in Bogotá. The test for children was standardized with 1166 children and youths in ages of 9 to 18 years. Additionally, there are data from university students. Results with different samples show that both test have an adequate reliability and that the test for adults discriminates between normal individuals and criminals.

Chapter 7 - Psychometric theory is the basis for the development of psychological assessment. However, the psychometric model appears to be inadequate in many clinical situations, because of the lack of sensitivity to change and its quest for homogeneous components. The term clinimetrics was introduced by Alvan R. Feinstein in 1982 to indicate a domain concerned with indexes, rating scales and other expressions that are used to describe or measure symptoms, physical signs, and other distinctly clinical phenomena in medicine. Clinimetrics offers a valuable alternative or integration to psychometrics, both from conceptual and methodological viewpoint. Current diagnostic entities in clinical psychology and psychiatry are based on clinimetric principles, but their use is still influenced by psychometric models. Clinical exemplifications of the clinimetric approach to psychological testing are illustrated, with particular reference to the concepts of macro-analysis and micro-analysis.

Chapter 8 - The study of intelligence has been dominated for years by the study of abstract or academic intelligence. The emphasis on intelligence as it operates in a real world context led to the development of the study of practical intelligence (Stemberg, 1986). Practical intelligence (PI) refers to the cognitive underpinning of everyday function and has been variously defined either as an intellectual process or capacity (Mathias and Nettelback, 1992; Wagner and Kistner, 1990); as a product or outcome of behavior, mainly as manifested in adaptation (Luckasson et al, 1992; Stemberg et al. 1995); or as a set of intellectual abilities which contribute to adaptation (Gardner, 1993; Greenspan and Driscoll, 1997).

Preliminary studies exploring the construct of PI consisted mainly of anecdotal examples of specific tasks thought of as unique representations of PI (Carraher, Carraher, and Schliemann, 1985; Ceci, and Liker, 1988; Lave, Murtaugh, and de la Roche, 1984). Currently, the most comprehensive body of data stems from the exploration of the role of PI in the successful manifestation of various occupational pursuits (for review see Sternberg, et al. 2000; Wagner, 2000), with the accumulating data suggesting that PI is psychologically distinct from academic intelligence (Sternberg, et al. 2001).

Practical intelligence is not assessed in traditional intelligence (IQ) tests, and, while some claim it is easy to measure (Sternberg, et al. 1995) others question the reliability and validity of various PI measures developed (McDaniel, 2003) as well as their factor structure, methods, and item selection (Kyllonen, 2003). Measures of practical intelligence should attempt to tap the covert, underlying cognitive components that may contribute to competence, but are not synonymous with performance. Some of the obstacles encountered include (a) difficulty in devising stimulus materials (such as might be found in a test kit) that correspond to the nature and complexity of practical intelligence tasks in the everyday world, and (b) the fact that performance in a simulation test (such as would be created if an individual were to be presented with practical tasks to solve) runs the risk of confounding competence with performance and bringing into the equation various motivational, affective and other potential sources of error variance (Chang, 2000). This chapter presents a broad review of current measures of practical intelligence as well as suggestions for further research and test development.

Chapter 9 - Typus melancholicus (TM) as described by Tellenbach in Germany is one of the concepts of pre- and intra-morbid personality traits of depressive subjects. The core features of TM are a compulsive desire for orderliness, and conscientiousness in interpersonal relationships. Based on the descriptive and anthropological TM concept, one brief TM-questionnaire has been developed in Japan: Kasahara's Inventory for the Melancholic Type Personality (KIMTP). Sufficient reliability and validity of this psychological test evaluating MT were shown in a German sample population. And factor analysis of KIMTP revealed 2 distinct clusters of items, which represented "harmony in personal relationships" (Factor 1) and "social norms" (Factor 2).

As a next step for exploring the validity of KIMTP, the authors studied the correlation between KIMTP and the NEO-Five Factor Inventory (NEO-FFI), which is used worldwide as one of the standard psychological tests evaluating personality. They found that TM evaluating with KIMTP was characterized by high Conscientiousness($r=0.29$, $p=0.036$) and high Agreeableness($r=0.45$, $p=0.001$). These results indicate that TM is not a personality trait, but rather a constellation of personality traits, and consists of multiple dimensions. In conclusion, KIMTP as a short psychological test evaluating a personality trait of depressives may discriminate the TM personality with some degree of universality despite cultural differences and be useful in cross-cultural comparisons of TM.

Chapter 10 - This paper serves to emphasize that if psychological consulting based on Wechsler-like test-batteries is to be carried out - due to their content conceptualization - then certain economic test improvements are needed. It is a matter of administering items, whose solutions are neither too easily found by the testee, nor whose solutions are obviously highly improbable. What is being asked for here is adaptive testing. Although, it is quite routine to apply a psychometric foundation of adaptive testing, the common technique of computerized so-called tailored testing is in no way a proper means in the case of (material and social) interaction which Wechsler-like test-batteries focus on. However branched testing can be applied without the online use of a computer. Such an approach has already been established in the AID 2 test-battery since 1985. This paper deals with the illustration of item generation and administration, psychometric quality checks, error of aimed-for ability parameter estimation, and last but not least it's handling by practitioners. There is evidence that adaptive testing as realized in AID 2 is superior to pertinent conventional testing, particularly with respect to administration duration and error of estimation.

Chapter 11 - Osman and colleagues (1998) developed the Reasons for Living Inventory for Adolescents (RFL-A) to assess five domains of reasons adolescents give for not killing themselves. Each domain closely matches the theoretical conceptualization of the target construct of reasons for living. We conducted two studies to further research with the RFL-A. Study 1 evaluated invariance of the 5-factor oblique solution across nonclinical high school ($N = 300$) and adolescent psychiatric inpatient ($N = 320$) samples. The objectives of Study 2 were to examine estimates of internal consistency reliability, known-groups validity, and differential correlates of the total RFL-A score in the separate samples of youths with diagnoses of posttraumatic stress disorder ($N = 90$) and conduct disorder ($N = 98$). The findings of Studies 1 and 2 provided additional strong support for the structural dimensions and psychometric properties of the RFL-A when used in clinical and nonclinical settings.

In: Leading-Edge Psychological Tests and Testing Research   ISBN: 978-1-60021-571-1
Editor: Marta A. Lange, pp. 1-25   © 2007 Nova Science Publishers, Inc.

Chapter 1

ASSESSMENT OF COGNITIVE PROCESSES: THE BASIS OF INTELLIGENT BEHAVIOR

F. Pérez-Álvarez[*,1,3] *and C. Timoneda-Gallart*[2,3]

[1]Pediatric Neurology /Developmental – Behavioral Neurology
Hospital Universitari ICS Dr J Trueta de Girona
[2]Educational Psychology
[3]Fundació Carme Vidal Xifre
University of Girona, Spain

ABSTRACT

Introduction. Neurological foundation of both cognitive and emotional phenomena has not yet been conclusively defined. However, nobody denies the interactive functioning of cognition and emotion. Understanding this interaction involves the understanding of behavior on a neurological basis. Both cognition and emotion, internal processes, can be assessed by means of external behavioral expression. Since 1994, we count on the PASS theory of intelligence, and since the 1980s we know part of the painful emotional-feeling processing. From a holistic perspective, we have integrated both concepts to explain, at least partially, the reason of human behavior in both a normal condition and dysfunctional condition.

Method. Since 1994, we conduct a line of research based on this framework, using both quantitative and qualitative method.

Results. Our results have to do with normal and non-normal subjects. We have translated and factor-analysis validated the DN:CAS battery for assessing PASS processing (*P*lanning, *A*ttention, *S*imultaneous, *Su*ccessive). In general, we have concluded that mixed processing deficits are more frequently found than single ones. We have defined characteristic DN:CAS profiles in dyslexia, attention deficit hyperactive disorder, and childhood benign epilepsy. Likewise, the profile of vulnerable gifted children. Of particular relevance is the finding of a DN:CAS profile related to dysfunctional emotional behavior. Furthermore, we have established the relationship

* Address: F Pérez-Álvarez, Neuropediatria / Neuroconducta, Servei de Pediatria, Hospital Universitari Dr. J Trueta de Girona, 17007 Girona. Tel. + 34 972 940200 Fax + 34 972 940270; E-mail: fpereza@comg.es

between planning and emotional processing, using functional magnetic resonance image methodology. A significant success rate in dysfunctional emotional behaviors that includes conduct disorder, among others, oppositional defiant disorder, asocial – aggressive behavior, bullying, teasing, and intimidation, drug abuse, but also somatization and other behavioral dysfunctions have been accomplished by using a procedure based on the cognitive-emotional concept mentioned.

Discussion and conclusions. Neurobiologically speaking, behavior must be considered as any body expression, whether verbal or non-verbal. In this sense, any behavior fulfills the PASS processing principle that says input, neurological central processing, and output or behavior itself must be differentiated. So, behavior is what we can directly observe, but the neurological central processing, non-directly observable, is what we must diagnose and treat. Beyond any concrete behavior, which we can call it, gifted child, dyslexic, ADHD, epileptic, dissocial behavior and so on, there is always a neurological central mechanism based on both cognitive and painful emotional-feeling processing, that is, both the cognitive component and the feeling-sensitive component of personal beliefs memorized throughout. The PASS mental operations, put in action to process any information entering central nervous system, account for the personal beliefs. The main conclusion is that this conception has proved to be useful to diagnose and treat any dysfunctional behavior.

INTRODUCTION

Strictly speaking, behavior must be considered anything an organism does, that is, any observable activity directly correlated with mental-psychic processes supported by neurological networks. In this sense, behaviors are motion, speaking, learning, crying, aggression, and so on. At least, two mental processes are operating whenever a behavior is put in action, the cognitive processing of information and the feeling processing and, in particular, painful feeling processing.

Cognitive functioning has not yet been unequivocally defined. The heterogeneity reported so far is again and again argued to be due to methodological difficulties. However, the first difficulty to solve is to define what cognitive function is about. For instance, learning difficulties are different in nature depending on whether they are due to tremor because of cerebellar dysfunction (somatic neuronal network), or due to exactly failure in mental cognitive processing (cognitive neuronal network) or, maybe, failure in social affective adjustment (feeling neuronal network). So scholarly failure can be due to cognitive failure, but also to emotional-affective disturbance and even to physical somatic-visceral disorder. The cognition concept deserves an appropriate clarification. We claim the cognitive function term to be referred to the scientifically validated mental-neurological function supported by a neurological network, whether known or supposed, and obtained by means of a validated cognitive test.

From the point of view of medical clinical neuropsychology, any test by itself can be considered useful on a psychometric basis if it allows us to diagnose a neurological disease. In this case, the test is a useful measure as part of the signs and symptoms of the disease and nothing else is intended. For instance, in some way, something similar to a sphygmodynamometer, an instrument for measuring the force of the pulse. From the point of view of cognitive etiopathogenesis, instead, the test being used not only must be conveniently validated but also validated in the sense of scientifically demonstrating that the results obtained convey the central neurological functioning, but not simply the result as signs and symptoms of something unknown. Etiopathogenic diagnosis is an advantage on treatment basis. This conception is satisfied by the PASS theory of cognitive processing of information [Das et al. 1979, 1994, 1996, 1999[a]; Timoneda and Perez-Alvarez, 1994].

What a test assesses depends on the concepts it is based on, which determines how it is constructed. Traditionally, a test has been constructed on the basis of knowing from observation that any human being is able to perform something (ability), then the test is standardized and the quantitative limits of normality are defined. Everybody assumes that there is a mental process behind the resolution capacity. According to this, what is measured (the resulting score) is a behavior produced by a particular human being at that time and on that day. In fact, this is equivalent to measuring any other corporal behavior like, for instance, motion capacity. We can create a test to score the performance in a concrete movement. The DN:CAS battery [Das and Naglieri, 1997] for assessing the PASS processing measures a resulting behavior in a test, but also tells us, by knowing the results in all the tests and how the tests are performed (qualitative assessment), that a particular bad result in a concrete test of the battery can be changed for better if the inefficient mental operation now applied is later applied in another different way. This implies a dynamic concept of intelligent behavior. This mental operational fluctuation can be facilitated by a convenient remediation program [Das, 1999b]. In other words, the DN:CAS gives us a profile that is non-static but dynamic, that is, changeable.

This battery informs us how efficiently four identified mental cognitive programs work, namely, Planning, Attention, Simultaneous, and Successive. These four programs are always working whenever any cognitive activity takes place independently of how information is both entering (input) or leaving (output) central nervous system (CNS). In fact, this is not different from what the CNS does with any kind of information being processed. For instance, ataxia must be considered a resulting behavior that can be due to failure in the cerebellar neuronal network (program), but also in the vestibular neuronal network (program). The same output can be due to different central programs. The four PASS programs were identified by taking into account how the CNS works the cognitive information according to Luria's studies of lesions [Luria,1980; Das, 1999a]. In essence, the basic idea consisted of observing that the same neurons produced different results (signs and symptoms) and vice versa, that is, different neurons produced the same result. Arising from this, concrete tests were created first and then factor analysis validated by comparing PASS tests with non-PASS tests earlier known. This way, we have got to know the non-verbal tests of K-ABC, Wechsler, Binet 4, and McCarthy assess PASS simultaneous and something else non-equivalent to PASS processing, while the tests of these previously mentioned batteries measure some PASS processing and sometimes something else non-comparable to. Likewise, the Forward Span assess PASS successive, while the Backward Span measures PASS successive and planning. In addition, the Wisconsin test measures PASS planning, but also something else non-PASS. And, the Stroop test measures PASS attention. This process lead to isolate the tests specifically measuring each of the four PASS processes [Das et al. 1994].

In sum, the PASS concept can be exemplified as follows: to remember the input 633435, you may do so by recalling the series with no other association (relationship) but only the lineal association, one digit after the following. Something like rote memorization of the kind of subvocal rehearsal for recalling a series, for instance. If so, you are operating with successive processing that works whenever working memory is operating. Instead, you can do it by recalling it as 63 34 35 in which case you are using the successive processing for recording three units, that is, 63 / 34 / 35, but each unit has been mentally elaborated with simultaneous processing, which allows us to establish the relationship $6 + 3 = 63$. The simultaneous also works whenever working memory works, but it is more relevant for long-term-memory. On the other hand, you can think as previously mentioned but, also, you can think 63 / 34 / 35 is as if 34, 35 and 36 in consecutive order, but turning 36 into 63 and translating the last unit to the first one in the series. In such a case planning allows you to operate with this mental strategy. Attention processing is always present and it is different from attention behavior. For example, inattentive behavior involves the attention processing when mental activity is focussed on another someone / something. This concept means that the same individual can resolve the problem of the sequence presented, now using his/her bad successive, for instance, with bad result (low intelligence ?), but, may be, hours later, using his/her good simultaneous, with excellent result (high intelligence ?). Similarly, an inattentive child (description of the behavior observed) can be an excellent PASS attentive processor, when we assess the PASS mental operation of being attentive. Or a disorganized child (description for an unplanned observed behavior) can be a very good PASS mental planner. In this line, for instance, knowing a supposed negative effect of a drug on a particular memory test is not so relevant as knowing the result in memory performance was due to the use of an inefficient PASS program that can be left out and substituted for another more efficient PASS program in order to achieve a better result. The PASS processing programs can be related to some particular regions in the brain, namely, *P*lanning to prefrontal cortex, *A*ttention to prefrontal cortex and reticular system (arousal), *S*uccessive to prefrontal cortex and temporal cortex, and *S*imultaneous to posterior brain, namely, parietal and occipital cortices.

To date, emotional phenomenon has not scientifically defined either. Above all, a clear distinction, if any, between emotion and cognition has not been definitely established. In the past, the emotion has been considered just a sensitivity independent of any cognitive phenomenon [Schachter, and Singer, 1962]. Later on, the physiological reaction associated to painful-emotional processing was proposed to be unspecific, independently of the concrete painful experience [Lyons, 1980]. More recently, the called "appraisal" of the processed painful sensitivity has been claimed to be the primary-determinant reason for any emotional behavior, which points to sensitivity rather than cognition as causal explanation; however, "appraisal" involves belief processing and beliefs are cognitive knowledge supposed to be cognitively processed. Additionally, this last notion is claimed to be applicable to emotional "order" and emotional "disorder" [Power and Dalgleish, 1997] without distinction.

Putting aside the conceptual dualism emotion-cognition, other important notions have to be noted. First, unconscious feeling processing is a generally assumed reality and, so, anger can be considered a reactive painful behavior unconsciously triggered [Lyons, 1980]. Second, reactive painful behaviors can be also considered a protective-defensive mechanism beyond any psychodynamic conceptualization [Lazarus, 1966; Horowitz, 1990]. Third, body language and, in particular, the facial expression is universally accepted to automatically-unconsciously express the feeling state of any person [Darwin, 1965; Ekman, 1973; Adolphs et al., 2000], although body language can also conveys informative cognitive content undoubtedly. And fourth, a substantial evidence is that verbal language incoherent with both body language and physiological reaction proves to be characteristic of the painful emotional-feeling behavioral response [Lang, 1984].

We claim that any theoretical framework to explain both cognition and emotion needs to be coherent with the neurological processing evidence we count on at present. Regarding emotion, the first evidence is that physical pain processing and painful emotional processing share, at least in part, anatomical areas and physiological functions. So, it is well known the shared ACTH – endorphin physiological reaction to both physical and emotional stress, which allow us to suppose that both the physical and the emotional stress are codified by the neurons as the same entity, in particular, as a danger signal [Selye, 1974; Buchsbaum, 1982]. The second evidence is that nowadays we know, although from animal experimentation, the pathways of painful-feeling processing from input to output of information [LeDoux et al., 1984, 1986, 1990; LeDoux, 1996]. According to this, painful-fearful sensitivity is unconsciously processed and, more relevantly, controlled by the temporal amygdala, the second gate in the pathway that triggers unconsciously uncontrolled automatic protective-defensive response. The prefrontal cortex knows what is going on later and does not avoid the behavioral reaction, already triggered by the amygdala, to a supposed life-threatening situation. The third evidence, from human lesion investigation, is that two prefrontal cortex, the emotional and the cognitive, have been dissociated and, strikingly, decision-making and planning faculty seems to basically depend on the emotional prefrontal rather than on the cognitive prefrontal [Damasio, 1994] when painful processing occurs, which allows us to reasonably deduce that the emotional sensitivity processing is a priority, even though the higher cognitive function is on. And a fourth subsequent evidence is that planning and feeling are interactive processing [Goldberg, 2001].

METHOD

Since 1994, our research has been focussed on both normal children and non-normal children. So, dyslexic children but also learning problems in general [Perez-Alvarez and Timoneda, 1999d, 1999e, 2000, 2004a; Das et al. 2000], children suffering from attention deficit hyperactive disorder [Perez-Alvarez and Timoneda, 1999c, 1999d, 2001, 2004a, 2004b] and epilepsy [Perez-Alvarez and Timoneda, 1996; Perez-Alvarez et al.2002; Pérez-Álvarez et al, 2006a] have been preferred focus of our published research. On the other hand, among our unpublished results, gifted children, autism and other developmental disorders, children with Down syndrome, Klinefelter syndrome, Williams syndrome and other chromosomal anomalies, as well as children with encephalic lesion due to cranial traumatism, and neurofibromatosis among heredodegenerative diseases have been all studied by us. Furthermore, we have diagnosed and treated children with different kind of behavioral problems [Perez-Alvarez and Timoneda, 1999a, 1999b, 2002].

Our research is based on both quantitative and qualitative investigation method. Within the quantitative method, the multivariate analysis as principal component factorial analysis with a maximum likelihood method of extraction and VARIMAX rotation was used, for instance, to validate the PASS cognitive DN:CAS battery. Apart from generalized tests widely used for assessing differences between both means and proportions, as well as for assessing correlations, particularly cluster analysis proved to be an useful tool.

The qualitative investigation method [Crabtree and Miller, 1992; Creswell, 1994] was the only one possible, we think, to face the behavioral analysis based on our theoretical framework that makes it useless "rating scales" , for instance, the "Child Behavior Rating Scale of Achenbach" or the "Facial Action Coding System" or the "Differential Emotional Scale". This method has been applied to a non-probabilistic sample (N = 1333), aged 5 – 15, recruited from patients pertaining to the normal socioeconomic community that usually uses our center, during the period January 1994 – December 2003 [Perez-Alvarez, 1999a, 1999b, 2002]. Our center is open to any kind of demand independently of the nature of the problem, benign or non-benign. Being diagnosed as suffering any non-organic "disease" was the inclusion criterion. Different symptoms were initially reported, for instance, "having sleeping trouble", "feeling unhappy or sad", "having headache or stomachache", "wetting the bed", "eating without appetite", or, simply, behavioral conflict at home and/or at school or scholar failure and so on. Exhaustive medical investigation was made as needed. The diagnose-intervention procedure was carried out by the same professional for each case. We think that the sample of the population is large enough to deduce valid conclusions.

Medical checking was carried out in order to rule out any pathological condition or frank neurological or psychiatric disorder. The protocol carried out included interview to the child and his/her parents, interview to his/her teacher and tutor, inquiry on background of his/her from his/her familiar doctor, detailed clinical anamnesis and exploration with attention to both general and neurological condition, as well as ophthalmologic and otorhinolaryngologic medical condition. Any subject given any medication was excluded. Also, either personal or by-phone contact with family doctor as well as contact with other professionals potentially working in parallel on the case were systematically carried out.

Qualitative data are both the verbal-linguistic behavior and the body-gesture language. From this point of view, behaviors are what we say and/or do as reading (straying onto lines above and below the one he/she is reading, for instance), speaking, learning,. Likewise, being interested in, attentive or inattentive attitude, being motivated, a smiling unconcerned attitude, face puzzled on hearing something or seeing something, showing hesitation, interest, effort, enthusiasm, anxious behavior, uncertainty, yawning, face of indifference, of affliction, depressing face, happy face, discomfort with affectionate aggression, doing at a hurried pace, answering impulsively, hysterical quality in the voice, calm tone of the voice, loudness of voice, nodding movement to express agreement or disagreement or understanding, looking away when uncomfortable and so forth. Body language allows us not only, and first of all, to assess feeling like happiness, affliction, anger and so on, but also to interpret the cognitive mental processing of idees or concept. So, in particular, the eye position allows us to know simultaneous processing is working and the eye scanning tells us planning is working. Likewise, a repeated verbal or sub - vocal rehearsal to facilitate recalling tells us the successive is working. Counting on his/her fingers may tells us mental counting is difficult.

Data ("dependent variables") are obtained from the patient or subject, the family, the teachers and any other members in inter-relationship with the case. Likewise, the data involving both linguistic and body language are clearly defined and collected via audio-video recording, implying an observation-registration process to get the utmost accuracy. Also, data are spontaneously collected without directive intervention to avoid the bias derived from the personal beliefs of the interviewer who follows a non-structured interview-like system. It is about an external observational procedure without direct participation, the researcher not being part of the observed universe.

The raw observed and collected data allow the investigator to interpret the beliefs linked to bad feeling forming part of the memorized information (cognitive beliefs + feeling) that constitutes the personal identity, that is, self - concept, self – esteem, self – confidence in psychological terms. The "independent variable" is the normalized procedure of diagnosis – intervention clearly defined and previously published [Perez-Alvarez and Timoneda, 1998]. Usually, 1 hour sessions, 1 per week, during 3 to 6 months were carried out. Diagnosis and Treatment work together since the beginning, the therapeutic effect consisting of making the person change the memorize painful feeling linked to personal cognitive beliefs to an extent enough as to decrease the threshold of triggering in the cerebral temporal amygdala, according to the most recent neurological evidence. Treatment is based on communication techniques focussed on getting a change of beliefs (from destructive to constructive beliefs) and associated feeling, with the always present aim of avoiding the non-constructive response to painful feeling processing in learning and behavior.

The instrument for "measuring" or assessing the data is the observer-investigator. His/her judgement, making inferences, is the instrument for interpreting the data. To control and avoid the inaccuracy (bias) characteristic of the intra-observer variability that produces subjective individual error, triangulation technique that produces the called "alien independent investigator effect" was carried out systematically. On purpose, every case was discussed in clinical session and inter – investigator agreement of 80% on any controversial question was needed.

To minimize the called "effect of the observer on the observed", each case was carried out by the same professional from the beginning to the end. The confounding effect and subsequent bias attributable to the empathic effect must be considered controlled, as far as possible, taking into account that the procedure implies empathic communication, but not sympathetic identification. As a further control to the bias arising from the observed-observer interaction, it must be emphasized that even though the observed subject knows he/she is observed and he/she could introduce the confounding effect of not willing, the involuntary masked painful emotional behaviors are involuntarily triggered, not susceptible therefore to be avoided by the will.

A very important methodological point is defining the criterion of success of the procedure in the sense we assume that the procedure is successful because it is able to eliminate the reactive painful emotional behaviors to a caertain extent. That means that the cerebral memorization of pain linked to memorized personal beliefs has changed enough to make unnecessary to be reacting with masked painful-emotional behaviors to the same degree as before. So the success was defined as not only the disappearance of the dysfunctional behavior causing the demand, but also the disappearance to enough extent of the profuse associated masked painful-emotional behaviors. It was considered "enough" improvement the reduction of , at least, 50% of the set of masked painful emotional behaviors, which was linked to a more satisfactory living. For accepting this last condition, the investigator contrasted it with the fathers, the other family members, the friends, the teachers, and so on, as possible. A follow-up consisting of yearly phone contact was carried out, being successful in 54 % of cases on the average.

Since 1998, all the cases (n = 703), independently of his/her nature, whether cognitive or non-cognitive, are administered the translated and validated PASS cognitive battery DN:CAS (Das Naglieri Cognitive Assessment System)[Naglieri and Das, 1997] in order to know the particular cognitive functioning. Later, we would see its diagnostic utility even to diagnose emotional dysfunctional behavior.

The method explained is subject to the limitations of qualitative investigations, but meets sufficient criteria of both validity and reliability to guarantee results and conclusions excluding the chance or placebo effect.

Concerning methodological aspects, finally, we have made a magnetic resonance image (fMRI) study [Perez-Alvarez et al. 2006b] consisting of investigating the fMRI pattern in 15 subjects as they make decision on painful feeling dilemmas [Greene et al. 2001] in comparison with non-painful feeling dilemmas with the aim of identifying neurological areas involved in decision-making (planning) when painful feeling processing is involved.

RESULTS

First of all, we have carried out the translation and factorial analysis validation of the DN:CAS battery in order to be used in Spanish and Catalan population [Das et al. 2000]. From the sample of validation study we extracted a normal control group (n = 300) for further studies that we will comment next.

We have found that the children who were administered the DN:CAS, whatever the reason (cognitive/learning or non-cognitive), showing underscoring (-1SD) in PASS processing more frequently showed mixed deficiencies than single one in the following scheme: planning, attention, and successive tend to be associated in different ways, such that we have not seen isolated attention deficiency, but we have seen any combination of attention with planning and successive. The most frequently isolated deficiencies are planning or successive. An infrequent isolated deficiency we have seen is PASS simultaneous deficiency (Figures 1-9).

As we have previously reported, dyslexic children scored under 85 (-1SD) in PASS successive in a frequency higher than expected by chance [Perez-Alvarez and Timoneda, 2000, 2004a]. Also, children with attention deficit hyperactive disorder according to DSM-IV criteria scored under 85 (-1SD) in PASS planning in a frequency higher than expected by chance [Perez-Alvarez and Timoneda, 2001, 2004b].

Developmental dyslexia has been explained to suffer temporal and, mainly, phonemic processing dysfunction as well as cognitive dysfunction. To test whether temporal, phonemic, and cognitive processing are interrelated we designed a study. After medical screening, 36 subjects, 7 to 14 years-old, boy/girl ratio of 2:1, were selected with phonemic processing tests. For every subject, two normal controls were also selected with the same phonemic tests. DN:CAS cognitive battery for diagnosing of cognitive processing was administered to subjects, and both subjects and controls were examined with a temporal processing test, made in laboratory, consisting of two kind of items, syllables with transition period of 40 milliseconds and other ones longer. Proportions and means were statistically analyzed. Factorial analysis was applied to scores in DN:CAS and syllabic acoustic tests. We saw (Table 1) that the dyslexics, compared to controls, made more errors in acoustic test (z = 6.73; p < 0.000). The DN:CAS mean obtained by the dyslexics was lower than controls (t = 6.73; p = 0.001). The factorial analysis accounting for 77% of the variance identified the acoustic test as a sequential processing test. We concluded that, on the basis of the cognitive psychology of information processing and neuroscience, the phonemic, temporal, and cognitive processing may be different expressions of the same central neurological mechanism.

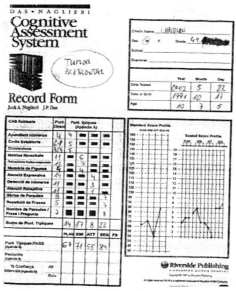

A case of prefrontal tumor. Note that successive and simultaneous are less affected than planning and attention. Planning and attention depend basically on prefrontal, whereas successive depends also on temporal, and simultaneous depends on posterior brain, that is, parietal and occipital. In fact, simultaneous is affected more than expected. Note that although "en" pattern is observed, however "imbalance" pattern is not.

Figure 1. DN:CAS: prefrontal tumor.

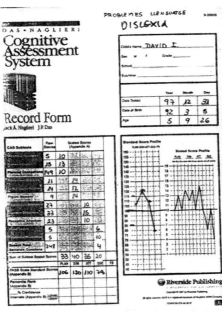

Isolate dysfunctional successive. We see this profile characteristically associated with dyslexia, reading-writing difficulties, and childhood benign epilepsy. Note "imbalance" pattern in attention and successive sub-scales that denotes emotional component.

Figure 2. DN:CAS: isolated successive deficit.

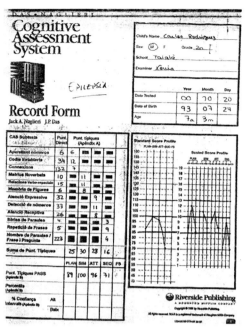

Isolated dysfunctional successive pertaining to a case of childhood benign epilepsy. Note also "imbalance" pattern in sub-scales.

Figure 3. DN:CAS: childhood benign epilepsy.

Associated dysfunction (-1SD) of planning + attention in a girl with learning problems. The most frequently dysfunctional (-1SD) processes are planning and successive. The most frequently associated dysfunctional (-1SD) processes are planning and/or attention and/or successive. In fact, all of them depend on anterior brain, instead, simultaneous depends on posterior brain, and its dysfunction is very rare. In our practice, isolated attention dysfunction is not seen. Practically, it is always seen associated with dysfunctional planning and/or successive. Note also the "en" and "imbalance" pattern in this example.

Figure 4. DN:CAS: associated dysfunction.

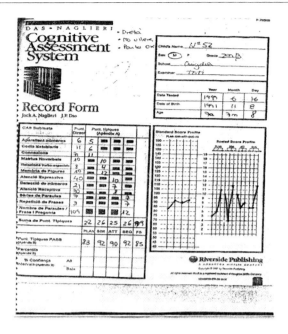

A case of learning, behavioral problems, and ADHD. We can see isolated dysfunctional (-1SD) planning + "en" and "imbalance" pattern. The dysfunctional processing most frequently found in ADHD is planning.

Figure 5. DN:CAS: isolated planning deficit.

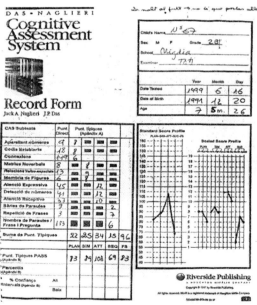

A case of learning and behavioral problems with associated dysfunctional (-1SD) planning + successive. Note "imbalance" pattern in successive. This is also an example of planning – attention dissociation, which denotes these two processes are different entities, although they are considered part of the called executive function.

Figure 6. DN:CAS: planning - attention dissociation.

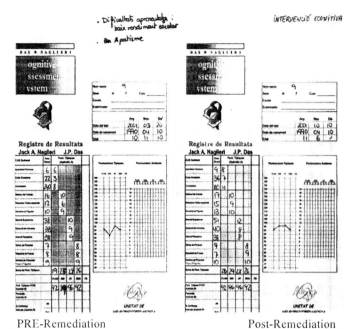

PRE-Remediation   Post-Remediation

A case of learning and behavioral problems as an example of isolated dysfunctional (-1SD)
    simultaneous. After PASS-PREP cognitive intervention, simultaneous has recovered.

Figure 7. DN:CAS: before - after PREP cognitive intervention.

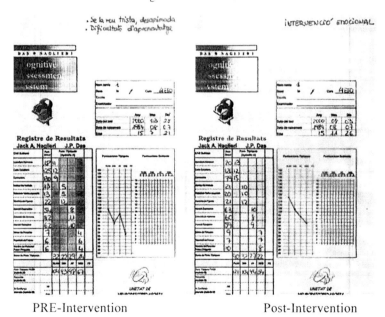

PRE-Intervention   Post-Intervention

A case of learning and behavioral problems with a very rare associated dysfunction (-1SD) successive +
    simultaneous. Although not represented in the graphic, "imbalance" pattern was also present. After
    emotional, but not cognitive, intervention, simultaneous, but mainly planning improved. This may
    be considered a typical case of mental block.

Figure 8. DN:CAS: before - after emotional intervention.

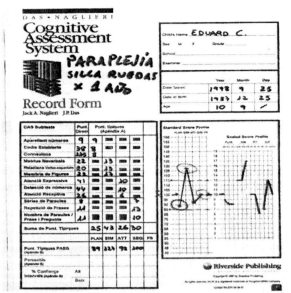

This is one of the most relevant cases with "en" pattern we have seen. "Imbalance" pattern is also present. He was categorized as gifted child; in fact, his simultaneous was excellent, as usual in this category. Instead, planning is low, as usual in gifted child with non-academic problems, but emotional disturb. This one lived one year in wheelchair because of psichogenic paraplegia. He had completely recovered after 6 months of successful emotional intervention.

Figure 9. DN:CAS: psichogeneic paraplegia / gifted.

This conception implies therapeutic considerations in the sense that dysfunctional reading can be trained without reading material . On the other hand, the acoustic test is suggested as a useful test to screen dyslexic children. Gifted children (n = 66) with behavioral problems scored under 85 (-1SD) in PASS planning (unpublished results) in a frequency higher than expected by chance when compared with a normal matched control group (n = 300) ($\chi^2 =$ 6.67 ; $P < 0.01$). We must remark that DN:CAS measures planning, but other batteries does not, which must be taken into account [Perez-Alvarez and Timoneda, 2004b].

In the line of our previous results [Perez-Alvarez and Timoneda, 1996], epileptic children (n = 66) classified into idiopathic or cryptogenic benign epilepsy, but not symptomatic epilepsy or severe epilepsy, neither rolandic epilepsy nor typical absence ("petit mal), all of them with consciousness impairment to different degree and electrical paroxysm in interictal scalp routine and sleep-deprived EEG, scored under 85 (-1SD) in PASS successive in a frequency higher than expected by chance when compared with a normal control group (n = 300) ($\chi^2 = 6.64$; $P = 0.01$). Furthermore, the epileptic children's mean (81.75 with SD 16.40) was inferior to the normal control group's mean (93.76 with SD 15.78) at significant statistical level (t = 3.29 ; $P= 0.001$) [Perez-Alvarez et al, 2006a].

Finally, we have seen that planning underscoring (-1SD) in emotional behavioral disorders (n = 1333) (Table 2) is more frequent than expected by chance ($\chi^2 = 7.00$; $P= 0.008$) when compared with a normal control group (n = 300). Moreover, we have identified a typical profile we call it "en" profile because the pattern is similar to the "en" letter (Figure 10), the frequency of which (n = 603)in children with emotional disorder is higher than expected ($\chi^2 = 8.00$; $P= 0.005$) by chance, compared with a normal control group (n = 300).

Table 1. Factorial analysis DN:CAS + acustic test

	Factor 1 Attention	Factor 2 Successive + Acustic test	Factor 3 Planning	Factor 4 Simultaneous
Acustic test	21895	*58134*	09375	28103
Attention				
ATT_G	*81882*	17171	30931	01208
ATT_EA	*52883*	07318	23828	02211
ATT_RA	*82188*	13217	12883	01135
ATT_NF	*71283*	07282	22438	12871
Planning				
PLN_G	33298	10236	*73232*	18312
PLN_VS	27383	05237	*78383*	23371
PLN_MN	22208	19121	*62288*	22832
PLN_PC	28323	08372	*83486*	18234
Successive				
SCC_G	14223	*98862*	13282	21833
SCC_NR	28283	*73548*	15488	18575
SCC_WO	17882	*68257*	08733	13323
SCC_SRQ	08227	*82342*	12211	21438
Simultaneous				
SMT_G	23238	28226	22423	*82317*
SMT_FM	28113	13133	18213	*62823*
SMT_MA	08282	05412	12233	*85283*
SMT_SV	18541	22838	11332	*88354*

Table 2. DSM-IV diagnostic approach

Diagnosis	N
Learning problem	144
Only communication problem (language)	91
Stuttering	14
Attention deficit disorder with / without hyperactivity	96
Selective mutism	7
Conduct disorder [a]	107
Anorexia / Binge eating disorder	106
Enuresis / Encopresis	79
Tics[b]	24
Depression	81
Anxiety	236
Somatization	348
Total	1333

[a] Conduct disorder: It includes, among others, oppositional defiant disorder, asocial – aggressive behavior, bullying, teasing, and intimidation, drug abuse.

[b] Tourette disorder excluded.

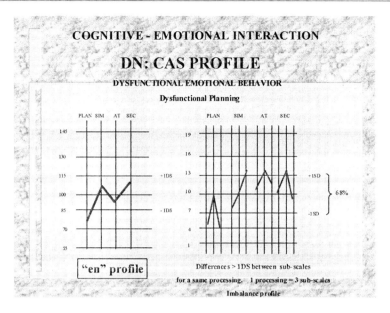

Figure 10. DN:CAS: "En" pattern.

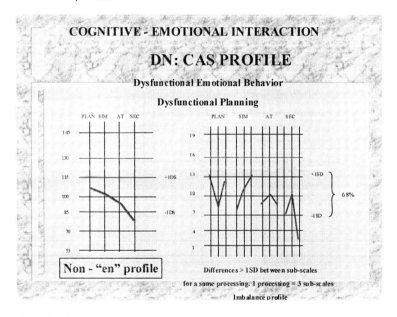

Figure 11. DN:CAS: "Imbalance" pattern.

This profile is due to the fact that planning and attention, in this turn, are the most sensitive processes to emotional disturb. This profile is associated with the fact that the sub-scales (each scale has three sub-scales) show differences between them superior to 1 SD. We must remember that emotional behavioral disorder, according to our concept, is defined as any dysfunctional behavior reactive to painful-feeling. Although the "en" profile is very characteristic, however any profile showing differences in score between subscales superior to 1 SD is suggestive of dysfunctional emotional behavior. We call it "imbalance" profile. (Figure 11). This "imbalance" profile (n = 397) compared with a normal control group (n = 300) shows a higher frequency at significant statistical level (χ^2 = 6.64 ; $P=0.01$) In fact, there is no cognitive reasonable argument to justify differences higher than 1 SD in three subscales that are assessing the same cognitive entity.

Regarding fMRI study [Perez-Alvarez F et al, 2006b], it has been suggested that decision making (planning) depends on sensitive feeling associated with cognitive processing rather than on cognitive processing alone. From human lesions, we know the medial anterior inferior ventral prefrontal cortex processes the sensitivity associated with cognitive processing, it being essentially responsible for decision making (planning). In this fMRI (functional magnetic resonance) study 15 subjects were analyzed using moral dilemmas as probes to investigate the neural basis for painful-emotional sensitivity associated with decision making. We found that a network comprising the posterior and anterior cingulate (classic limbic structures) and the anterior medial prefrontal cortex was significantly and specifically activated by painful moral dilemmas, but not by non-painful dilemmas. These findings provide new evidence that the cingulate and anterior medial prefrontal are involved in processing painful emotional sensibility, in particular, when decision making takes place. We speculate that decision making (planning) has a cognitive component processed by cognitive brain areas and a sensitivity component processed by emotional brain areas. The structures activated suggest that decision making depends on painful emotional feeling processing rather than cognitive processing when painful feeling processing happens. In psycho-educational words, this fMRI study tells us that cognitive performance depends on emotional state, when painful feeling processing occurs. In fMRI language, this finding makes plausible emotional mental block that we assume we can unveil as in "en" DN:CAS profile or "imbalance" DN:CAS profile.

Trying to verify once again the interrelationship between cognition and emotion we designed the study we show in Tables 3 and 4. We selected two pre and post treatment groups. One group was only emotionally treated (Table 3). The other was only cognitively treated (Table 4). As you can see, both groups responded with improvement in planning, but strikingly although the cognitively treated group improved in planning and simultaneous, the emotionally treated group improved in planning at a higher statistical level of significance. See also Figures 7 and 8.

Table 3. DN:CAS assessment before and after emotional intervention

	Before Emotional Intervention	After Emotional Intervention	
	n σ SD	n σ SD	t P
Planning	35 83.9 11.2	35 89.6 13.3	2.9 0.008
Attention	35 86.1 14.3	35 88.3 13.5	0.0 NS
Simultaneous	35 92.9 15.1	35 95.1 15.0	1.1 NS
Successive	35 88.7 13.0	35 92.5 15.3	1.5 NS

Perez-Alvarez and Timoneda (1998) *Neuropsicopedagogia. ¿Es como parece?*. Barcelona: Editorial Textos Universitarios Sant Jordi.

Table 4. DN:CAS assessment before and after PREP cognitive intervention

	Before PREP	After PREP	
	n σ SD	n σ SD	t P
Planning	35 81.5 13.4	35 89.1 11.4	2.6 0.047
Attention	35 88.3 14.3	35 90.3 13.3	0.7 NS
Simultaneous	35 86.3 13.5	35 94.0 14.5	3.0 0.029
Successive	35 79.8 08.6	35 80.8 11.3	2.7 NS

JP Das (1999b) PREP: PASS Reading Enhancement Program. Deal. NY: Sarka Educational Resources.

DISCUSSION

Long ago, it was established that cognitive performance, but not emotional "performance", is susceptible to be assessed, although it was likewise assumed that the emotional state influences the cognitive performance. The results of our research allow us to conclude that the practical procedure we utilize based on the theoretical framework already summarized is a useful one to diagnose and treat cognitive - emotional dysfunctions. The procedure has two components, the diagnosis and the treatment, simultaneously taking place and focussing on two basic mechanisms responsible for any behavior, one the cognition and the other the emotion in the sense of painful-feeling sensitivity. In neurological terms, behavior is both learning and any other act of human being. First of all, we must say that an emotional intervention without using instructional cognitive material is practically always needed in those cases where the learning problem is the principal concern, for instance, dyslexia.

First, we will explain how the emotional procedure works without dealing with the cognition of emotion. The key concept is that, whenever and whatever behavior is put in action, both cognitive (ideas) and feeling (sensitivity) processing happen at the neurological level. The behavior in action is essentially the consequence of feeling processing rather than of cognitive processing, which is what our fMRI study [Perez-Alvarez et al. 2006b] seems to tells us. It is also what lesion studies tells us [Damasio, 1994; Camile et al. 2004, Perez-Alvarez et al. 2006c] . For instance, a patient with an emotional prefrontal lesion behaves unsociably because his/her emotional medial-ventral-inferior prefrontal is not processing-codifying the painful feeling associated to an unsociably behaving, but not because his/her cognitive dorsolateral prefrontal along with his/her temporal, parietal and occipital external cognitive cortices are incapapable of understanding which consequence follows which behavior. In other words, if I behave sociably, I do it because I will feel badly otherwise, but not for any reason of understanding, learning, or reasoning. In other words, the behavior is coherent with feeling, but not with good logical reasoning, if the painful-feeling takes place.

Then, the next notion to keep in mind is that the painful-feeling sensitivity is neurologically experienced in countless circumstances we call them with nearly countless linguistic terms describing them, namely, anxiety, depression, stress, fear, anger, worry, uncertainty, fatigue and so on, but also in unthinkable circumstances like aggression, violence, and so on that we can include in the impulsive behavior category. That is, painful-feeling processing provokes a reactive impulsive behavior (fight behavior), although the opposite can be also possible (flight behavior). We will see that the painful feeling processing becomes equal to the impulsivity processing, this last term conveying the behavioral reaction in particular. Striking evidence from animal experimentation [LeDoux et al., 1984, 1986, 1990; LeDoux, 1996] suggests that the impulsive processing responsible for impulsive behavior is not different from the painful-fearful feeling processing we are talking about. That is, all evidence points to the conclusion that all live beings hold an anatomical-biochemical-physiological neurological mechanism in charge of processing countless situations or experiences that are codified as dangerous events. This is because the involved neurological structures are not able to discriminate the real danger from the unreal one on an evolutionary basis.

Sometimes the painful feeling, neurologically codified as danger, is consciously experienced, but sometimes it is unconsciously-subconsciously experienced, although painful sensation is a linguistic term linked to consciousness. For instance, the person aggressively behaving is not simultaneously aware of his/her conscious bad feeling, but he/she is unconsciously feeling badly and, in fact, the aggressive behavior should be considered a compensatory reactive behavior to the bad feeling being unconsciously processed, which allows him/her to feel better, doing the behavior as opposed to not doing it. In this condition, the cognitive neocortex of this person is aware of the unconsciously triggered verbal or/and gesture aggressive behavior, but not of the real reason (painful feeling) responsible for it.

To follow, we must emphasize that the neurons similarly codify as danger what we call the countless linguistic terms we have earlier mentioned. More and more neurological evidence points to the fact that the painful-feeling sensitivity processing network count on neurons processing and codifying sensitivity, but not cognitive informative data, even for the prefrontal and the cognitive cerebral lobe par excellence. In fact, this described functional mechanism compares with what we now know about painful-feeling sensitivity processing in animals [LeDoux et al., 1984, 1986, 1990; LeDoux, 1996].

Having said that, we must clarify that any person, either consciously or unconsciously experiencing a painful feeling, is processing two kinds of bad feeling. One, the past memorized bad feeling linked to what psychologists calls personal identity, and other one the current bad feeling that is generally associated with a concrete current painful event (triggering factor). The memorized painful feeling (sensitivity) is associated with the corespondent cognitive component (informative data) that constitutes the learned and memorized personal beliefs. We will see later that the personal beliefs work basically at a central subconscious level beyond what we externally can see, hear, etc. between input of information (event or events as precipitant factors) and output of information (behavioral response) [Das, 1999; Das et al. 1994, 1996, 2000; Perez-Alvarez and Timoneda, 2004a, 2004b]. For instance, someone argues: "Well, I get so nervous... But you see, the children... the traffic jam... my inefficient secretary... my unbearable boss..." Or: "I hit him, he insulted me" Or, for instance, the case of someone known as a very impressive person for his/her impressive determination, showing no doubt at all in front of whatever situation. Here, we can see three different behavioral outputs in PASS information processing terms. These examples show several triggering causal painful events, namely, "children/traffic/secretary/boss" or "insult" . The adjustment of the particular reactive behavioral response-output to a good logical reasoning will tell us if the behavioral response must be justified by just the triggering causal events or, rather, must be justified by the memorized past bad feeling (personal identity in sensitive neurological terms). If so, we will call it masked (because of unconscious mechanism) painful behavior [Goleman, 1986].

Poor logical reasoning appears whenever the behavior being expressed is not the consequence of logical reasoning supported by the cognitive neocortex, but of the unconscious bad feeling supported by subneocortical amygdala network processing a danger signal due to past painful experiences. This is in accordance with the non-physical painful-fear processing in animal experimentation [LeDoux et al., 1984, 1986, 1990; LeDoux, 1996]. Turning to the third example, the impressive determination might potentially be a masked painful behavior like whatever behavioral output. Again, the presence of poor logical reasoning will tell us. In general, poor logical reasoning is uncovered because of: (a) Contradiction between verbal language and body language. For instance, "I am well", but with uncontrolled body manifestation of suffering. Verbal production is not the consequence of reasonable and reflexive arguments, but of bad feeling unconsciously triggering the verbal response. Likewise, the person that verbally manifests to be very worried, but his/her body tell us otherwise. Or, the person with impressive determination that unhappily behaves in a suffering way, without relaxation, to compensate his/her personal painful feeling memorized in the past. In fact, he/she paradoxically behaves according to a pattern of auto-confidence, but he/she is unconsciously suffering from the lack of auto-confidence. His/her neurons are unconsciously processing danger. This behavior is contradictory in logical terms. Alternatively, non-contradiction would be the behavioral impressive determination without an unconscious suffering component. (b) Contradiction in arguments of verbal language, frequently expressing itself as exaggerated-disproportional arguments or overacting body behavior, because again the produced behavior is mainly not the consequence of any reason at all. In earlier mentioned examples, on a different day the same person with the same triggering factors will not behave similarly, or this hitting person, likewise, will not behave this way long after.

In any case, contradiction assessment requires us to unveil the cognitive-feeling beliefs at central neurological level of processing between the input and the output [Das, 1999; Das et al. 1994, 1996, 2000; Perez-Alvarez and Timoneda, 2004a, 2004b]. We claim that this central processing we are talking about happens by support of the emotional prefrontal. Let's turn to one of the examples; someone tells me "idiot" (event-input triggering-precipitant causal factor) and I respond by hitting him (behavioral output response), but the magnitude of my response depends more on my personal unconscious belief and associated bad feeling in the sense of "I'm not able / I'm worthless / I feel badly", than on the particular bad feeling provoked by "idiot" itself. At this point, we must say that, whenever "I feel badly" , this situation corresponds frequently to the experience of blame sentiment in psychological terms. This scheme is always operating in such a way that you can substitute the causal factor "you are an idiot" for any other factor, for instance, "you are not intelligent" or, simply, "a bad experience at school" or "a bad experience at home", with verbal language not being necessary at all. So, at the input level, we can differentiate external input or internal input, for instance, a thought such as "I am a failure". The data content can be classified into linguistic data (propositional data) via visual or auditory channels and non-linguistic data (analogic data) as it is "somebody laughing or shouting" via visual, auditory or tactile channels. At central processing, propositional data (thought, language) or/and analogic data (images, sounds, smells, tastes) are processed. We must emphasize that the bad feeling is more frequently processed and memorized implicitly-unconsciously than consciously.

In sum, good logical reasoning consists of using only valid arguments and true premises, for only in this way does an argument give a reason to the conclusion being true. But, according to our framework, the good logical reasoning must be analyzed by considering unconscious beliefs forming part of the premises. For example, a child is presented with single separated letters, concretely, *u b s*. He/she is asked to pronounce the successive combination *b u s*, and he/she answers correctly. Later, he/she is asked to pronounce the sequence *q u s*, and the answer is also /bπ s/ . Apparently, an incorrect answer. However, if the mentally processed knowledge is the symbol "b" is "b" independently of placing it right side up or not, then good logical reasoning has happened, because "a chair remains a chair whether its feet are on the floor or pointing toward the ceiling". For the child in the example to be able to learn further, it will be necessary condition the educator, the therapist, to know this. Similarly, in the above mentioned example someone tells me "idiot" (input of information like "tell me how *b u s* is pronounced) and the answer is a verbal and non-verbal aggressive behavior (output) . What matters is the central mental processing, supporting the personal identity, in terms of beliefs that can be formulated as follows: "idiot is worthless and painful; I'm unable and worthless and I feel badly if/because I feel idiot" . Really, the neurons at the amygdala are supposed to be codifying danger in a situation like this one. This way, both cognitive processing and emotional processing work interactively.

To conclude, a substantial component of a good logical reasoning has to do with planning function [Stuss and Benson, 1986; Fuster, 1989; Damasio, 1994; Das et al. 1996; Goldberg, 2001]. Only a good logical reasoning allows us both to make decisions and to plan any action, which basically implies us to foresee and feel the consequences derived from the action in question, and take the best option. Otherwise, a masked planning causes us to make masked decisions, as it is the case in the "en" DN:CAS profile, for instance. The cognitive and emotional therapeutic effect is based on discovering personal beliefs and intending to change them by means of inductive learning and indirect communication and, in particular, the metaphor [Grinder et al. 1978; Erickson and Rossi, 1981] as prototype of indirect communication. The educator or therapist acts as a mediator but not as an instructor in the sense that the decision of changing is on the part of the patient. The therapeutic effect is conveyed by means of both the verbal language and the body language, this one being a priority. The gold rule is communicating what we want to communicate without conveying a painful feeling; that is why indirect communication techniques that avoid any communicative reference to the "you" (patient), "you are ...", "you must ...", and so on is mandatory.

Now, we will focus on cognitive training according to this conception [Das, 1999b]. First of all, we must remark that the PASS cognitive intervention is oriented to train the central neurological processing but not the resulting external product. According to the PASS concept, central neurological processing is diagnosed and trained by means of the behavior at the intake and output of information, but specifically the intake and output of information are neither diagnosed nor trained. Taking into account that the PASS processes will intervene with whatever the task put in action, we can cognitively train a dyslexia problem without using reading material [Das, 1998; Das et al. 2000] or an ADHD case without focussing on attentional behavior, for instance. The PASS cognitive intervention is based on training the planning (strategies) to reach a maximal efficiency in simultaneous, reducing to a minimum the requirement in successive. Concretely, the job of planning training involves diagnosing the less efficient planning (strategies) being used by the patient first, and secondly to cause him/her to consciously experience the inefficiency of the strategy being used and, later, a new more efficient planning (strategies) based on a more efficient use of the simultaneous. The diagnosis of strategies involves one to be looking for accessing cues like the eyes up and to the lateral position, for instance, that allows us to know simultaneous processing is working, or the eyes scanning that tells us planning is working. Likewise, repeated verbal or sub - vocal rehearsal to facilitate remembering tells us the successive is working. The intervention itself has two components. One, and first, implies him/her to be aware of the inefficient strategy and, secondly, be aware of a more efficient strategy susceptible to be used to resolve the same task. Both interventions are made using indirect communication. In concrete terms, the use of "you" is avoided and the following question is formulated: How did Jimmy (for instance) do to resolve the task? More than less frequently, he/she will be unable to consciously know it. If so, next, we will do the task such that the inefficient strategy can be caught by him/her, avoiding direct instruction. Then, we will ask: How could/can we do ? Again, the formulation with "we" instead of "you". At this point, we are intending him/her to discover the new efficient strategy. This process of inductive "metacognitive" learning involves him/her to experience the "I'm able / I'm worthy / I feel very well" as an expression of personal autonomy. Furthermore, it is well known that inductive learning has a more powerful memorizing effect than deductive learning. After a reasonable time without success, the educator – therapist will mediate, making some procedure without direct instruction that allows him/her to be aware of a possible strategy to be put in action. Direct verbal instruction is the least desirable method, because it is difficult to describe a mental procedure and explanations may serve only to confuse children. Moreover, do not pursue the matter. It may only frustrate the child, who may eventually discover the strategy later anyway. We must remark that any strategy to be indirectly induced has to meet the principle that any new concept to be learned by anyone has to be incorporated and related to his/her previous base of acquired knowledge, keeping in mind that concrete but not abstract concepts must be utilized. It is about creating opportunities for the child to discover a general rule. This is true, also, for the personal beliefs. In so doing, not only near transfer linked to the context of learning but also far transfer (beyond the context of a particular learning) of strategies has been demonstrated [Das et al. 1994]. The far transfer involves the internalization of a principle rule applicable to multiple contexts, producing not only an immediate effect but also a sustainable effect. We must remember that rote memorization, reinforced by repetition, is not comprehension. Meaningful knowledge happens by learning relationships and forming associations and comparisons (PASS simultaneous), which is inherent to memorization laws for long term memory as it is the case in chunking, space-time contiguity, acrostics and acronyms, "sing-song" learning, etc. A successive strategy is needed in a similar way to working memory. Planning allows us the maximal efficiency in simultaneous with the successive available. Attention is always working to allow us a conscious operation.

On diagnosing and treating, some golden rules must be taken into account. 1. A child should be rewarded for *trying* , not for coming up with the right answer. 2. Initially, lead the child around to the right answer by easy questions. Even if you have to provide the answer, make it look as though he/she really knew the answer but couldn't think of it ! 3. For starting a session, always begin by using material so absurdly simple that your child couldn't possibly fail, allowing the child a few initial triumph. 4. For stopping a session, always stop a session while your child wants to continue a little longer. 5. For speed of session, "hurry ahead slowly" if possible. For remediation, too fast a pace slows learning !

Neurologically, human clinical evidence [Teuber, 1964; Luria, 1980; Stuss and Benson, 1986; Fuster, 1989; Thatcher, 1991, 1992] had informed us that, indeed, planning [Das et al. 1996] depends on the prefrontal cortex. Recently [Damasio, 1994], it was stated that two dissociable prefrontal cortex could be differentiated-dissociated, namely, the cognitive dorsolateral prefrontal cortex and the "emotional" medial-ventral-inferior prefrontal cortex in charge of processing the feeling-sensitivity of the data (informative cognitive content), processed by the more external cognitive cortex, which is convergent with the last evidence reported by fMRI studies [Greene et al. 2001; Singer et al, 2004; Camille et al. 2004, Perez-Alvarez et al. 2006c]. Furthermore, human clinical evidence suggests that decision-making process linked to planning process, which is supposed to be exclusively dependent on the cognitive deliberative prefrontal cortex, nowadays, in fact, is thought to be dependent on the feeling prefrontal cortex, which accounts for a subject with lesion in the feeling prefrontal cortex, dorsolateral cortex being intact, to behave unsociably without remorse or, likewise, gamble without concern for the painful consequences [Damasio, 1994; Perez-Alvarez and Timoneda, 2005]. Therefore, painful-feeling sensitivity and, equally, the subsequent impulse control [Hollander, 2001, 2003] seems to be neurologically dependent on the balanced function of both planning processing and impulsive processing, such that any cause acting on either neurocircuitry can produce impulsive neurological activity with variable external behavioral expression. In other words, planning dysfunction activates painful feeling-impulsive processing and vice versa, painful feeling-impulsive dysfunction makes planning function difficult [Goldberg, 2001]. In sum, recent evidence in animals and old anatomical evidence and recent fMRI evidence in humans increasingly suggest that the painful feeling processing, in general, is supported by a network integrated by the thalamus, amygdala, anterior and posterior cingulate cortex, insula, and anterior-ventral-medial prefrontal cortex, whereas the most external cortical structures, namely, dorsolateral prefrontal, temporal, parietal and occipital are responsible for the processing of concepts or ideas. We postulate that the interaction between these two neurological networks takes place according to the explanation we have argued. So far, our fMRI study [Perez-Alvarez et al. 2006b] has allowed us to count on a fMRI normal pattern we are now comparing with different dysfunctional situations like, for instance, attention deficit hyperactive disorder . We have hypothesized that these children will show a pattern different from normal children, susceptible to be correlated with DN:CAS profiles.

Along the discussion, to conclude, we have tried to argue how human behavior can be explained according to what nowadays the CNS tell us about both the processing of cognitive information and the processing of the painful sensitivity. Whether or not you are persuaded by the arguments we are expressed, we hope you may at least to reconsider some of your own assumptions about the human behavior and the role of cognition and emotion, and their psychological assessment. The procedure we have discussed is useful for special populations, that is, disadvantaged children, learning disabled, mentally handicapped, special education children, slow learners, low achievers, environmentally deprived, brain-injured, gifted and handicapped children, socially and emotionally disturbed children, etc. Remember, these general labels may be prejudicial, giving the impression that the child cannot be helped.

ACKNOWLEDGEMENTS

We are indebted to J Alabau, J Baus, J Hernández and S Mayoral, for his/her professional dedication, and to the children, and their parents for their invaluable collaboration in the research presented here.

This work has been partially supported by grants of the University of Girona (Spain).

REFERENCES

Adolphs RH, Damasio D, Tranel G, Cooper A, Damasio AR. (2000). A role for somatosensory cortices in the visual recognition of emotion as revealed by 3 – 0 lesion mapping. *Journal Neuroscience* , 20, 2683-2690.

Buchsbaum MS. (1982). Role of opioid peptides in disorders of attention in psychopathology. *Proceedings New York Academy Science*, 82, 352-365.

Camille N, Coricelli G, Sallet J, Pradat-Diehl P, Duhamel JR, Sirigu A.(2004). The involvement of the orbitofrontal cortex in the experience of regret. *Science,* 304, 1167-1170.

Crabtree BF, Miller WL. (1992). *Doing qualitative research.* Newbury Park, CA: Sage Publications.

Creswell JW. (1994). *Research design. Qualitative and quantitative approaches.* Thousand Oaks, CA: Sage Publications.

Damasio AR.(1994). *Descartes'Error.* Putnam: New York.

Darwin C. (1965). *The expression of the emotions in man and animals.* Chicago: Chicago University Press.

Das JP, Kirby JR, Jarman RF. (1979*). Simultaneous and successive cognitive processes.* New York: Academic Press.

Das JP, Naglieri JA, Kirby JR. (1994). *Assessment of cognitive processes. The PASS theory of intelligence.* Massachussets: Allyn and Bacon, Inc.

Das JP, Kar R, Parrila RK. (1996). Cognitive planning. The psychological basis of intelligent behavior. London: Sage Publications Ltd.

Das JP, Garrido MA, Gonzalez M, Timoneda C, Pérez-Álvarez F. (2000). *Dislexia y dificultades de lectura.* Barcelona: Paidós Editorial.

Das JP, Naglieri JA. (1997). Cognitive Assessment System. Illinois: Riverside Publishing.

Das J.P. (1998). *Dyslexia and Reading difficulties.* Edmonton, Canada: University of Alberta.

Das JP. (1999a). A neo-Lurian approach to assessment and remediation. *Neuropsychology Review,* 9, 107-115.

_____ . (1999b). PREP: PASS Reading Enhancement Program. Deal, NY: Sarka Educational Resources.

Das JP.(2003). Theories of intelligence: Issues and applications. In G Goldstein and SR Beers. (Eds), *Comprehensive handbook of psychological assessment.* Vol I *Intellectual and neuropsychological assessment.* John Wiley and Sons, Inc.

Ekman P. (1973). Cross-cultural studies of facial expression. In P Ekman. (Ed), *Darwin and facial expression : A century of research in review.* New York: Academic Press.

Erickson MH and Rossi E. (1981). *Experiencing hypnosis: Therapeutic approaches to altered states.* New York: Irvington.

Fuster JM. (1989). *The prefrontal cortex.* New York: Raven Press.

Goldberg E. (2001). *The executive brain.* Oxford University Press.

Goleman DP. (1986). *Vital Lies, Simple Truths: The Psychology of Self-Deception.* New York: Touchstone Books.

Greene JD, Sommerville RB, Nystrom LE, Darley JM, Cohen JD. (2001). An fMRI investigation of emotional engagement in moral judgment. *Science* 293:2105-8.

Grinder J, DeLozier J, Bandler R.(1978). *Patterns of the Hypnotic Techniques of Milton H Erickson.* Vol.II Cupertino, CA: Meta Publications.

Hollander E. (2001). New developments in impulsivity. *Lancet,* 358, 949-50.

Hollander E, Posner N, Cherkasky S.(2003). *The neuropsychiatry of aggression and impulse control disorders.* In Yudofsky SC and Hales RE. (Eds), Washington DC: American Psychiatric Press, Inc.

Horowitz M.J. (1990). A model of mourning: Changes in schemas of self and others. *J American Psychoanalytic Association* , 38, 297-324.

Lang PJ. (1984). Cognition in emotion. In Izard CE, Kagan J, Zajonc RB. (Eds), *Emotions, cognition and behavior.* New York: Cambridge University Press.

Lazarus RS. (1966). *Psychological stress and the coping process.* New York: McGraw-Hill.

LeDoux JE, Sakaguchi A, Reis DJ. (1984). Subcortical efferent projections from the medial geniculate nucleus mediate emotional responses conditioned by acoustic stimuli. *Journal Neuroscience,* 4, 683-698.

LeDoux JE, Sakaguchi A, Iwata J, Reis DJ. (1986). Interruption of projections from the medial geniculate body to an archi-neostriatal field disrupts the classical conditioning of emotional responses to acoustic stimuli in the rat. *Neuroscience,* 17, 615-627.

LeDoux JE, Farb CF, Ruggiero DA. (1990). Topographic organization of neurons in the acoustic thalamus that project to the amygdala. *Journal Neuroscience,* 10, 1043-1054.

LeDoux JE. (1996). *Emotional brain.* New York: Simon and Schuster.

Luria AR. (1980). *Higher cortical functions in man.* New York: Basic Books.

Lyons W. (1980). *Emotion.* Cambridge UK: Cambridge University Press.

Pérez-Alvarez F, Timoneda C. (1996). Epilepsia y aprendizaje. *Rev Neurol,* 24, 1128-9.

_____. (1998). *Neuropsicopedagogia. Es como parece?.* Barcelona: Editorial Textos Universitarios Sant Jordi.

_____ . (1999a). Cognición, emoción y conducta. *Rev. Neurol.,* 29, 26-33.

_____ (1999b). Fenotipos conductuales: Explicación cognitiva y emocional. *Rev. Neurol.,* 29, 1153-1159.

_____ (1999c). El hiperquinético a la luz del PASS. *Rev. Neurol.,* 28, 472-475.

_____ (1999d). El PASS y la disfasia, dislexia e hiperquinético. *Rev. Neurol.,* 28 (Supl.), 193.

_____ (1999e). La disfasia y la dislexia a la luz del PASS. *Rev. Neurol.,* 28, 688-69.

_____(2000). Disfunción del procesamiento secuencial PASS en la dislexia. *Rev. Neurol.,* 30, 614-619. http://www.revneurol.com/3007/i070614.pdf.

_____ . (2001). Disfunción neurocognitiva PASS del déficit de atención *Rev. Neurol.,* 32, 30-37. http://www.revneurol.com/3201/k010030.pdf

_____ . (2002). Conductas emocionales como disfunción neurológica. *Rev. Neurol.,* 35, 612-624. http://www.revneurol.com/LinkOut/form MedLine.asp?Refer=2001110

_____.(2004a). Learning Both in Attention Deficit Disorder and Dyslexia in the light of PASS Neurocognitive Dysfunction. In HD Tobias (Ed), *Focus on Dyslexia Research.* pp. 173-179. Hauppauge, NY: Nova Science Publishers, Inc.

_____.(2004b). Attention Deficit / Hyperactive Disorder as Impulsivity Disorder according to PASS Neurocognitive Function. In P. Larimer (Ed), *Attention Deficit Hyperactivity Disorder Research Developments.* pp 173-184. Hauppauge, NY: Nova Science Publishers, Inc.

_____. (2005). La función intelectual: De qué se trata? *Acta. Pediatr. Esp.,* 63,101-4.

Perez-Alvarez F, Timoneda C, Baus J. (2002). Topiramate monotherapy in children with newly diagnosed epilepsy. *Epilepsia,* (Supl. 8), 187.

Perez-Alvarez F, Timoneda C, Baus J.(2006a) Topiramato y epilepsia a la luz del Das-Naglieri Cognitive Assessment System. *Rev. Neurol.,* 42, 3-7.

Perez-Alvarez F, Timoneda C, Reixach J. (2006b). An fMRI study of emotional engagement in decision-making. *Transaction Advanced Research,* 2, 45-51.

Perez-Alvarez F, Peñas A, Bergada A, Mayol Ll. (2006c). Obsessive-compulsive disorder and acute traumatic brain. *Acta Psychiatr. Scand.,* 114, 295.

Power M and Dalgleish T. (1997). *Cognition and Emotionv.from order to disorder.* UK: Psychology Press, Publishers.

Schachter S and Singer JE. (1962). Cognitive, social, and physiological determinants of emotional state. *Psychological Review,* 69,379-399.

Selye H. (1974). *The Stress of My Life: A Scientist's Memoirs.* New York: Van Nostrand Reinhold.

Singer T, Seymour B, O'Doherty J, Kaube H, Dolan RJ, Frith CD.(2004). Empathy for pain involves the affective but not sensory components of pain. *Science,* 303, 1157-1162.

Stuss DT, Benson DF. (1986). *The frontal lobes.* New York: Raven Press.

Teuber HL. (1964). The riddle of frontal lobe function in man. In Warren JM and Akert K. (Eds), *The frontal granular cortex and behavior.* New York: Mc Graw-Hill. P. 410-444.

Thatcher RW.(1991). Maturation of human frontal lobes: Physiological evidence for staging. *Developmental Psychology,* 7, 397-419.

_____. (1992). Cyclic cortical reorganization during early childhood. *Brain and Cognition,* 20,24-50.

Timoneda Gallart C, Perez-Alvarez F. (1994). *Successive and simultaneous processing in preschool children.* Madrid: Proceeding Book 23rd International Congress of Applied Psychology. pp 156.

In: Leading-Edge Psychological Tests and Testing Research   ISBN: 978-1-60021-571-1
Editor: Marta A. Lange, pp. 27-50   © 2007 Nova Science Publishers, Inc.

Chapter 2

THE ITALIAN VERSIONS OF THE BECK ANXIETY INVENTORY AND THE BECK DEPRESSION INVENTORY-II: PSYCHOMETRIC PROPERTIES AND DISCRIMINANT POWER

Claudio Sica[*] *and Marta Ghisi*[**]

[*]Department of Psychology, University of Firenze, Italy
[**]Department of General Psychology, University of Padova, Italy

ABSTRACT

Background: Epidemiological evidence suggests that anxiety and depressive disorders are the most common mental disorders. A common way to assess anxiety and depressive symptoms is through self-reports. Relevant to the aims of the present study is the fact that content validity of self-reports can vary across different cultures. As a consequence, validity should be established when the instrument is used with cultural groups on which it has not been standardized. Therefore, the purpose of this study was to present data on the Italian versions of the Beck Anxiety Inventory (BAI) and Beck Depression Inventory-II (BDI-II), probably among the most common self-reports that measure the severity of anxiety and depressive symptoms.

Method: the Italian version of the BAI was administered to a sample of 831 individuals belonging to the general population and to a sample of 122 patients with either anxiety or depressive disorders. The Italian version of the BDI-II was administered to a sample of 723 college students and to a sample of 72 depressed patients. Alpha and test-retest reliabilities were computed along with associations with age and education. The BAI and BDI-II were also subjected to a Confirmative Factor Analysis and a second-order factor analysis. Convergent validity was ascertained by computing the product-moment correlations with other conceptually-related self-report measures. Lastly, to ascertain the discriminative power of the BAI and BDI-II, normal and clinical samples were compared by means of ROC analysis.

---

[*] Author for correspondence: Claudio Sica, Dipartimento di Psicologia, University of Firenze Via San Niccolò, 93, 50125, Firenze, Italy. Phone: 055-2491618 Fax: 055-2345326. E-mail: claudio.sica@unifi.it

Results: Overall, demographic variables did not influence the scores of the BAI and the BDI-II. Confirmative factor analysis for both measures showed the best fit for a multi-factor solution; however, a second-order factor analysis showed strong support for a higher order unidimensional structure of the BAI and BDI-II. Validity was confirmed by the significant association with other measures of anxiety or depression. Lastly, ROC curves indicate excellent discriminative power of the BAI and BDI-II for distinguishing patients from non clinical individuals.

Conclusions: The BAI and BDI-II proved a reliable and valid measure of anxiety and depressive symptoms in the Italian context. The present study confirmed the excellent psychometric properties of the BAI and BDI-II on Italian individuals and supported its use in both normal and clinical individuals.

INTRODUCTION

Epidemiological evidence suggests that anxiety and depressive disorders are the most common mental disorders in Italy, with a twelve-month prevalence rate as high as, respectively, 7.1% and 3.5% (The WHO World Mental Health Survey Consortium, 2004). Given that an optimal mental health care policy aims to treat effectively existing cases of mental illness and reduce future cases by means of early detection and treatment, a correct assessment of symptoms appears critical for an effective intervention on clinical disorders.

One of the most common way to assess anxiety and depressive symptoms is through self-reports. In this case, clinical judgements are strongly influenced by the construct validity of such instruments. In particular, content validity is an important component of construct validity because it provides evidence about the degree to which the elements of the assessment instrument are relevant to and representative of the targeted construct (Haynes, Richard and Kubany, 1995). However, domain and facets of many constructs change over time and across contexts; in other words, the relevance and representativeness of the elements of a self report are unstable and conditional in nature (De Vellis, 1991; Ebel and Frisbie, 1991). Relevant to the aims of present study is the fact that content validity of self-reports can vary across different cultures. As a consequence, validity should be established when the instrument is used with cultural groups on which it has not been standardized. Without evidence of translation and psychometric adequacy and appropriate normative data, the use of assessment instruments with different cultural groups is of concern (Kinzie and Manson, 1987).

In this chapter we present two studies concerning the psychometric characteristics of two of the most common self-report measures of anxiety and depressive symptoms: the Beck Anxiety Inventory (BAI)[1], and the Beck Depression Inventory-II (BDI-II)[2] Since such instruments were developed in the USA, it required an in-depth analysis to demonstrate their reliability and validity on an Italian population. As we will see, our studies showed that the Italian versions of the BAI and BDI-II have excellent properties and can undoubtedly enhance the quality of clinical research and practice in Italy and therefore contribute to international investigation in the clinical psychology field.

STUDY 1: PSYCOMETRIC PROPERTIES OF THE ITALIAN VERSION OF THE BECK ANXIETY INVENTORY

An instrument which can improve the assessment of anxiety in the Italian context - both for clinical research and applications - is the Beck Anxiety Inventory (BAI; Beck, Epstein, Brown and Steer, 1988). The BAI is a 21-item self-report inventory that measures the severity of anxiety symptoms. Each BAI item is rated on a 4-point scale ranging from 0 (not at all) to 3 (severely-I could barely stand it). The BAI was developed to assess symptoms specific to anxiety and with a goal of minimizing overlap with depressive items. For this reason, the authors obtained a high correlation between the content of BAI and the symptom criteria presented in the Diagnostic and Statistical Manual of Mental Disorders-Third edition Revised (DSM III-R; American Psychiatric Association, 1987) for diagnosing patients with panic (PAD) and generalized anxiety disorders (GAD). Nevertheless, the inventory was moderately related (r=.48) to the Beck Depression Inventory (BDI; Beck, Ward, Mendelson, Mock and Erbaugh, 1961), even though this correlation was lower compared to those obtained with other measures of anxiety (Beck et al., 1988).

The BAI has been used with adolescents, adults and older people with anxiety or affective disorders, showing good psychometric properties (Beck, Steer, Ball and Ranieri, 1996; Jolly, Aruffo, Wherry and Livingstone, 1993; Kabacoff, Segal, Hersen and van Hasselt, 1997). In these studies the internal consistency (Cronbach's alpha) typically ranged from .90 to .94. The one week test-retest correlation coefficient was acceptable (rs from .62 to .73; Beck et al.,1993; Creamer, Foran and Bell, 1995). The BAI manual (Beck et al.,1993) reported moderate correlations with other anxiety measures (rs from .47 to .58) and a correlation of .41 with a measure of obsessive and compulsive symptoms. In reference to criterion-validity, Beck and colleagues (1993) reported that patients with panic disorder scored higher than the patients with GAD and social phobia, whereas patients with obsessive compulsive disorder (OCD) did not differ from patients with other types of anxiety disorders (GAD, social phobia, panic disorder with and without agoraphobia) in the mean BAI score. Regarding the factorial structure of the BAI, both two and four factor solutions were found in exploratory factor analytic studies (Beck et al., 1988; Beck and Steer ,1991; Creamer et al., 1995; Hewitt and Norton, 1993; Steer, Rissmiller, Ranieri and Beck, 1993). Noteworthy, Osman, Hoffman, Barrios, Kopper, Breitenstein and Hahn (2002) extracted a higher order factor by specifying only one factor in the final solution of their exploratory factor analysis. In three recent studies, confirmatory analyses revealed a good fit for a 4-factor model consisting of subjective, autonomic, neurophysiological, and panic symptoms (Enns, Cox, Parker and Guertin,1998; Osman, Kopper, Barrios, Osman and Wade, 1997; Wetherell and Areán, 1997) whereas the two-factor model proved inadequate when tested using a confirmatory factor analytic approach (Osman et al., 1997; Osman, Barrios, Aukes, Osman and Markway, 1993). Lastly, Osman and colleagues (1997) and Wetherell and colleagues (1997) showed that a second-order analysis of the primary factors provided support for a single-factor structure of the BAI.

The BAI is a very popular anxiety measure. During the years 1991-1998, it ranked third, behind the STAI and the Fear Survey Schedule, in terms of use in research (Piotrowski,1999). The BAI has been translated into French (Freeston, Ladoucer, Thibodeau and Gagnon, 1994), Spanish (Novy, Stanley, Melinda, Averil and Daza, 2001) and German (Margraf and Ehlers,

1998). Moreover, there are Arabic (Al-Issa, Al-Zubaidi, Bakal and Fung, 2000), Mexican (Robles, Varela, Jurado and Paez, 2001), Korean (Yook and Kim, 1997) and Turkish versions (Ulusoy, Sahin, and Erkmen, 1998). All the versions presented good psychometric properties and resulted in useful findings in non-clinical as well as clinical research.

The present study aimed to evaluate the psychometric properties of the BAI for the Italian population. We examined the internal consistency, the gender differences, the concurrent and discriminant validity, and its factorial structure. In addition, we ascertained the discriminant power of the BAI by contrasting clinical individuals and community controls with ROC curves (Receiver Operating Characteristic method; Metz, 1978; Swets, 1996).

Participants and Procedure

The subjects were 831 individuals belonging to community (418 male and 413 female) enrolled in different towns of Northern Italy. Males did not differ from females in age (Total Mean=38.1; SD=16.2), years of education (Total Mean= 14.9; SD=3.7), marital status (Total figures: 43% single, 46.5% married or cohabitant, 8% separated or divorced, 2.5% widow or widower) whereas a higher proportion of males had a full time job (53.6% Vs. 41.7%) and a higher proportion of females were full time homemaker (7.3% Vs. 1.7). The employment profile of the total sample was: 22.3% students, 47.7% full- time job, 10.9% part time job, 4.5 % full time homemaker, 2.2% unemployed, 8.5% retired, 0.2 not working because of disability, 3.7% other. The participants were enrolled during free access conferences about psychological topics of general interest. At the end of each conference, participants were requested to complete a battery of self-report measures. The questionnaires were counterbalanced in order to control the order effects. All individuals participated on a voluntary basis and gave their written consent before entering into the study.

Clinical individuals were patients with either DSM-IV diagnosed obsessive-compulsive disorder or generalized anxiety disorder as their most severe problem (anxious group, AG) and patients with DSM-IV major depressive disorder as their most severe problem (depressed group, DG). Anxious and depressed individuals were all outpatients recruited from mental health clinics or private settings. To establish DSM-IV diagnoses all patients were interviewed by Ph.D. level psychologists experienced in diagnosing psychiatric disorders, using the Structured Clinical Interview for DSM-IV (First, Spitzer, Gibbon and Williams, 1996). Although inter-rater reliability for the main diagnosis was not examined formally, each case was audio-recorded and carefully reviewed in supervisory meetings and all diagnoses were reached by inter-rater consensus.

After being assessed, suitable patients were invited to participate in the study. Non-suitable patients were those with a current or past psychotic disorder, dementia, mental retardation or a current substance use disorder. Eligible participants were requested to complete a battery of self-report measures. Administrations of measures were undertaken individually and the sequence of measures was rotated in order to control for order effects. All individuals participated on a voluntary basis and gave their written consent before entering into the study. The final sample consisted of 64 anxious patients and 58 depressed patients. Table 1 provides descriptive statistics on various demographic variables for the two clinical groups as well as for a third group of 69 individuals, randomly selected from the sample of 831 subjects belonging to community (Community Controls, CC), for comparative purposes.

Table 1. Demographic data of the three groups

	AG (64)	DG (58)	CC (69)	Chi^2 or F probability	Significant SNK Post-hoc comparison (p<.05)
Age	34.5 (9.6)	35.3 (10.7)	35.7 (15.8)	NS	-
Years of education	13.8 (3.4)	11.5 (3.2)	13.2 (2.4)	.001	DG<AG, CC
% of females	51.9	51.7	49.3	NS	-
% of married/ cohabitant	41.6	30	44.9	NS	-
% of employed	59	52	63	NS	-
% of unemployed	6.3	9	3	NS	-
BDI	19.2 (9.2)	27.8 (12)	5.5 (6.3)	.001	DG>AG>CC

Notes: NS= non significant; standard deviations in brackets; SNK= Student Newman Keuls;
AG= Anxious group; DG= Depressed group; CC= Commmunity controls; BDI= Beck Depression Inventory

The three groups were equivalent with respect to demographic variables with the exception of education that was slightly lower in the DG. This difference was not considered a problem since in a previous study by our group, the BAI scores showed to be insensitive to education (Coradeschi, Sica, Ghisi, Sanavio, Dorz, Novara and Chiri, in press). Noteworthy, the three groups differed in a theoretical meaningful way on the Beck Depression Inventory (BDI; Beck and Steer, 1987) scores, in that the DG had significant higher scores than the other two groups and the AG had significant higher scores than CC.

Measures

Translation of the BAI

Standard steps outlined in the psychology literature guided the translation process used in this study. (e.g., Brislin, 1986). In the first step, three independent researchers translated the questionnaire from English to Italian and then reached agreement on a common version. Idiomatic Italian at the sixth-grade level was used for this step. Moreover, the researchers reviewed the common version to ensure there were no colloquialisms, slang, or esoteric phrases that would make interpretations difficult. The shared form was then back-translated by a bilingual person with an extensive knowledge in psychological research. The back-translation proved to be nearly identical to the original one. As a final step, the BAI items of the Italian version were rated by 5 experts in anxiety disorders. Each expert rated the items on a 5-point scale (1=not at all, 5= extremely) for clarity (the extent to which the item is clearly described).The ratings from the experts indicated the strength of the clarity (mean across all items=4.4; DS=0.4) . This last step showed that further item refinement was unnecessary.

Other Measures of Psychopathology

All participants completed a background information questionnaire and the following measures:

The *Penn State Worry Questionnaire* (PSWQ; Meyer, Miller, Metzger, and Borkovec, 1990) is a 16-item inventory designed to assess trait worry and to capture the generality, excessiveness, and uncontrollability characteristics of pathological worry. Each item is rated on 1 (no at all typical of me) to 5 (very typical of me) Likert-type scale. The internal consistency of the Italian version of the PSWQ (Morani, Pricci and Sanavio, 1999) was good (Cronbach's alpha = .85). Other studies reported a 2-10 week retest reliability ranging from .74 to .93 (see Meyer et al., 1990). In the present study, the alpha coefficient for the PSWQ Total was .88.

Obsessive Compulsive Inventory (*OCI*; Foa, Kozak, Salkovskis, Coles, and Amir, 1998) is a 42-item self-report in which patient rate separately the frequency and the distress of particular obsessions and compulsions. The instrument generates a total score and scores for seven separate subscales. The Italian version of the OCI showed good psychometric properties (Sica, in preparation). In the present study only the distress total score was utilized and the alpha estimate was .92.

Social Interaction Anxiety Scale (*SIAS*; Mattick and Clarke, 1998) is a widely used measure to assess fears of social interaction. It contains 19 items describing cognitive, affective, and behavioral reactions to interactional situations. The Italian version of the SIAS proved very reliable and stable measure; convergent validity was confirmed by the significant associations with measures of assertive behaviour and psychopathology (Sica, Musoni, Bisi, Lolli, Sighinolfi, in press). In the present study only a subsample of 432 individuals completed the SIAS and the alpha estimate was .87.

Beck Depression Inventory (*BDI*; Beck and Steer, 1987) is a widely used 21-item self-report inventory that measures the presence and severity of affective, cognitive, motivational, psychomotor, and vegetative manifestations of depression. The Italian version of the BDI was administered to about 900 Italian adults (Centomo and Sanavio, 1992). The findings indicated a good internal consistency (Cronbach's alpha=.82) and a 30-days retest reliability of .74. In the present study the alpha estimate for the BDI was .86.

Results

Internal Consistency

The internal consistency was .87 (Cronbach's alpha) and the corrected item-total correlations typically ranged from .31 to .61 (Table 2).

BAI Scores and Association with Gender, Age and Education

The average BAI score in our sample was 7.6 (SD=7.2), consistent with a minimal level of anxiety. The BAI total score did not correlate significantly with age (r=.05) and education (r=-.08).

Table 2. Means, standard deviations, percentages symptomatic, and corrected item-total correlations of the BAI administered to 831 Italian individuals from community

Item	M	SD	%	r_{tot}
Item 1	.31	.62	24.2	.31
Item 2	.42	.73	29	.40
Item 3	.25	.56	20.2	.37
Item 4	.78	.86	54.2	.57
Item 5	.54	.83	36.2	.55
Item 6	.24	.57	18.5	.42
Item	M	SD	%	r_{tot}
Item 7	.55	.79	39.4	.60
Item 8	.15	.45	12.3	.43
Item 9	.17	.51	12.2	.50
Item 10	.94	.86	65	.62
Item 11	.18	.54	12.4	.45
Item 12	.20	.51	17	.46
Item 13	.45	.73	33.7	.61
Item 14	.28	.61	21.9	.42
Item 15	.21	.54	16.5	.48
Item 16	.20	.55	14.6	.38
Item 17	.33	.61	26.6	.53
Item 18	.58	.81	42.2	.34
Item 19	.12	.44	9.5	.39
Item 20	.35	.67	26.2	.36
Item 21	.39	.70	28.9	.46

Notes: %= total percentage endorsing response choices 1, 2, or 3; r_{tot}= Corrected item-total correlations.

A one way ANOVA was performed to compare the BAI score by gender. Results showed that significant differences between male and females were observed ($F_{(1, 816)}$=8.6, p<.003). The mean BAI score was higher for the females (M=8.4; SD=7.7) compared to the males (M=6.9; SD=6.7). The differences on the BAI total score across gender were similar to that reported by Beck and Steer (1993, p.5) who found that women with anxiety disorders had higher scores than men with anxiety disorders.

To further evaluate the magnitude of differences across gender eta squared value (η^2) was computed. According to Cohen (1977), η^2=0.1 corresponds to a small effect size, η^2=0.6 to a medium effect and η^2=1.4 to a large effect size. The η^2 value (.01) suggested that the magnitude of the differences across gender was rather low. This finding is corroborated by other studies which found none or small differences across gender on the BAI total score when used to adults (Hewitt et al., 1993; Gillis, Haaga and Ford, 1995; Wetherell et al., 1997).

Validity

Concurrent validity was ascertained by correlating the BAI with a series of anxiety-related measures (Table 3). There was a significant positive correlation between BAI and PSWQ, OCI and SIAS. Correlations with all these measures remained significant (although lower) after controlling for depression (Table 3). Overall, the BAI showed a pattern of specific association with anxiety-related measures.

Table 3. Zero-order and partial correlations between the BAI and other anxiety-related constructs

Measures	Zero-order	Partial r*
PSWQ	.50	.33
OCI	.50	.15
SIAS	.33	.20

*controlling for depression as measured by the Beck Depression Inventory
Notes: all correlations are significant at critical alpha of .01.

We also examined by means of zero-order correlation between the BAI and the BDI. The BAI correlated significantly with BDI (r=.59, p<.001) confirming the overlap between measures of anxiety and measures of depression (Creamer *et al.*, 1995; Dent and Salkovskis, 1986; Gotlib and Cane, 1989). Since it has been hypothesized that worry is an important mediator in the association between anxiety and depression (Borkovec, Ray and Stöber, 1998), we also computed the correlation between BAI and BDI controlling for the worry effect (as measured by PSWQ). In fact, the association between BAI and BDI dropped from .59 to .43.

Factors Structure of the BAI

A Confirmatory Factor Analysis (CFA) was performed for four model of BAI factorial structure. The first model was composed by four factors (Neurophysiologic, Subjective, Panic and Autonomic), proposed by Beck *et al.* (1988) and Beck and Steer (1991); the second model is composed by four factors (Cognitive, Autonomic, Neuromotor and Panic), proposed by several authors such as Enns, Cox, Parker and Guertin (1998), Osman *et al.* (1997), Osman *et al.* (2002) and Wetherell and Areán (1997). The third model is composed by two factors (Cognitive and Somatic), proposed by Creamer *et al.* (1995), Hewitt and Norton (1993), and Steer, Rissmiller, Ranieri and Beck (1993). The fourth model is a unifactor solution, proposed by Osman and colleagues (1997; 2002) and by Wetherell and colleagues (1997).

The comparison was done using a maximum likelihood CFA and the goodness of fit was evaluated by the following criteria recommended by Cole (1987): Goodness of Fit (GFI) ≥ .85; Adjusted Goodness of Fit (AGFI) ≥ .80, Root Mean Square Error of Approximation (RMSEA) ≤ 0.10. We also evaluated the Normed Fit Index (NFI), Comparative Fit Index (CFI), Incremental Fit Index (IFI) and a Chi-square (χ^2) to degree of freedom ratio of less than 3.00 (Kline, 1998). To compare the fitness of the four models Akaike's Information

Criterion (AIC) (Akaike, 1987) was used. The model that yields the smallest value of AIC is considered the best (Kojima et al., 2002). The CFA was performed with LISREL 8.54 (Jöreskog, and Sörbom, 2003). Approximately all the models met the criteria for adequacy of fit, with the exception of the Chi-square (χ^2) to degree of freedom ratio (perhaps due to the large size of the sample or the non normal distribution of the scores). The AIC for the model 1 was slightly lower than other three models, indicating the best fit for the Italian community sample (Kojima et al., 2002; Table 4). This final model along with standardized parameter estimates is presented in Figure 1.

Table 4. Summary of the fit statistics for the different factor structures of the BAI

	GFI	AGFI	RMSEA	NFI	CFI	IFI	χ^2/df	AIC
BAI model 1 (4 factors)	0.87	0.83	0.086	0.90	0.91	0.91	6.59	1389.80
BAI model 2 (4 factors)	0.87	0.83	0.087	0.90	0.91	0.91	6.55	1402.00
BAI model 3 (2 factors)	0.87	0.84	0.086	0.90	0.91	0.91	6.53	1401.40
BAI model 4 (unifactor)	0.83	0.79	0.10	0.87	0.89	0.89	7.96	1842.79

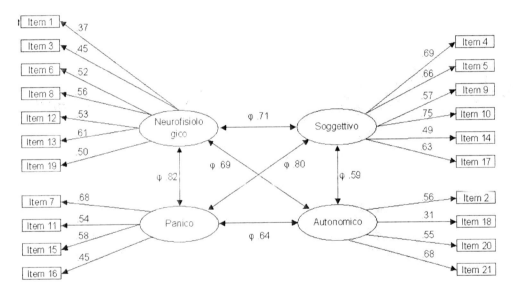

Figure 1. The four-factor model of the BAI with standardized parameter estimates.

Since the BAI was designed to measure a single construct, anxiety, that may comprise several latent factors, we hypothesized that a second-order model might also describe well the data. Actually, the substantial correlation among the four factors warranted the examination of a second-order solution. Toward this aim, a second-order principal axes factor analysis was performed using the four factors totals as raw data. The unrotated matrix yielded one factor with eigenvalues greater than 1.0, explaining 63.7% of total variance. All the primary factors loaded significantly on the single second-order factor (subjective symptoms=.76; panic symptoms=.75; neurophysiological symptoms=.75; autonomic symptoms = .61) providing support for a unidimensional measure of anxiety severity.

Discriminative Power

For clinical and research application may be of interest using the BAI also as a diagnostic tool. To ascertain the discriminative power of the BAI, ROC curves (Receiver Operating Characteristic method; Metz, 1978; Swets, 1996) were computed. The ROC analysis uses the association between sensitivity and specificity to derive an area under the curve which indicates how well overall a measure distinguishes between case positive (i.e., anxious individuals) and case negative (i.e., controls or depressed individuals) in a given sample, irrespective of the base rate. A value of .50 of the area under the curve indicates chance level and 1.0 indicates a perfect diagnostic tool.

The nonparametrically computed areas under the curve were indeed large: .95 when comparing anxious from normal individuals, and .63 when discriminating anxious from depressed patients. Overall, these results indicate excellent discriminative power of the BAI for distinguishing anxious from controls and a fair power for distinguishing anxious individuals from patients with depression.

Conclusion

The Italian version of the BAI showed very good psychometric properties when applied to Italian individuals. Alpha coefficient (.87) was comparable to that reported by Beck and Steer (1993) in the original version. Sex differences were found on the BAI total score. However, the evaluation of the magnitude of the effect sizes suggested that such differences had a low clinical significance. This finding is corroborated by other studies which found none to small differences across gender on the BAI total score when applied to adults (Hewitt *et al.*, 1993; Gillis *et al.*, 1995; Wetherell *et al.*, 1997). Therefore, our study provided further evidence that the nature of the anxiety as measured by the BAI does not appear to differ between men and women. Furthermore, the BAI scores resulted insensitive to age and education: overall, demographic characteristics seem not to affect the scores of the Italian version of the BAI.

The correlations of the BAI with other measures of anxiety revealed good concurrent validity. The correlation among the BAI and the Obsessive Compulsive Inventory confirmed the association between anxiety and obsessive-compulsive symptoms (e.g. Dent and Salkovskis,1986). Also, the significant association among the BAI and the Penn State Worry Questionnaire was in accordance with those studies showing an overlap between the construct of anxiety and worry (i.e., Andrews and Borkovec, 1988; Stöber, and Joormann, 2001).

The correlation between the BAI and the BDI (r=.59) was comparable to that reported by Beck et al. (1988) on a clinical sample (r= 0.48) and somewhat lower to that found by Dent and Salkovskis, (1986) on a British college sample (r= .61). Overall, such results confirm the presence of a partial overlap between measures of anxiety and depression which often coexist, especially in clinical individuals, (Enns *et al.*, 1998; Osman *et al.*, 2002). The overlap between anxiety and depression may be partially explained by the presence of a mediator variable like worry. Actually, when we considered the association between BAI and BDI without worry (as measured by the PSWQ), the overlap of anxiety and depression was reduced. Borkovec and colleagues (1998, p.569) contended that "...the content of worry may alternate between thoughts of future feared events (and thus generate anxiety) and thoughts of past negative events (and thus create depression)". Furthermore, the experimental induction of worry in normal subjects caused both anxious and depressive responses (Andrews and Borkovec, 1988).

On the other hand, our study showed that the correlations between the BAI and the other anxiety-related constructs remained significant even when the effect of depressive symptomatology was controlled. That is, the BAI proved to be specifically related to anxiety symptomatology. This is consistent with other studies which found the BAI and self-report measures of depression may assess distinct phenomena (Enns *et al.*, 1998; Hewitt *et al.*, 1993; Osman *et al.*, 2002; Wetherell *et al.*, 1997).

Concerning the BAI factorial structure, a four factor solution proved to be the most adequate our sample: the four factors extracted referred to neurophysiological symptoms (e.g. wobbliness in legs and faint), subjective anxiety (e.g., scared and terrified), panic (e.g., fear of dying and difficulty breathing) and autonomic aspects of anxiety (e.g., face flushed and feeling hot). In this study, data were also offered in support of an unidimensional structure of the BAI. This last result is consistent with both recent investigations carried out through Confirmatory Factor Analysis (Osman *et al.*, 1997; Osman *et al.*, 2002; Wetherell *et al.*, 1997) and with Beck and colleagues (1988) theoretical conceptualization and interpretation.

Lastly, the validity of the BAI was further confirmed from the ROC analysis: the BAI showed a very good power in discriminating between anxious individuals and controls and a fair ability in discriminating between anxious and depressive patients.

STUDY 2: PSYCHOMETRIC PROPERTIES OF THE ITALIAN VERSION OF THE BECK DEPRESSION INVENTORY-II

The BDI-II (BDI-II; Beck, Steer, and Brown, 1996) is the revised form of Beck depression Inventory Amended (BDI-IA; Beck and Steer, 1993); it was developed for the assessment of symptoms corresponding to criteria for diagnosing depressive disorders listed in the American Psychiatric Association's *Diagnostic and Statistical Manual of Mental Disorders*, 4th Edition (DSM-IV, American Psychiatric Association 1994). Furthermore the BDI-II was developed to provide a better discrimination between depression and anxiety.

Compared to the BDI-IA, in the BDI-II four items (Weight loss, Body image change, Work difficulty, and Somatic preoccupation symptoms) were dropped and replaced by Agitation, Concentration difficulty, Worthlessness, and Loss of energy. Other two items were changed to allow for increases as well as decreases in appetite and sleep. Also, many of the statements used in rating the symptoms were reworded. Lastly, the time frame for the BDI-II ratings was extended to two weeks to be consistent with the DSM-IV criteria for Major Depressive Disorder. In sum, the BDI-II constitutes a substantial revision of the original BDI.

The BDI-II consists of 21 items that measure the severity of depressive symptoms. Each BDI-II item is rated on a 4-point scale ranging from 0 to 3. The total score is calculated simply by summing the single item score, and it ranges from 0 to 63. The instructions ask the respondent to endorse, for each item, the most characteristic statement, covering the time frame of "the past two weeks, including today". In general, the BDI-II requires between 5 and 10 minutes to complete. Beck and colleagues (1996) stated that the BDI-II should not be sensitive to memory and response set.

The BDI-II has been used with college students, showing good psychometric properties (Al-Musawi, 2001; Beck et al.,1996; Dozois, Dobson and Ahnberg,1998; Storch, Roberti, and Roth, 2004; Whisman, Perez and Ramel, 2000). In these studies the internal consistency (Cronbach's alpha) was typically around .90 and ranged from .84 to .93 (Al-Musawi, 2001; Beck et al., 1996; Dozois et al., 1998; Osman, Downs, Barrios, Kopper, Gutierrez and Chiros, 1997; Storch et al., 2004; Whisman et al., 2000). The one and two week test-retest correlation coefficients were also good (respectively .74 and .75; Leigh and Anthony-Tolbert, 2001; Al-Masawi, 2001).

As far as convergent validity is concerned, the BDI-II has shown a good correlation value (r=.77) with the subscale Depression of the Depression Anxiety Stress Scale (Lovibond and Lovibond, 1993), and with two subscale of the Mood and Anxiety Symptom Questionnaire (MASQ; Watson, Clark, Weber, Assenheimer, Strauss and McCormick, 1995): r=.71 with MASQ Nonspecific Depression, and r=.70 with MASQ Anhedonic Depression (Osman et al., 1997).

In general, when administered to college students, the BDI-II seem correlate more with depressive measures than anxiety ones (Al-Musawi, 2001; Storch et al., 2004).

In reference to criterion-validity, Sprinkle, Lurie, Insko, Atkinson, Jones, Logan and Bissada, (2002) have found that the BDI-II discriminated between students with or without a depressed mood diagnosis as determined by Structured Clinical Interview for DSM-IV Axis I Disorders (First et al., 1996).

Regarding the factorial structure of the BDI-II, in samples of college students both two (Beck et al.,1996) and three (Al-Musawi, 2001) factor solutions were found in exploratory factor analytic studies. The two dimension model (Cognitive-affective and Somatic) was confirmed by confirmatory analysis (Dozois et al., 1998; Storch et al., 2004; Whisman et al., 2000;). Moreover, a three factor solution was confirmed both by Osman et al., (1997; Negative attitude, Performance difficulty and Somatic factors) and by Al-Musawi, (2001; Cognitive-affective, Overt emotional upset, Somatic-vegetative factors).

Aim of the present study was to provide with initial data to evaluate the psychometric properties of the BDI-II for the Italian individuals. Therefore, we examined the internal consistency, the gender differences, the concurrent and discriminant validity, and the factorial structure of the BDI-II in a sample of 723 college students. In addition, the discriminant power of the BDI-II was investigated by contrasting clinical individuals and college students with ROC curves (Receiver Operating Characteristic method; Metz, 1978; Swets, 1996).

Participants and Procedure

Seven-hundred and twenty-three undergraduates (343 male and 380 female) attending various psychology and engineering classes at the University of Padova (North Italy) completed a battery of self-report measures which included the BDI-II and questions about background information. Males (mean age=21.7 years; SD=1.6; range 19 to 31) were slightly older than females (mean age=20.98; SD=2.66; range 18 to 36; $F_{(1,720)}$ = 19.07; p<.0001). A percentage of 98.3% of participants was single. The questionnaires were counterbalanced to control the order effects. To ascertain the stability over time, a subsample of 60 students completed the BDI-II on two occasions one month apart.

Clinical individuals were patients with DSM-IV depressive disorders as their most severe problem (depressed group, DG). DG participants were excluded if they had a current or past psychotic disorder, dementia, mental retardation or a current substance use disorder. The depressed individuals were all outpatients recruited from mental health clinics. To establish DSM-IV diagnoses all patients were interviewed by Ph.D. level psychologists experienced in diagnosing psychiatric disorders, using the Structured Clinical Interview for DSM-IV (First, et al.,1996). Although inter-rater reliability for the main diagnosis was not examined formally, each case was audio-recorded and carefully reviewed in supervisory meetings and all diagnoses were reached by inter-rater consensus. After being assessed, suitable patients were invited to participate in the study. The final sample consisted of 72 depressed individuals. The main demographic and clinical characteristics of the 72 patients are shown in Table 5.

Table 5. Demographic and clinical characteristics of the 72 patients with depressive disorders

	Depressed Patients (72)
Age	41 (12.5)
Years of education	9.7 (3.4)
% of females	74
% of married/ cohabitant	48
% of singles	42
% of separated/divorced	6
% of employed	67
Type of disorder and %	Major Depressive Episode= 30
	Bipolar II Disorder= 20
	Major Depressive Disorder= 17
	Dystimic Disorder= 14
	Mood Disorder NOS=19
% of first appearance of disorder	More than five years ago = 44
	Between five and two years ago =11
	Less than two years ago = 45
% of patients with previous hospitalization	26
% of patients with a general medical condition	18.1

The scores on the BDI-II of the DG was compared to the scores of 72 individuals randomly selected from the sample of the 723 college students. The main demographic features of such group were: 74% of females, mean age=21.1 (DS=2.1), mean years of education=13.9 (DS=1.4) and 98% singles.

College students completed the questionnaires in small groups whereas in the case of clinical individuals administrations of measures were undertaken individually. All individuals participated on a voluntary basis and gave their written consent before entering into the study.

Measures

Translation of the BDI-II

Standard steps outlined in the psychology literature guided the translation process used in this study (e.g., Brislin, 1986). In the first step, three independent researchers translated the questionnaire from English to Italian and then reached agreement on a common version. Idiomatic Italian at the sixth-grade level was used for this step. Moreover, the researchers reviewed the common version to ensure there were no colloquialisms, slang, or esoteric phrases that would make interpretations difficult.

The shared form was then back-translated by a bilingual person with an extensive knowledge in psychological research. Comparison between back-translation and original version of the BDI-II revealed discrepancies for five items: (4) Loss of pleasure, (5) Guilty feelings, (7) Self-dislike, (13) Indecisiveness, (19) Concentration. In order to understand the sources of these differences, the original items and the corresponding back-translated ones were evaluated independently by three American scholars with a specific expertise in depressive disorders and test construction. The three experts all pointed out two basic problems in the back-translated items: a) they conveyed a less strong meaning compared to the original counterparts or b) they sounded more emotional. To illustrate, the back-translation of rating 2 of the item 13 (Indecisiveness) was "I have more difficulties in making decisions than usual" while the original formulation was "I have much greater difficulty in making decisions than I used to". An example of the second problem is the following: the back-translation of rating 1 of the item 7 (Self-dislike) was: "I've lost the faith in myself" whereas the formulation of the original counterpart was "I have lost confidence in myself".

Following the suggestions of the three experts, the five items were then reformulated and back-translated again. This time, the back translation proved to be nearly identical to the original one.

As a final step, the BDI-II items of the Italian version were rated by 5 experts in depressive disorders. Each expert rated the items on a 5-point scale (1=not at all, 5= extremely) for clarity (the extent to which the item is clearly described).The ratings from the experts indicated the strength of the clarity (mean across all items=4.2; SD=0.6). This last step showed that further item refinement was unnecessary.

Other Measures of Psychopathology

The *State-Trait Anxiety Inventory- form* Y (STAI-Y, Spielberger, Gorush, Lushene, Vagg and Jacobs, 1983; Italian version by Pedrabissi and Santinello, 1989) a structured self-report consisting of 20 descriptive statements assessing the anxiety as personality feature on the scale of frequency 1-4 (1=almost never, 2=sometimes, 3=often, 4=almost always). The one-month test-retest correlation coefficients ranged from .65 to .86. The concurrent validity was assessed with other measures of trait-anxiety and the correlations ranged from .52 to .80 (Spielberger *et al.*, 1983). In our sample the internal consistency was .89 (Cronbach's alpha).

The *Depression Questionnaire* (DQ; Bertolotti, Michielin, Sanavio, Vidotto and Zotti, 1997) is a 24 item self-report measure of depressive symptoms developed in Italy. Each item provides a statement (e.g., I often feel like crying), and respondents are requested to indicate in a yes/no format whether the statement correctly describes the way they feel "right now". Twenty-two the items represent the presence of a specific depressive symptom. The remaining 2 items are structured to allow the respondent to deny the presence of a depressive symptom, so that the answer "no" represents higher symptomatology. An estimate of the internal consistency of the DQ yielded a Cronbach's alpha of .86. Test-retest correlations were .88 with a 7-day laps between administrations and .72 with a 30-day lapse. Validity studies showed that the DQ discriminates between depressed patients and individuals without psychological problems (Bertolotti et al., 1997). In the present study, the alpha coefficient for the DQ was .77.

Results

Internal Consistency and Temporal Stability of the BDI-II

In the students sample the internal consistency was .80 (Cronbach's alpha) and the corrected item-total correlations typically ranged from .30 to .46 with the exceptions of item 9 (suicidal thoughts), item 14 (worthlessness) item 18 (changes in appetite) and item 21 (loss of interest in sex; see Table 6). The one-month test-retest correlation was good (r=.76).

Table 6. Means, standard deviations, percentages symptomatic, and corrected item-total correlations of the BDI-II administered to 723 Italian undergraduates

Item	M	SD	%	r_{tot}
Item 1	.25	.51	22.1	.39
Item 2	.29	.50	26.3	.40
Item 3	.18	.44	16.6	.31
Item 4	.34	.60	27.5	.37
Item 5	.40	.59	35.1	.34
Itcm 6	.26	69	15.5	.31
Item 7	.24	.50	21.2	.36
Item 8	.53	.69	43.8	.36
Item 9	.13	.41	11.2	.24
Item 10	.30	.73	19.2	.30
Item 11	.52	.62	46.7	.34
Item 12	.30	.58	24.9	.43
Item 13	.33	.59	19.8	.46
Item 14	.11	.39	8.3	.27
Item 15	.57	.60	51.6	.46
Item 16	.92	.76	70	.36
Item 17	.49	.68	40.5	.42
Item 18	.74	.81	57	.25
Item 19	.66	.71	52.8	.45
Item 20	.52	.59	47.3	.44
Item 21	.16	.49	11.8	.24

Notes: %= total percentage endorsing response choices 1, 2, or 3;
r_{tot}= Corrected item-total correlations.

BDI-II Scores and Association with Gender and Age

The average BDI-II score in our sample was 8.23 (SD=5.6), consistent with minimal depression according Beck *et al.,* (1996) criteria. The scores on the BDI-II total did not correlate significantly with age (r=-.03). Since epidemiological studies have found that women are most subjected to have depressive disorders than men (e.g., The ESEMeD/MHEDEA 2000 Investigators, 2004), we compared the BDI-II total score by gender.

Results from a covariance analysis, using age as covariate, showed that females reported higher depression scores (M=9.5; SD=5.5) compared to males (M=6.9; SD=5.4; $F_{(3, 714)}$=41.272; p<.0001). Interaction gender x age was also significant, meaning that the gender differences were circumscribed to specific age categories.

To further evaluate the magnitude of differences across gender, eta squared value (η^2) was computed. According to Cohen (1977), η^2=0.1 corresponds to a small effect size, η^2=0.6 to a medium effect and η^2=1.4 to a large effect size. The η^2 value (.006) suggested that the magnitude of the differences between sexes was rather low. This finding is corroborated by other studies which found none or small differences across gender and age on the BDI-II total score when applied to students (Beck *et al.,*1996; Dozois, *et al.*,1998; O'Hara, Sprinkle, and Ricci, 1998; Osman *et al.*, 1997).

Validity

Convergent validity was ascertained by correlating the BDI-II with a depressive-related measure. There was a significant positive correlation between BDI-II and DQ, with a value of .77 (p<.0001), that remained significant - even though lower in value - after controlling for STAI score (partial r =.59; p<.0001). This last evidence demonstrates that BDI-II is specifically associated with a depressive-related measure.

Discriminant validity was examined by means of zero-order correlation between the BDI-II and the STAI. The BDI-II correlated significantly with STAI (r=.66, p<.0001) confirming the overlap between measures of anxiety and measures of depression (Creamer *et al.,* 1995; Dent and Salkovskis, 1986; Gotlib and Cane, 1989).

Factors Structure of the BDI-II

We performed a Confirmatory Factor Analysis (CFA) for five models of BDI-II factor structure. The first model is composed by two factors and 19 items (Cognitive-Affective and Somatic), proposed by Beck *et al.*, (1996). The second model is composed by two factors and 19 items (Cognitive-Affective and Somatic), proposed by Dozois *et al.*, (1998). The third model is composed by two factors and 21 items (Cognitive-Affective and Somatic), proposed by Whisman *et al.,* (2000) and by Storch et al., (2004). The fourth model is composed by three factors and 21 items (Negative attitude, Performance difficulty and Somatic element), proposed by Osman *et al.*, (1997). The fifth and last model is a unifactorial solution.

For the comparison we employed a maximum likelihood CFA for each model and the goodness of fit was evaluated by the following criteria recommended by Cole (1987): Goodness of Fit (GFI) ≥ .85; Adjusted Goodness of Fit (AGFI) ≥ .80, Root Mean Square Error of Approximation (RMSEA) ≤ 0.10. We also evaluated the Normed Fit Index (NFI), Comparative Fit Index (CFI), Incremental Fit Index (IFI) and a Chi-square (χ^2) to degree of freedom ratio of less than 3.00 (Kline, 1998). To compare the fitness of the four models Akaike's Information Criterion (AIC) (Akaike, 1987) was used. The model that yields the smallest value of AIC is considered the best (Kojima *et al.*, 2002).The CFA was performed with LISREL 8.54 (Jöreskog and Sörbom, 2003).

Although the indices for the five models met the criteria for adequacy of fit and were similar each other, the AIC for the model 1, proposed by Beck *et al.*,(1996), was slightly lower than other four models (Table 7), indicating the best fit to the Italian student sample. This final model with standardized parameter estimates is presented in Figure 2.

Table 7. Comparison between the different models for factor structure of the BDI-II in the students sample

	GFI	AGFI	RMSEA	NFI	CFI	IFI	χ^2/df	AIC
BDI-II model 1 (2 factors)	0.93	0.92	0.055	0.88	0.92	0.92	3.08	556.99
BDI II model 2 (2 factors)	0.93	0.92	0.056	0.87	0.91	0.91	3.18	569.94
BDI II model 3 (2 factors)	0.93	0.91	0.054	0.88	0.92	0.92	2.96	667.97
BDI II model 4 (3 factors)	0.93	0.93	0.052	0.89	0.92	0.92	2.88	636.59
BDI II model 5 unifactor	0.92	0.90	0.065	0.86	0.89	0.89	3.74	691.13

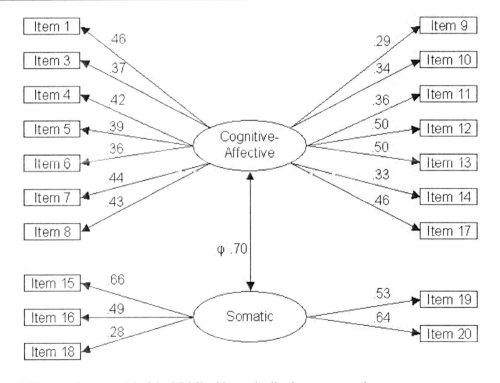

Figure 2. The two-factor model of the BDI-II with standardized parameter estimates.

Since the BDI-II was designed to measure a single construct, depression, that may comprise several latent factors, we hypothesized that a second-order model might also describe well the data. Actually, the substantial correlation among the two factors warranted the examination of a second-order solution. Toward this aim, a second-order principal axes factor analysis was performed using the two factors totals as raw data. The unrotated matrix yielded one factor with eigenvalues greater than 1.0, explaining 56% of total variance. All the two primary factors loaded significantly on the single second-order factor (Cognitive-Affective=.74 and Somatic=.74) providing support for a unidimensional measure of depression severity.

Discriminative Power

For clinical and research application may be of interest using the BDI-II also as a diagnostic tool. The use of BDI-II as a diagnostic tool requires to ascertain its discriminative power.

To ascertain the discriminative power of the BDI-II, ROC curves (Receiver Operating Characteristic method; Metz, 1978; Swets, 1996) were computed. The ROC analysis uses the association between sensitivity and specificity to derive an area under the curve which indicates how well overall a measure distinguishes between case positive (i.e., depressed individuals) and case negative (i.e., college students) in a given sample irrespective of the base rate. A value of .50 of the area under the curve indicates chance level and 1.0 indicates a perfect diagnostic tool.

The nonparametrically computed area under the curve was indeed large: .88 when discriminating depressed from college students. Overall, these results indicate excellent discriminative power of the BDI-II for distinguishing patients with depression from controls.

Conclusion

The BDI-II was translated in such a way to adhere as close as possible to the established guidelines provided in cross-cultural literature. Moreover, the contribution of three independent American scholars well-grounded in depressive disorders and test construction was particularly useful in refining the questionnaire. Lastly, ratings from five Italian experts in depressive disorders showed that items of the Italian version of the BDI-II were clearly formulated.

In fact, the Italian version of the BDI-II showed good psychometric properties. The internal consistency was .80 (Cronbach's alpha), comparable to that found by Al-Musawi, (2001), Beck et al.,(1996), Dozois et al., (1998), Osman et al., (1997), Storch et al., (2004), and Whisman et al., (2000).

Gender differences were found on the BDI-II total score. However, the evaluation of the magnitude of the effect sizes suggested that such differences had a low clinical significance. This finding is corroborated by other studies which found none to a small differences across gender on the BDI-II total score when applied to college samples (Dozois et al.,1998; O'Hara et al.,1998). Therefore, our study provided further evidence that the nature of the depression as measured by the BDI-II does not appear to differ significantly between male and female college students.

The positive correlations of the BDI-II with another measure of depression (DQ) revealed good concurrent validity (r=.77). The correlation between the BDI-II and a measure of anxiety (STAI; r=.66) was comparable to that reported by Storch et al.,(2004) (r=.69) on a student sample. Overall, such results confirm the presence of a partial overlap between measures of depression and anxiety which often coexist (Enns, et al.,1998; Osman et al.,2002). However, it is important to note that the STAI has been criticized because it contains several references to depressive symptoms and commonly it correlates more with depressive measures than anxiety measures (Bieling, Antony and Swinson, 1998). That is, the correlation shown in this study between the BDI-II the STAI may be inflated due to the depressive content of several STAI items.

In any case, our study showed that the correlations between the BDI-II and the other depression-related construct remained significant even when the effect of anxious symptomatology was controlled. That is, the BDI-II proved to be specifically related to depression symptomatology. This is consistent with other studies which found that self-report measure of depression and self-report measures of anxiety may assess distinct phenomena (Enns *et al.*, 1998; Hewitt and Norton, 1993; Osman *et al.*, 2002; Wetherell and Areán, 1997).

Concerning the BDI-II factorial structure, we performed a maximum likelihood Confirmatory Factor Analysis (CFA). The best fit of the BDI-II to the Italian student sample resulted in the model composed of two factors and 19 items (Cognitive-Affective and Somatic), proposed by Beck *et al.*,(1996). All the indices met the criteria for adequacy of fit: GFI=0.93, AGFI=0.92, RMSEA=0.055, NFI=0.88, CFI=0.92, IFI=0.92, and the Chi-square (χ^2) to degree of freedom ratio (χ^2/df=3.08). The bifactorial structure of the BDI-II found in the present study is consistent with many investigations (Beck *et al.*,1996; Dozois *et al.*, 1998; Whisman *et al.*, 2000, Storch *et al.*, 2004).

In this study, data were also offered in support of an unidimensional structure of the BDI-II. This is not surprising at all, since Beck and colleagues' (1996) theoretical conceptualization and interpretation considered the BDI-II as a global measure of depressive symptomatology.

Lastly, the validity of the BDI-II was further confirmed from the ROC analysis: the BDI-II showed a very good power in discriminating between depressed individuals and controls.

GENERAL CONCLUSION

The BAI and BDI-II proved a reliable and valid measures of anxiety and depressive symptoms on Italian individuals. Discriminant power was established, confirming that the BAI and BDI-II are a useful instrument for differentiating people with and without psychopathology. Moreover, the results concerning the BAI were obtained on a sample which may be approximately considered as representative of the Italian population.

Some limitations of the two studies need to be noted. In the first study, we did not collect data about the test-retest reliability of the BAI. However, in a previous study on Italian individuals, Coradeschi *et al.*, (in press) had 179 college students (70% females) to complete the BAI on two occasions one week apart. In that case the test-retest correlation figure was adequate (r = .62) for a state-like measure.

In the case of the BDI-II, results were based on a sample restricted in age, educational leve land socio-economic status. However, similar results were obtained on normal samples with broader demographic characteristics (Ghisi, Flebus, Montano, Sanavio, & Sica, 2006).

For both studies self-report measures were mainly used in determining the psychometric properties of the Italian versions of the two questionnaires. In addition, further studies need to address the capability of the BAI and BDI-II to detect therapeutic changes when applied to Italian individuals.

Despite this shortcomings, the two studies presented here are the first to inquire into the psychometric properties of the BAI and BDI-II on Italian individuals. Such studies offer a strong evidence that the BAI and BDI-II can be used to evaluate in a reliable way anxiety and depressive symptoms in the Italian population.

REFERENCES

Al-Issa, I., Al-Zubaidi, A., Bakal, D., and Fung, T. S. (2000). Beck Anxiety symptoms in Arab college students. *Arabian Journal of Psychiatry, 11*, 41-47.

Al-Musawi, N. (2001). Psychometric properties of the Beck Depression Inventory-II with university students in Bahrain. *Journal of Personality Assessment, 77*, 568-579.

American Psychiatric Association. (1987*). Diagnostic and statistical manual of mental disorders (3rd ed.-rev.).* Washington DC: American Psychiatric Association.

American Psychiatric Association (1994) *Diagnostic and Statistical Manual of Mental Disorders*, 4th ed. Washington, DC: APA.

Akaike, H. (1987). Factor analysis and AIC. *Psychometrika, 52*, 317-332.

Andrews, V. H., and Borkovec, T. D. (1988). The differential effects of induction of worry, somatic anxiety and depression on emotional experience. *Journal of Behavior Therapy and Experimental Psychiatry, 19*, 21-26.

Beck, A. T., Epstein, N., Brown, G., and Steer, R. A. (1988). An inventory for measuring clinical anxiety: psychometric properties. *Journal of Consulting and Clinical Psychology, 56*, 893-897.

Beck, A. T., and Steer, R. A. (1987*). Manual for the revised Beck Depression Inventory.* San Antonio, TX: The Psychological Corporation Harcourt Brace and Company.

Beck, A. T., and Steer, R. A. (1991). Relationship between the beck Anxiety Inventory and the Hamilton Anxiety Rating Scale with anxious outpatients. *Journal of Anxiety Disorders, 5*, 213-223.

Beck, A. T., and Steer, R. A. (1993). *Beck Anxiety Inventory Manual.* San Antonio, TX: The Psychological Corporation Harcourt Brace and Company.

Beck, A. T., and Steer, R. A. (1993). *Manual for the Beck Depression Inventory.* San Antonio, TX: The Psychological Corporation.

Beck, A. T., Steer, R. A., Ball, R., and Ranieri, W. F. (1996). Comparison of Beck Depression Inventories -IA and –II in psychiatric outpatients. *Journal of Personality Assessment, 67*, 588-597.

Beck, A. T., Steer, R. A., and Brown G. K. (1996). *Beck Depression Inventory Second Edition Manual.* San Antonio, TX: The Psychological Corporation.

Beck, A. T., Ward, C. H., Mendelson, M., Mock, J. E., and Erbaugh, J. K. (1961). An inventory for measuring depression. *Archives of General Psychiatry, 4*, 561-571.

Bertolotti, G., Michielin, P., Sanavio, E., Vidotto, G., Zotti, A. M. (1997). *CBA - 2.0, Cognitive Behavioural Assessment 2.0 : Scale Primarie: Manuale.* Firenze : O.S., Organizzazioni Speciali.

Bieling, P. J., Antony, M. M. and Swinson, R. P. (1998). The State-Trait Anxiety Inventory, trait version: Structure and content re-examined. *Behaviour Research and Therapy, 36*, 777-788.

Borkovec T. D., Ray W. J., Stober J. (1998). Worry: a cognitive phenomenon intimately linked to affective, physiological, and interpersonal behavioral processes. *Cognitive Therapy and Research, 22,* 561-576.

Brislin, R. W. (1986). The wording and translation of research instruments. In W.J. Lonner and J.W. Berry (Eds.), Field methods in cross-cultural research. Beverly Hills, CA: Sage.

Centomo, C. and Sanavio, E. (1992). Padua Inventory e Beck Depression Inventoy: indagine su studenti di scuola media superiore. *Manuscript not published.*

Cohen, J. (1977). *Statistical power for the behavioral sciences.* New York: Academic Press.

Cole, D. A. (1987). Utility of confirmatory factor analysis in test validation research. *Journal of Consulting and Clinical Psychology*, 55, 584-594.

Coradeschi, D., Sica, C., Ghisi, M., Sanavio, E., Dorz, S., Novara C. and Chiri, L. (in press). Studi preliminari sulle proprietà psicometriche del Beck Anxiety Inventory. *Bollettino di Psicologia Applicata.*

Creamer, M., Foran, J., and Bell, R. (1995). The Beck Anxiety Inventory in a non-clinical sample. *Behaviour Research and Therapy, 33,* 477-485.

De Girolamo, G., Polidori, G., Morosini P. L., Mazzi, F., Serra, G., Scarpino, V., Reda, V., Visonà, G., Falsirollo, F., Rossi, A. (2005). Prevalenza dei disturbi mentali comuni in Italia, fattori di rischio, stato di salute ed uso di servizi sanitari: il progetto ESEMED-WMH. *Epidemiologia e Psichiatria Sociale*, 14, Supplemento al n. 4.

Dent, H. R., and Salkovskis, P. M. (1986). Clinical measures of depression, anxiety and obsessionality in nonclinical populations. *Behaviour Research and Therapy, 24,* 689-691.

De Vellis, R. F. (1991). *Scale development: Theory and applications.* Newbury Park, CA: Sage.

Dozois, J. A., Dobson, K. S., Ahnberg, J. L. (1998). A psychometric evaluation of the Beck Depression Inventory-II. *Psychological Assessment*, 10, 83-89.

Ebel, R. I. and Frisbie, D. A. (1991). *Essentials of educational measurement. (5th ed.).* Englewood Cliffs, NJ: Prentice-Hall.

Enns, M. W., Cox, B. J., Parker, J. D. A. and Guertin, J. E. (1998). Confirmatory factor analysis of the Beck Anxiety and Depression Inventories in patients with major depression. *Journal of Affective Disorders*, 47, 195-200.

The ESEMeD/MHEDEA 2000 Investigators (2004). Prevalence of mental disorders in Europe: results from the European Study of the Epidemiology of Mental Disorders (ESEMeD) project. *Acta Psychiatrica Scandinavica*, 109 (Suppl. 420), 21-27.

First, M. B., Spitzer, R. L., Gibbon, M. and Williams, J. B. W. (1996). *Structured Clinical Interview for* DSM-IV - Patient Edition (SCID-I/P). New York: Biometrics Research Department. New York State Psychiatric Institute.

Foa, E., Kozak, M. J., Salkovskis, P. M., Coles, M. E., and Amir, N. (1998). The validation of a new obsessive compulsive disorder scale: The Obsessive Compulsive Inventory. *Psychological Assessment*, 10, 206-214.

Freeston, M. H., Ladouceur, R., Thibodeau, and N., Gagnon F. (1994). L'inventaire d'anxiete de Beck. Proprietes psychometriques d'une traduction francaise./The Beck Anxiety Inventory: Psychometric properties of a French translation. *Encephale, 20*, 47-55.

Ghisi, M., Flebus, G. B., Montano, A., Sanavio, E. & Sica (2006). *Beck Depression Inventory-II. Manuale.* Firenze: Organizzazioni Speciali.

Gillis, M. M., Haaga, D. A., and Ford, G. T. (1995). Normative values for the Beck Anxiety Inventory, Fear Questionnaire, Penn State Worry Questionnaire, and Social Phobia and Anxiety Inventory. *Psychological Assessment, 7,* 450-455.

Gotlib, I. H., and Cane, D. B. (1989). Self-report assessment of depression and anxiety. In P. C. Kendall and Watson (Eds.). *Anxiety and depression: Distinctive and overlapping features* (pp. 131-169). New York: Academic Press.

Haynes, S. N., Richard, D. C. S. and Kubany, E. S. (1995). Content validity in psychological assessment: A functional approach to concepts and methods. *Psychological Assessment,* 7, 238-247.

Hewitt, P. L. and Norton, G. R. (1993). The Beck Anxiety Inventory: A psychometric analysis. *Psychological Assessment,* 5, 408-412.

Jolly, J. B., Aruffo, J. F., Wherry, J. N., and Livingstone, R. (1993). The utility of the Beck Anxiety Inventory with inpatient adolescents. *Journal of Anxiety Disorders, 7,* 95-106.

Jöreskog, K., and Sörbom, D. (2003). LISREL 8 (Version 8.54). Chicago: Scientific Software International.

Kabacoff, R. I., Segal, D. L., Hersen, M., and van-Hasselt, V. B. (1997). Psychometric properties and diagnostic utility of the Beck Anxiety Inventory and the State-Trait Anxiety Inventory with older adult psychiatric outpatients. *Journal of Anxiety Disorders, 11,* 33-47.

Kinzie, J. D., and Manson, S. M. (1987). The use of self-rating scales in cross-cultural psychiatry. *Hospital and Community Psychiatry,* 38, 190-196.

Kline, R. B. (1998). *Principles and practice of structural equation modeling.* New York: Guilford Press.

Kojima, M., Furukawa, T. A., Takahashi, H., Kawai, M., Nagaya, T., Tokudome, S. (2002). Cross-cultural validation of the beck depression Inventory-II in Japan. *Psychiatry Research,* 110, 291-299.

Leigh, I. W., Anthony-Tolbert. S. (2001). Reliability of the BDI-II with deaf persons. *Rehabilitation Psychology,* 46, 195-202.

Lovibond, S. H., and Lovibond, P. F. (1993). *Manual for the Depression Anxiety Stress Scales (DASS),* Psychology Foundation Monograph. New South Wales, Australia: University of New South Wales.

Margraf, J., and Ehlers, A. (1998). *Das Beck-Angstinventar (The Beck Anxiety Inventory).* Bern, Switzerland: Huber.

Mattick, R. P. and Clarke, J. C. (1998). Development and validation of measures of social phobia scrutiny fear and social interaction anxiety. *Behaviour Research and Therapy, 36,* 455-470.

Metz, C. E. (1978). Basic principles of ROC analysis. *Seminars in Nuclear Medicine,* 8, 283-298.

Meyer, T. J., Miller, M. L., Metzger, R. L., and Borkovec, T. D. (1990). Development and validation of the Penn State Worry Questionnaire. *Behaviour Research and Therapy,* 28, 487-495.

Morani, S., Pricci, D., and Sanavio, E. (1999). "Penn State Worry Questionnaire" and "Worry Domains Questionnaire": Italian versions and reliability. *Psicoterapia Cognitiva e Comportamentale, 5,* 195-209.

Novy, D. M., Stanley, M. A., Averill, P., and Daza, P. (2001). Psychometric comparability of English and Spanish-language measures of anxiety and related affective symptoms. *Psychological Assessment, 13,* 347-355.

O'Hara, M. M., Sprinkle, S. D., Ricci, N. A. (1998). Beck depression Inventory-II: college population study. *Psychological Reports,* 82, 1395-1401.

Osman, A., Barrios, F. X., Aukes, D., Osman, J. R., and Markway, K. (1993). The Beck Anxiety Inventory: Psychometric properties in a community population. *Journal of Psychopathology and Behavioral Assessment, 15,* 287-297.

Osman, A., Downs, W. R., Barrios, F. X., Kopper, B. A., Gutierrez, P. M., Chiros, C. E. (1997). Factor structure and psychometric characteristics of the Beck Depression Inventory-II. *Journal of Psychopathology and Behavioral Assessment,* 19, 359-376.

Osman, A., Hoffman, J. Barrios, F.X., Kopper, B.A., Breitenstein, J.L., and Hahn, S.K. (2002). Factor structure, reliability, and validity of the Beck Anxiety Inventory in adolescent psychiatric inpatients. *Journal of Clinical Psychology,* 58, 443-456.

Osman, A., Kopper, B. A., Barrios, F. X., Osman, J. R., and Wade, T. (1997). The Beck Anxiety Inventory: Reexamination of factor structure and psychometric properties. *Journal of Clinical Psychology, 53,* 7-14.

Pedrabissi, L., Santinello, M. (1989). Inventario per l'ansia di "Stato" e di "Tratto" dello STAI Forma Y: Manuale. Firenze: Organizzazioni Speciali.

Piotrowski, C. (1999). The status of Beck Anxiety Inventory in contemporary research. *Psychological Reports, 85,* 261-262.

Robles, R., Varela, R., Jurado, S., and Paez, F. (2001). Version Mexicana del Inventario de Ansiedad de Beck: Propriedades Psicometricas./The mexican version of the Beck Anxiety Inventory: Psychometric properties. *Revista Mexicana de Psicologia, 18,* 211-218.

Sica, C., Musoni, I., Bisi, B., Lolli, V., and Sighinolfi, C. (in press). Social Phobia Scale (SPS) e Social Interaction Anxiety Scale (SIAS): traduzione ed adattamento italiano. *Bollettino di Psicologia Applicata.*

Spielberger, C. D., Gorush, R. L., Lushene, R., Vagg, P. R., and Jacobs, G. A. (1983). *Manual for the State-Trait Anxiety Inventory STAI Form Y.* Palo Alto, CA: Consulting Psychologists Press.

Sprinkle, S. D, Lurie, D, Insko, S. L., Atkinson, G., Jones, G. L., Logan, A. L., Bissada, N. N. (2002). Criterion Validity, Severity Cut Scores, and Test-Retest Reliability of the Beck Depression Inventory-II in a University Counseling Center Sample. *Journal of Counseling Psychology,* 49, 381-385.

Steer, R. A., Rissmiller, D. J., Ranieri, W. F., and Beck, A. T. (1993). Structure of the computer-assisted Beck Anxiety Inventory with psychiatric inpatients. *Journal of Personality Assessment, 60,* 532-542.

Stöber, J., and Joormann, J. (2001). Worry, procrastination, and perfectionism: differentiating amount of worry, pathological worry, anxiety and depression. *Cognitive Therapy and Research, 25,* 49-60.

Storch, E. A., Roberti, J. W., Roth, D. A. (2004). Factorial structure, concurrent validity, and internal consistency of the Beck Depression Inventory-Second Edition in a sample of college students. *Depression and Anxiety,* 19, 187-189.

Swets, J. A. (1996). *Signal detection theory and ROC analysis in psychology and diagnostics: Collected papers,* Hillsdale, NJ, England: Lawrence Erlbaum Associates, Inc. xv.

Ulusoy, M., Sahin, H., and Erkmen, H. (1998). Turkish version of the Beck Anxiety Inventory: Psychometric properties. *Journal of Cognitive Psychotherapy, 12,* 153-162.

Watson, D., Clark, L. A., Weber, K., Assenheimer, J. S., Strauss, M. E., and McCormick, R. A. (1995). Testing a tripartite model. IL Exploring the symptom structure of anxiety and depression in student, adult, and patient samples. *Journal of Abnormal Psychology, 104,* 15-25.

Wetherell, J. L. and Areán, P. A. (1997). Psychometric evaluation of the Beck Anxiety Inventory with older medical patients. *Psychological Assessment, 2,* 136-144.

Whisman, M. A., Perez, J. E., Ramel, W. (2000). Factor structure of the Beck Depression Inventory-Second Edition (BDI-II) in a student sample. *Journal of Clinical Psychology, 56,* 545-551.

The WHO World Mental Health Survey Consortium (2004). Prevalence, severity and unmet need for treatment of mental disorders in the World Health Organization World Mental Survey. *Journal of the American Medical Association, 291,* 2581-2590.

Yook, S. P., and Kim, Z. S. (1997). A clinical study on the Korean version of the Beck Anxiety Inventory: A comparative study of patient and non-patient. *Korean Journal of Clinical Psychology, 16,* 185-197.

In: Leading-Edge Psychological Tests and Testing Research ISBN: 978-1-60021-571-1
Editor: Marta A. Lange, pp. 51-70 © 2007 Nova Science Publishers, Inc.

Chapter 3

THEORY AND TEST VALIDATION: A PRACTICAL EXAMPLE

Gregory T. Smith, Agnes M. Annus and Tamika C. B. Zapolski
University of Kentucky, KY USA

ABSTRACT

Many psychological constructs cannot be directly observed. The first challenge for the psychological researcher, then, is to develop ways to measure unobservable traits in convincing ways. One builds evidence for the validity of one's measurement by showing that a measure relates to measures of other psychological constructs in theoretically predictable, consistent ways. Thus, to argue for the validity of a measure is to show that the measure conforms to a theory, of which the target construct is a part. Since the validity of each measure is similarly dependent on theory and on empirical relations with other imperfect measures, there is no single, final test establishing the validity of a measure. Instead, validation is an ongoing process. The authors provide a concrete example of this process, using a theory of their own: they first consider the evidence supporting the theory, and then they criticize their own work to explore the uncertain, provisional nature of validity evidence. They emphasize that appreciating the nature of this ongoing, critical process contributes to scientific advancement.

INTRODUCTION

The aim of this chapter is to advance psychological researchers' ability to test the validity of their theories. We will first review basic aspects of construct validation, along with current philosophy of science perspectives that can inform the validation process. We will then make the discussion more concrete by offering a critical evaluation of one of our own programs of research. In doing so, we intend to illustrate that even well-developed validity evidence is provisional in nature and appropriately subject to ongoing criticism. It is crucial that researchers appreciate that theory validation is an ongoing process that involves the consideration of both the identified, core theory under consideration and the numerous other, related theories (including measurement theories) one must invoke to test the core theory.

CONSTRUCT VALIDITY

Many, perhaps most, psychological constructs are not directly observable. We cannot observe, in a direct, unmediated way, psychological constructs such as intelligence, extraversion, negative affectivity, perseverance or many others. Instead, we infer their existence because doing so enables us to develop sophisticated, precise theories that are useful for the explanation and prediction of behavior. This reality defines the first, and perhaps central, challenge facing psychological researchers: how can one determine whether one's measure of an unobservable, inferred entity is valid?

Since Cronbach and Meehl's (1955) classic paper on construct validity, researchers have come to understand that the only way to evaluate the validity of a measure of an inferred construct is to demonstrate that the measure relates to other measures of inferred constructs in theoretically predictable ways. For example, one might hold the theory that individual differences in intelligence should predict individual differences in school performance, in achievement test scores, in number of years of education completed, and even in future jobs attained. One might further hold that individual differences in intelligence are unlikely to be related to traits such as agreeableness or sensation seeking. When one then develops a measure of intelligence, one must evaluate the validity of the measure from the standpoint of that theoretical starting point. To the degree that one's predictions are confirmed empirically, one develops growing confidence that one's measure is an accurate, valid measure of intelligence.

It is clear that this process yields indeterminate results. Although one's confidence in the validity of one's measure certainly should grow in the face of a series of positive results, one has hardly proven that one is measuring intelligence. Suppose, for example, that there are individual differences in test-taking ability that are, to some degree, independent of intelligence. Suppose further that one has inadvertently developed a measure of test-taking ability, not a measure of intelligence. Such a measure could easily correlate with various measures of school performance and achievement, and since measures of school performance and achievement can heavily influence one's ultimate career options, it would not be surprising if one's test predicted career outcomes. And, of course, it would not be surprising if test-taking ability was unrelated to both agreeableness and sensation seeking.

The general implication from this hypothetical example is that positive, theory-confirming results should not be understood to constitute proof of the validity of one's measure. Even with the positive results imagined here, one's measure could lack validity, as we have described. In fact, positive results could even occur in a situation in which both the theory and the measure lack validity. Suppose sensation seeking was actually related to intelligence (perhaps intelligent people seek stimulation, as part of a general need for cognition), but was not related to test-taking ability. The apparently positive results described above could thus have been obtained with an invalid measure and an invalid theory.

The situation becomes even more complex in the face of unexpected findings. Suppose that one's putative measure of intelligence correlated with achievement test scores and career outcome, but not with school performance. There are many possible explanations for such a pattern. Perhaps one's theory is correct, but one's measure is not a sufficiently valid measure of intelligence. Perhaps one's measure is valid, but one's theory is incorrect. Perhaps one's theory is valid, one's measure is valid, but the measure of school performance lacks validity (imagine that, to some degree, school grades are assigned in biased ways, such as by race or gender). Perhaps one's theory is correct and one's measure is somewhat valid, but is contaminated by just enough invalid items to attenuate correlations with criterion measures, thus obscuring the possible correlation with school performance.

One can readily appreciate that there are many other sources of uncertainty in this enterprise. A test of the validity of a measure of a construct is, inevitably, a test of the validity of some theory concerning that inferred construct: one cannot validate a measure without a theory, and each test of a theory pertains to the validity of that theory (Landy, 1986; Smith, 2005). In the above example, when one tests whether one's new measure of intelligence correlates with achievement test scores, one is simultaneously testing the validity of one's measure and the validity of the theory driving the test. Clearly, an unexpected finding could result from either inaccuracies in one's measure or inaccuracies in one's theory. In fact, as we have demonstrated above, even expected results could follow from mistakes in both measurement and theory.

In the next section of this chapter, we offer a very brief review of relevant advances in the philosophy of science and relate them to the current understanding that theory tests are indeterminate. We then make the discussion more concrete, by considering a practical example from our own research.

PHILOSOPHY OF SCIENCE, HISTORY OF SCIENCE, AND IMPLICATIONS OF THIS UNCERTAINTY

One of the most important contributions made by Cronbach and Meehl (1955) when they introduced the concept of construct validity was their description of the inextricable intertwining of measure validation and theory testing. They famously referred to the nomological network of relationships among constructs and behaviors: they argued that there is a lawful set of relationships between sets of constructs and between constructs and behavior. Therefore, one validates one's measure by demonstrating its place in the nomological network: if the measure is a valid representation of a construct, it should relate to constructs in ways specified by theory. At the time, their critical advance was to describe how one could validate measures—and theories—in ways that did not require immediate, direct observation of behavior. The concept of a nomological network provided an apparently clear, empirical anchor for the enterprise of validating measures of unobservable entities.

There have, however, been advances in philosophy of science, informed in part by studies of how science actually operates, that suggest that the classic, Cronbach and Meehl (1955) view of construct validity may need to evolve in a subtle but important way. The concept of lawful relationships among constructs and behavior implies a level of certainty: in a given study, lawful relationships can be observed, thus supporting the validity of a measure or theory, or they can fail to be observed, presumably thus invalidating either the measure or the theory in question. One can readily imagine, from this perspective, definitive tests: an empirical result counter to one's theory could disprove the theory.

The idea that a theory can be disproved with a single, negative result is consistent with a philosophy of science referred to as *justificationism* (Duhem, 1914/1991; Lakatos, 1968). Familiar concepts consistent with justificationism are the idea of a critical experiment, that itself could disprove a theory, and logical positivism (Blumberg and Feigl, 1931), which uses the concept that theories are straightforward derivations from observed facts, and so tests of theories are, essentially, observations of facts.

During the past 50 or 60 years, advances in both philosophical work (Bartley, 1987) and in historical studies of how science operates (Weimer, 1979) have converged on a set of theories referred to as *nonjustificationist* (Bartley, 1987; Campbell, 1987; 1990; Feyerabend, 1970; Kuhn, 1970; Lakatos, 1968; Weimer, 1979). From the nonjustificationist perspective, there are no critical experiments that can, by themselves, disprove a theory. More generally, the nonjustificationist perspective holds that the very concept of lawful relations among constructs fails to consider the conditional and provisional nature of scientific findings, and hence of knowledge itself.

To illustrate the basis for this perspective, consider this set of implications of nonjustificationism. The test of any theory presupposes the validity of several other theories that also influence the empirical test (these include measurement theories, theories of the relationships among other variables, and so on; they are often referred to as auxiliary theories: Lakatos, 1999; Meehl, 1978, 1990). A negative empirical result, then, could reflect the failure of an auxiliary theory, rather than a failure of the core proposition that led to the empirical test.

It follows that no theory is ever fully proved or disproved. At any given moment in the empirical process, evidence tends to favor some theories, or research programs, more than others. Empirical evidence that appears to be disconfirming evidence can be evaluated in terms of whether it most likely results from problems in the core theory under consideration or one of the auxiliary theories invoked to conduct the test, such as theories concerning measurement or theories concerning the independence of two other constructs involved in the test (Lakatos, 1968, 1999; Meehl, 1990). Clearly, then, one must make judgments concerning the likely explanations for various empirical test results, and there is no agreed-on system for doing so. Thus, the evaluation of research findings is less exact than was imagined under the justificationist perspective. Lakatos (1999) has discussed the need to evaluate research programs as a whole (given the many theories operative in any set of empirical tests), and has used the general framework of considering whether a given research program is progressing or degenerating.

Nonjustificationism appreciates that any empirical test requires one to invoke multiple theories simultaneously. It follows that each component of a research program, i.e., each component of theory derivation, hypothesis formation, and empirical test, must be open to critical evaluation. For scientific knowledge to advance, researchers must appreciate that each result can, and should, be evaluated critically with respect to multiple assumptions reflecting multiple theories. Weimer (1979) thus argues that what characterizes science is "comprehensively critical rationalism:" the idea that every aspect of a research program must be open to critical evaluation and potential revision. One can view each proposition, and each piece of empirical evidence, as contributing to an argument for one theory or against another

(Weimer, 1979). The hallmark of science, from this perspective, is that scientists embrace critical evaluation, whether in the form of theoretical argument or empirical test.

It is easy to see that advocates for a theory can almost always defend the theory by arguing that a negative result reflected a weakness in an auxiliary theory or hypothesis (such as measurement). It follows that the process of theory validation is ongoing, as researchers test hypotheses designed to evaluate either a core theory or one or another auxiliary theory that has been involved in prior tests of the core theory. Each study provides evidence relevant to the validity of several theories that were relied on for the study (Landy, 1986; Smith, 2005). In light of this advanced understanding of the scientific process, Cronbach and Meehl's (1955) original version of construct validity, with its reliance on relatively certain, lawful relationships among constructs, may have been a bit more justificationist than now seems warranted. Indeed, Meehl (1990) made that observation himself. In a sense, the current, nonjustificationist appreciation for the ongoing process of theory and measure validation represents a further extension of their core understanding of the provisional nature of validity evidence (Smith, 2005).

The concepts reviewed so far in this chapter have been discussed elsewhere (Cronbach and Meehl, 1955; Messick, 1981; Landy, 1986; Smith, 2005). The intent of this chapter is to describe something of the "real-life" implications of the current, nonjustificationist understanding of construct validity. In general, to the degree that researchers can appreciate the ongoing nature of the validation process and can remain attentive to the auxiliary theories they invoke in their research, the more likely they will be to develop rigorous, critical tests of their theories. We believe it is essential for researchers to be able to evaluate their own work from this perspective. In this chapter, we intend to provide an example of such an effort: we will address the practical implications of validation theory by critically evaluating aspects of our own program of research.

We will describe a program of research developed to further understanding of the risk process for eating disorders. We will begin by articulating the theory and then reviewing the current evidence in support of the theory. That review will indicate that our theory is well supported empirically. We will then subject our theory to critical evaluation, both with respect to the core aspects of the theory and with respect to the auxiliary theories on which the theory depends. We hope thus to demonstrate that even well-validated theories rely on numerous other theories and assumptions, and so should be subject to ongoing critical scrutiny.

EATING DISORDER EXPECTANCY THEORY

Eating disorder expectancy theory is an application of basic expectancy theory to the problem of eating disorders. What we refer to as basic expectancy theory is the learning theory developed by Tolman (1932) and elaborated on by many authors, including MacCorquodale and Meehl (1953) and Bolles (1972). Like other learning theorists of the time, Tolman taught rats to run mazes in order to obtain rewards. A unique contribution of his work, though, was that he then demonstrated that rats appeared to form memories of the layout of the maze, leading them to form expectancies for the consequences of different routes through the maze. He did this in various ways. For example, he did experiments showing that the rats could find the reward whether they were asked to run through the maze, swim through the maze, or even ride a trolley car through the maze (Tolman, 1932).

Tolman's point was that rats were not learning a sequence of motoric responses, but rather were developing cognitive maps of the maze. Essentially, as a result of learning, they knew how the maze was laid out, so they could get to the end by any number of motoric acts: they could rely on their memories, or their expectancies concerning the maze. From this point of view, the mechanism of learning is that, as a result of one's learning history, one forms cognitive expectancies, and those expectancies then guide one's future behavioral choices. One's expectancies summarize one's learning history, and so are the cognitive mechanism by which prior learning leads to subsequent behavior.

It has become clear that invocation of the expectancy construct has proven valuable in applied learning paradigms. For example, understanding of risk for alcohol abuse has been advanced by the use of expectancy theory (Goldman, 1999; Goldman, Brown, Christiansen, and Smith, 1991; Smith, Goldman, Greenbaum, and Christiansen, 1995). A series of studies has shown that alcohol expectancies appear to be formed prior to drinking onset (presumably by modeling), they predict early onset problem drinking, and reducing expectancies can lead to reduced drinking, at least among men (Darkes and Goldman, 1993; Dunn and Goldman, 1996; Miller, Smith, and Goldman, 1990; Smith et al., 1995). Thus, at present, there appears to be both basic and applied support for the notion that learned expectancies are one mechanism by which learning shapes subsequent behavior.

The central idea in applying expectancy theory to eating disorders is that individuals are exposed to different learning experiences concerning eating, dieting, and thinness. As a result, they form different expectancies for the consequences of those behaviors and states. Their different expectancies lead them to engage in different behaviors.

Hohlstein, Smith, and Atlas (1998) offered two clinical hypotheses. First, learned expectancies for reinforcement from eating are a means by which one's learning experiences lead to overeating and binge eating. To the degree that some women have come to associate eating with powerful reinforcers, they hold unusually strong expectancies for reinforcement from eating, and so pursue food in order to obtain those reinforcers. Second, learned expectancies for reinforcement from dieting and thinness are a mechanism by which one's learning history leads to an emphasis on thinness and dieting (Hohlstein et al., 1998). If one comes to associate thinness with powerful, perhaps overgeneralized reinforcers, one holds strong expectancies for reinforcement from thinness, and hence pursues thinness more strongly than do others, and, in the extreme case, to pathological levels. Eating and thinness/dieting expectancy theory holds that a woman's learned expectations are the cognitive summaries of her learning history, and they operate to shape her subsequent behaviors, including maladaptive behaviors.

Evidence Supporting Eating Disorder Expectancy Theory

We have sought to validate this theory, and our measures of eating and thinness/dieting expectancies, in a series of steps. In the first study (Hohlstein et al., 1998), we began by interviewing both disordered and non-disordered women. We sought to determine what kinds of reinforcement women expected to experience from eating, as well as from dieting and thinness. We then engaged in a series of test development steps, including item content evaluation, exploratory factor analysis on one sample to determine whether there were underlying dimensions to women's expectancies, and confirmatory factor analysis on an independent sample to verify the obtained dimensionality (Hohlstein et al., 1998).

We identified five scales to the 34-item Eating Expectancy Inventory (EEI) and one, global scale to the 44-item Thinness and Restricting Expectancy Inventory (TREI). The EEI scales included two negative reinforcement scales ("Eating helps manage negative affect" and "Eating alleviates boredom"), two positive reinforcement scales ("Eating is pleasurable and useful as a reward" and "Eating enhances cognitive competence") and a fifth scale measuring the expectancy that "Eating leads to feeling out of control." The five-factor structure fit the data well in that original, confirmatory sample, and it fit significantly better than did any alternative factor structure.

The TREI's one factor solution also fit the data very well. Although multifactor solutions also fit well, intercorrelations among putative subscales were all greater than .80, suggesting the merit of describing one, overall factor ("Thinness and restricting food intake lead to overgeneralized self-improvement"). Important content domains included in the TREI are reflected in these sample items: "I feel like I could conquer things more easily if I were thin," "I would feel more capable and confident if I were thin," "I would cope better with failures at work or school if I were thin," and "I would be more attractive if I were thin."

Since that original study, we have replicated both the five-factor structure of the EEI and the one-factor structure of the TREI on nine independent samples (four early adolescent female samples: MacBrayer, Smith, McCarthy, Demos, and Simmons, 2001; Simmons, Smith, and Hill, 2002; one late adolescent female sample: Simmons et al., 2002; one college female Caucasian sample and one college female African American sample: Atlas, Smith, Hohlstein, McCarthy, and Kroll, 2002; and two more college samples, one female and one male: Boerner, Spillane, Anderson, and Smith, 2004).

A core aspect of the theory is that individual differences in expectancies cause individual differences in eating disorder symptomatic behavior. The first step toward validating this theory was to show that eating and thinness expectancies covaried with various forms of symptomatology. We have provided a great deal of evidence for the cross-sectional covariation of expectancies and symptoms. In college, late adolescent, and early adolescent samples (including men, women, Caucasians, and African Americans), and in an eating disordered sample, expectancies that eating helps manage negative affect, alleviate boredom, and leads to feeling out of control, and the expectancy that thinness/dieting lead to overgeneralized self-improvement, consistently account for substantial variance in measures of bulimic symptom levels and measures of maladaptive dietary restraint, with correlations generally ranging from $r = .40$ to $r = .62$ (Annus, Smith, Fischer, Hendricks, and Williams, in press; Atlas et al., 2002; Boerner et al., 2004; Hohlstein et al., 1998; MacBrayer et al., 2001; Simmons et al., 2002).

Eating and thinness expectancy profiles discriminated among anorexic patients, bulimic patients, psychiatric controls, and normal controls. There were no differences between psychiatric and normal controls, and classification accuracy among the three groups of anorexics, bulimics, and controls was 96%. Bulimic patients simultaneously held expectancies that eating helps alleviate negative affect and boredom, and that thinness leads to overgeneralized self-improvement. Anorexic patients held strong expectancies for the benefits of thinness, and unusually low expectancies for the benefits of eating.

We believe one value of eating disorder expectancy theory is that it can help identify those elements of a situation that are active in influencing symptom levels. In another cross-sectional study, Annus and Smith (2006) studied college women who were heavily involved in dance training. We found the following: (a) lifetime amount of time spent in dance class was unrelated to adult eating disturbance; (b) women's reports of learning experiences concerning thinness during their dance classes significantly and substantially predicted adult disordered eating; (c) reports of learning experiences about thinness in dance class predicted endorsement of thinness expectancies; and (d) thinness expectancies appeared to mediate the relationship between learning about thinness and adult eating disturbance. Although this study relied on retrospective reports, it suggests that dance experience may relate to eating disorder symptom development only when there is an emphasis on thinness that leads to thinness expectancy development.

Other cross-sectional evidence further supported eating disorder expectancy theory. Hohlstein et al.'s (1998) finding that neither eating nor thinness expectancies differentiated between normal women and psychiatric control women indicated that expectancies were not simple markers of disturbance. Simmons et al. (2002) found that expectancies accounted for different symptom variance from that explained by EDI-2 personality risk factors (perfectionism, interpersonal distrust, and ineffectiveness); expectancies are distinct from those factors. Fischer and Smith (2006) found that eating and thinness expectancies were disorder-specific: they related to eating disorder symptoms but not to drinking behavior or gambling behavior. MacBrayer et al. (2001) found evidence consistent with the hypothesis that various expectancy scales mediate the influences of negative maternal modeling regarding eating and family teasing about weight, in their influence on bulimic symptoms among middle school girls. Annus et al. (in press) reported findings supporting the same hypothesis with adult, eating disordered women: expectancies appeared to mediate the influence of retrospectively recalled family learning experiences on current symptom levels.

Of course, findings of cross-sectional covariation between expectancies and symptom levels is only minimally informative with respect to the core contention of the theory: that eating and thinness expectancies cause eating disorder symptomatic behavior. Although it was necessary to establish covariation, because the hypothesized causal relationship would be extremely unlikely in its absence, covariation certainly does not demonstrate causality. The next step in our program of research was to test whether eating and thinness expectancies predict the subsequent onset of, and subsequent increases in, symptomatic behavior.

Smith, Simmons, Flory, Annus, and Hill (in press) studied middle school children longitudinally. We began by developing developmental trajectories of binge eating and purging across three years, beginning with the first year of middle school. Not surprisingly, the vast majority of girls were neither binge eating nor purging during middle school. There were also two trajectories of initially symptomatic girls: one maintained high levels of binge eating (or purging) across the three years, and the other maintained moderate levels of binge eating (or purging). For each behavior, there was a fourth trajectory group, which was of particular importance for us. These groups were characterized by significant increases in binge eating (or purging) across the three years. The "binge eating increase" group went from a mean score .08 standard deviations below the sample mean at year 1 to a mean score 1.65 standard deviations above the sample mean at year 3 (8th grade). The "purging increase" group went from a mean score .63 standard deviations above the sample mean to a score 2.18 standard deviations above the sample mean by year 3.

We then conducted two sets of empirical tests. First, we tested whether initial expectancies could differentiate between members of the continually asymptomatic group and the symptom-increase group (for both behaviors). Second, we identified girls who were asymptomatic at year 1 and tested whether initial expectancies predicted which girls began to binge eat (or purge) during the three-year longitudinal period.

Concerning binge eating, initial expectancies that eating helps alleviate negative affect and dieting/thinness lead to overgeneralized life improvement differentiated the continually non-binge eating group from the "binge eating increase" group significantly. Concerning purging, the expectancy that dieting/thinness lead to overgeneralized life improvement differentiated between the continually non-purging group and the "purging increase" group.

Among originally asymptomatic girls, the same two expectancies predicted subsequent symptom onset. Thus, the expectancies of 7th grade girls predicted the subsequent onset of binge eating and purging as well as subsequent increases in binge eating and purging across the following three years. In a similar vein, Stice and Whitenton (2002) showed that thinness/dieting expectancies held by 11-15 year old girls predicted subsequent body dissatisfaction.

This demonstration of time-lagged prediction adds further support to eating disorder expectancy theory. If eating and thinness expectancies represent summaries of girls' learning histories, and if learning shapes future behavior, then it should be true that (a) the expectancies covary with indices of binge eating and purging and (b) they predict the onset of those behaviors over time. Our empirical demonstration of both covariation and time-lagged prediction constitutes evidence for the validity of eating disorder expectancy theory, as well as evidence for the construct validity of our expectancy measures. Of course, there is another crucial step in the process of supporting a causal model such as this one: the experimental manipulation of expectancies should influence subsequent symptom reports.

Fister and Smith (2004) conducted the first experimental manipulation of expectancies. We manipulated college women's thinness expectancies simply by showing them pictures of attractive but normal weight models. We asked one group of women to view these models and another group to view pictures of attractive and very thin models. We focused on women identified as high risk for the development of eating disorders, based on their responses to other risk measures. High risk women in the two experimental conditions did not differ in their ratings of the attractiveness of the models, thus supporting the validity of our effort to match models on attractiveness while varying them in weight. However, the high risk women who viewed the normal weight models were less likely to endorse expectancies for reinforcement from thinness and dieting than were women who viewed the thin models. It appeared that exposure to attractive, normal weight models may have disrupted the risk process for these women. This finding that expectancies can be manipulated, and that their manipulation can have this effect, was important. Our next step was to test whether an expectancy manipulation altered symptom levels.

Annus, Smith, and Masters (2006) conducted just such a study. We developed a three-stage intervention to undermine expectancies for reinforcement from thinness. In two studies, we compared the success of our intervention with that of psychoeducation. Psychoeducation has been well-established as a successful intervention, particularly for women with moderate levels of symptomatology (Laessle, 1991; Olmsted, 1991; Ordman and Kirschenbaum, 1986), but it does not address expectancies directly. We chose this comparison because we wanted a rigorous test of expectancy manipulation: we sought to determine whether our manipulation of expectancies produced greater drops in symptom levels than did psychoeducation. In the first study, we compared the two approaches on a sample of symptomatic college women. In the second study, we compared them on a general sample of high school girls.

For both samples, both interventions produced substantial, linear drops in body dissatisfaction, overall disordered eating, purging frequency, and binge eating frequency. Most importantly, the thinness expectancy manipulation produced greater drops in body dissatisfaction in both samples, and a greater drop in overall disordered eating among the high school girls (Annus et al., 2006). Thus, expectancy manipulation produced significant declines in symptom levels, and in some cases those declines were greater than those produced by a well-established intervention.

Taken together, these studies constitute strong evidence for the validity of eating disorder expectancy theory and for the construct validity of the eating and thinness expectancy measures that were used in this research. We have shown clear, consistent factor structures to the expectancy measures, covariation between expectancies and symptom levels, evidence of discriminant validity, evidence consistent with the view that expectancies mediate the influence of learning events on symptom levels, temporal precedence of expectancies, and isolation of the putative cause (thinness expectancies) from other causes, with a demonstrated effect on subsequent symptom levels.

However, the theme of this chapter is that evidence for the validity of theories, and for the measures used to test them, is always provisional and always subject to scrutiny and criticism. We next offer criticisms of our own theory and work, in order to demonstrate the reality and practical importance of this proposition.

CRITICAL EVALUATION OF EATING DISORDER EXPECTANCY THEORY

The Validity of Expectancy Theory

We view the success of expectancy theory in the basic science literature as important evidence for the validity of eating disorder expectancy theory. We have argued that learned expectancies can be used to explain behavior in general, so surely they would help explain the specific behaviors that make up eating disorders (Smith et al., in press). From our point of view, we have simply been applying well-established learning theory to one specific domain.

It is important to appreciate, though, that basic expectancy theory is not universally accepted as valid. Indeed, there are many alternative perspectives to explain learning, behavior acquisition, and choice. Space precludes a detailed consideration of several such alternative models, but we will briefly refer to a few possibilities. We do so to illustrate that our decision to apply basic expectancy theory to eating disorders reflected a choice, at the beginning of the research program, of one of many possible starting models.

From a classic behavioral perspective, behavior is a function of both the contingencies of reinforcement and environmental circumstances (Baum, 1973). Organisms respond based on the reinforcement available within the environmental context. This perspective is famously summarized by Herrnstein's (1961) matching law: the proportion of behavior allocated to each of two choices is proportional to the amount of reinforcement available from those two choices. Behavioral theorists emphasize the need to focus on observable behavior, and they have identified theoretical mechanisms to explain behavior across long delays that, in their view, does not rely on the inference of unobservable, internal cognitive entities (Rachlin, Logue, Gibbon, and Frankel, 1986). From their perspective, the invocation of cognitive maps and expectancies adds an unnecessary, non-confirmable step to the explanatory process. Instead of relying on expectancy theory, one should rely strictly on behavioral models. Thus, eating disorder expectancy theory involves the application of an invalid model to a new problem.

There are also many criticisms of expectancy theory from a cognitive perspective. One of the most common theories of attitudes is the expectancy-value model (Ajzen, 2001). In this model, expectancies are understood to be beliefs. One forms expectancies or beliefs concerning the attributes of an object or behavior (such as anticipated consequences of a behavior, in the present case), and then one's attitude toward the object or behavior is a function of both one's expectancies/beliefs and the subjective value one places on those expected attributes. From this point of view, it is not sufficient simply to know one's expectancies; one must also know the degree to which one values the expected consequences of a behavioral option before one can predict whether a person would choose that option. Thus, expectancy theory is incomplete: it considers only one part of the causal mechanism.

One can perhaps readily see that an expectancy-value model of attitudes itself may be incomplete. In the more fully elaborated theory of planned behavior (Ajzen, 1985; Schifter and Ajzen, 1985), one considers an individual's attitudes (expectancy times value), one's subjective norms (in this case, one's perceived social pressure to lose or not to lose weight), and the perceived control one has over the prospective behavior. These factors cause one to form behavioral intentions, such as to diet, and those behavioral intentions are the proximal cause of the behavior (Schifter and Ajzen, 1985; Ajzen, 2001). To the degree that this model is valid, and indeed numerous supportive studies have been reported (Ajzen, 2001), one might conclude that eating disorder expectancy theory is flawed in its focus on only one part of the process.

It is important to appreciate that each of these two perspectives, and many other perspectives as well, are supported by considerable research and they have strong supporters. One can see, then, that advocates of either behavioral or cognitive/attitude models would find reasons to object to eating disorder expectancy theory, despite the impressive evidence that has accrued in support of it.

As advocates for eating disorder expectancy theory, it is incumbent on us to consider these alternative models and respond to them, whether to incorporate aspects of their perspectives or not. In a nutshell, our perspectives are these. Concerning classic, behavior theory alternatives, we simply find the work of Tolman and others compelling. We have concluded that there is simply no straightforward, parsimonious, behavioral way to explain phenomena such as the immediate generalization of learning that Tolman and others have documented. In our view, the use of concepts such as memory, cognitive maps, and expectancy is necessary to explain experimentally observed phenomena. There are other reasons for our support of the need to infer concepts such as memory and cognition, many grounded in evolutionary theory, but we cannot address those here, due to space limitations.

Concerning the theory of planned behavior, we have both theoretical and empirical reasons to question the utility of including the concepts of value, subjective norms, perceived control, and behavioral intentions. One way to view the theory of planned behavior is that humans make behavioral choices following a series of considerations: they consider the outcomes they expect, the value they place on those outcomes, the norms they perceive governing such behavioral choices, whether they believe they have control over the choices and outcomes, and then form intentions, which result in behavior. We find that implausible. Human behavior is far more rapid, immediate, and even automatic than can be captured by such a model.

Thus, an alternative view is that those steps happen in a kind of automatic way, without conscious reflection. If that is true, then we wonder about the value of measuring each step, as though they were independent. If it all happens in an immediate, non-reflective way, perhaps what one measures is the strength of the association between the behavior and the outcome, and it is the strength of the association that is predictive. Perhaps expectations of a given outcome, valuing that outcome, and judging its position in relation to social norms, are all components of the strength of one's association between the behavior and the outcome.

If this loosely-sketched, alternative perspective is accurate, (a) how do we explain the apparent empirical success of the theory of planned behavior, and (b) why, still, are we just measuring expectancies? We do not have space to conduct a comprehensive, critical evaluation of the theory of planned behavior. It may be, though, that with each component one adds in, one is simply adding additional indicators of the strength of the association. If so, adding variables such as value and perceived norms will increase predictive power, but not for the reasons that were supposed. As we showed above, it is certainly quite possible to obtain results supporting a theory even when the theory is not fully accurate.

We measure expectancies because we believe they are an excellent way to capture the strength of the association between the behavior and the anticipated outcome. We believe that the expectancies that women initially provided us very likely had value and subjective norms "built in." By definition, a reinforcer has value: a reinforcer is anything that increases the likelihood of that behavior in the future. When we ask women what kinds of reinforcement they expect from eating, or from dieting, it makes no sense to then ask whether they value those reinforcers. We can apply similar logic to the concept of subjective norms and to perceived control. From a theoretical standpoint, then, we view the measurement of expectancies for reinforcement (or, where appropriate, expectancies for punishment) as relatively direct measures of the associations between a behavioral choice and its consequences: the "pull" of the behavior, in terms of its reinforcement, is, we believe, captured by expectancy measurement. Relatedly, our theory does not depend on the view that women calculate and consider their expectancies before they act; rather, we believe, in the measurement process we are inserting ourselves and measuring the strength of the association that influences the act.

There is some empirical evidence consistent with our claim in the study of two other addictive behaviors. In the study of alcohol use and smoking, researchers have conducted studies in which they included a value component along with their expectancy measurement. In each case, concurrent prediction was slightly increased by including measurement of values and of the product of expectancies and values (Copeland and Brandon, 2002; Fromme and D'Amico, 2000). Advocates of the theory of planned behavior would likely see that evidence as in support of their perspective. On the other hand, Copeland and Brandon (2002) described the improvement in smoking prediction as very modest in magnitude, and Fromme and D'Amico (2000) concluded that the prediction with and without the value component was "remarkably similar." Our guess is that prediction improved very slightly because one was adding additional predictors of the same set of associations. We consider it unlikely that it was the measurement of an actual, valuing process that was added and that improved prediction.

It is easy to see that there is a great deal of room for healthy, informative debate among these different perspectives. We are certainly not in a position to claim that our favored perspective has been proved true. Eating disorder expectancy theory, then, simultaneously has impressive validity evidence behind it and is subject to important criticisms concerning the underlying basic theory.

Do Eating Disorder Expectancies Actually Explain Disorder?

One important concern for any attempt to identify risk factors for disorders is whether the putative risk factors truly play a causal role, or are, instead, mere non-causal correlates of a disorder. In the case of anorexia nervosa, there may in fact be good reason to believe that thinness expectancies are, essentially, culturally based epiphenomena, not causally active agents.

Recently, Keel and Klump (2003) conducted a cross-cultural review of the disorder and concluded that it seems to occur in roughly the same frequency in different cultures, and has done so through recent history. If they are right, then the Western cultural emphasis on thinness is unlikely to be the basis of anorexia nervosa. Many of the presumed risk factors studied in the West, such as societal emphasis on thinness (Heinberg, Thompson, and Stormer, 1995; Stice, 2002) and expectancies for overgeneralized reinforcement from thinness (Hohlstein et al., 1998), may be artifacts, because they do not exist in other cultures with similar prevalence rates of anorexia nervosa. Instead, these supposed risk factors are likely culture-bound, post hoc explanations women construct for themselves in order to try to explain behavior that is actually driven by a biological cause.

Anorexic women in other cultural contexts may have constructed other explanations for their disorder. For example, some Catholic nuns in the 17th and 18th centuries reportedly fasted for religious purity. Some of those nuns may have been anorexic, as it is reported that they appear to have been unable to control their refusal of food (Keel and Klump, 2003). In these cases, fasting for religious purity may have been a post hoc explanation for an endogenous disorder. In Western cultures, then, the societal emphasis on thinness and the resulting expectations for reinforcement from thinness may be an analogous, post hoc explanation for an endogenous disorder. Thus, what may be universal is the disorder itself, and what may be culturally specific are the causal explanations constructed by patients and the researchers who study them (Smith, Spillane, and Annus, 2006). It may well be true, then, that in the case of anorexia nervosa, expectancies are only markers for the disorder when the true underlying cause is genetic.

Of course, it may still be true that eating disorder expectancies play a causal role in non-endogenous, anorexia-like extreme dieting, purging, and preoccupations with weight. There is clear evidence that a very high percentage of women in the United States and other Western countries experience, at some point in their development, maladaptive eating and dieting-related behaviors that are subclinical with respect to formal DSM-IV diagnosis but that bring serious harm (Franko and Omori, 1999; Mitchell and Eckert, 1987). It is likely that difficulties at this subclinical level tend only to be present in Western cultures or cultures which are heavily influenced by Western cultures; they may well, therefore, have a learning or environmental component to them. Thinness expectancies, as summaries of women's learning histories, may play an active, causal role in the emergence of those problems. That possibility is supported by the findings that thinness expectancies predicted subsequent changes in purging behavior (Smith et al., in press) and manipulation of thinness expectancies reduced symptom levels (Annus et al., 2006): neither of those studies examined clinically diagnosed anorexia nervosa patients.

In contrast to the case with anorexia nervosa, Keel and Klump (2003) reported clear evidence that bulimia nervosa appears to be a culturally specific disorder. If the disorder only occurs in certain cultural contexts, then environment, and hence learning, must play an important role. It therefore seems likely that one's learning history, summarized as expectancies, plays an active, causal role in this disorder (see Smith et al., 2006, for a more in-depth treatment of this issue). Bulimia nervosa patients may have learned to expect negative reinforcement from eating and overgeneralized reinforcement from thinness. As likely as this prospect is, though, we know of no experimental manipulations of eating expectancies. At this point, then, the theory that eating and thinness/dieting expectancies cause the emergence of bulimia nervosa needs further validation.

Is Eating Disorder Expectancy Theory Culture-Specific?

If eating and dieting expectancies represent one's learning history, and if individuals learn different things about eating and about thinness in different cultures, expectancies may well vary across cultures. Indeed, they may well vary across cultural subgroups within the umbrella of Western/American culture. One possibility that has received some attention in the literature is whether Caucasians and African Americans differ in their eating and thinness expectancies. African American women typically have lower prevalence rates of thinness/purging-related eating disorders than do Caucasian women (Striegel-Moore and Smolak, 2000); does this difference stem from different learning histories and different expectancies?

In one study (Atlas et al., 2002), we showed that Caucasian and African American college students produced the same factor structures of eating and dieting expectancies, and that those expectancies correlated with symptom reports to the same degree for both groups. Although the risk factors appeared to operate in similar ways, it was also true that African American women had lower mean levels of both expectancies and symptomatology. We have offered that study as evidence for the cross-cultural usefulness of our eating and thinness expectancy measures. However, our conclusion is very much open to criticism. We used an etic approach to compare the groups on the expectancy measures: we tested the same expectancy dimensions in both groups, and those dimensions were created from previous Caucasian samples.

We did show that expectancy scales developed from interviews with Caucasian women performed comparably for Caucasian and African American women. However, one can make a strong argument that we did not actually show that those scales reflected the dimensions of learned expectations from eating and dieting that were most central to the experiences of African American women. Perhaps if we had used an emic approach, in which we would have repeated the test construction process anew with African American women, we might have found different expectancies than those we found with Caucasian women. With an emic approach, we would not have presumed the dimensionality of expectancies, but instead we would have asked African American women what expectancies they had about eating and thinness. We then would have developed a new measure, based on their responses. We did not do so, so existing research does not address the possibility that there are cultural differences in which expectancies are most important to women.

The same argument can be made concerning our study of the expectancies of men (Boerner et al., 2004): perhaps an emic approach would have revealed different dimensions of importance for men than those identified for women. More broadly, we have not examined the cross-cultural validity of eating disorder expectancy theory in relation to any other groups. We do not know if similar expectancies would be identified with other ethnic minorities, such as Asian-Americans, Hispanic-Americans, Native Americans, or others. Of course, at this point we know nothing about the nature of expectancy theory in cultures that value heavy weight. It is apparent that the issue of culture has not been adequately examined in relation to eating disorder expectancy theory; a great deal of additional work is necessary before we understand how culturally general and how culturally specific the theory is.

Are Eating Disorder Expectancies Age Specific?

Most research that has been done with eating disorders has focused on college or adolescent women. That focus has certainly been present in eating disorder expectancy theory research. At this point in the evaluation of the theory, we have very little information concerning whether eating and/or thinness expectancies change with age. There is evidence that levels of neuroticism or negative affectivity decline during the middle age years (Teachman, 2006); perhaps expectancies that eating helps manage negative affect become less important for middle aged women. It may be that the extreme pursuit of thinness becomes less normative among middle aged individuals. If so, perhaps thinness expectancies decline, and their decline is consistent with declines in symptomatology among those women. In other words, the theory may still be accurate, but learning, context, and resulting behavior have changed. There are many possibilities, and we simply do not know. We therefore do not know the age range of relevance for eating disorder expectancy theory. These issues require considerable further investigation.

EATING DISORDER EXPECTANCY MEASUREMENT

To date, we have only measured expectancies with questionnaire responses. Following Campbell and Fiske's (1959) discussion of method variance, and the need to measure constructs in ways that are as free as possible from method variance, our exclusive reliance on questionnaire expectancy reports is an important limitation of this research. Although we have measured criterion variables using both questionnaires and interviews, we have not yet measured expectancies by other forms of self-report, such as interviews, or by other means (observation, implicit assessment, peer report). We therefore do not know the degree to which our assessment of expectancies is confounded by the means of assessment: we do not know how different true expectancies are from "expectancies as measured by questionnaire." As encouraging as our validity findings are, they can be skeptically viewed as evidence only for the validity of one method of assessing expectancies.

Another criticism of our measures is that the items vary in terms of specificity versus generality. For example, the item "I would be happy if I were thin" is general: it does not refer to the specific form of reinforcement that thinness would bring. One can be happy for many reasons; a positive response to this item does not tell us exactly what reinforcer the individual is expecting. Another such item is "If I were thin, there would be one less thing to worry about;" an obese individual may endorse this item because they would not have to worry about their health if they were thin while an already thin individual may endorse this item for completely different reasons. A more specific item is, "I would be more attractive to the opposite sex if I were thin." The presence of items of varying levels of specificity introduces uncertainty into the measurement process. Expectancy measurement could, perhaps, be made more specific and more precise.

SUMMARY AND CONCLUSIONS

We have sought to provide a concrete demonstration of the observation that evidence for the validity of theories, and for the validity of measures used in testing theories, is always provisional and subject to continual scrutiny and criticism. After reviewing the basic literature on construct validity and theory validity, we have provided an example of this reality using our own research. We reviewed eating disorder expectancy theory and the impressive body of empirical evidence in support of the theory. The supportive evidence includes all the kinds of evidence thought necessary to validate a causal process: we showed covariation, temporal precedence of the putative cause, time-lagged prediction, and change in symptom level following experimental manipulation of expectancies. We then went on to articulate numerous criticisms of our own theory. Those criticisms ranged from the fundamental (is expectancy theory valid?), to its clinical relevance (does eating disorder expectancy theory really explain disorder?), to the measurement of the constructs, to needs for further research on possible cultural and age influences on the value of the theory. We could have identified many more possible criticisms.

We have not offered these criticisms to argue that our theory is invalid. On the contrary, we believe most readers would find the supportive evidence convincing. Instead, our goal has been to show that even strong evidence for the validity of theories and measures can be, and should be, subject to ongoing, critical scrutiny. Researchers should bring a critical eye to their own research. Doing so can help advance knowledge by identifying problems in existing theories, improving theories to respond to potential problems, and improving tests of theories by sparking more critical tests of both core and auxiliary propositions. The degree to which researches can do each of these things is the degree to which scientific knowledge can advance at a more rapid rate.

REFERENCES

Ajzen, I. (1985). From intentions to actions: A theory of planned behavior. In J. Kuhl and J. Beckman (Eds.), *Action-control: From cognition to behavior* (pp. 11-39). Heidelberg: Springer.

Ajzen, I. (2001). Nature and operation of attitudes. *Annual Review of Psychology, 52,* 27-58.

Annus, A. M., Smith, G. T., Fischer, S., Hendricks, M., and Williams, S. F. (in press). Associations among Family and Peer Food-Related Experiences, Learning about Eating and Dieting, and the Development of Eating Disorders. *The International Journal of Eating Disorders.*

Annus, A.M., and Smith, G.T. (2006). Thinness expectancies help clarify the relationship between dance study and eating disturbance. Manuscript in preparation.

Annus, A. M., Smith, G. T., and Masters, K. (2006). Manipulation of Thinness and Restricting Expectancies: Further Evidence for a Causal Role of Thinness and Restricting Expectancies in the Etiology of Eating Disorders. Manuscript submitted for publication.

Atlas, J. G., Smith, G. T., Hohlstein, L. A., McCarthy, D. M., and Kroll, L. (2002). Similarities and differences between Caucasian and African American women on eating disorder risk factors and symptoms. *The International Journal of Eating Disorders, 32(3),* 326-334.

Bartley, W.W. III (1987). Philosophy of biology versus philosophy of physics. In G. Radnitzky and W.W. Bartley III (Eds.), *Evolutionary Epistemiology, Rationality, and the Sociology of Knowledge.* (pp. 7-46). La Salle, IL: Open Court.

Baum, W.M. (1973). The correlation based law of effect. *Journal of the Experimental Analysis of Behvior, 20,* 137-153.

Blumberg, A.E., and Feigl, H. (1931). Logical positivism. *Journal of Philosophy, 28,* 281-296.

Boerner, L.M., Spillane, N.S., Anderson, K.G., and Smith, G.T. (2004). Similarities and differences between women and men on eating disorder risk factors and symptom measures. *Eating Behaviors,* 5, 209-222.

Bolles, R.C. (1972). Reinforcement, expectancy, and learning. *Psychological Review, 79(5),* 394-409.

Campbell, D.T. (1987). Evolutionary epistemology. In G. Radnitzky and W.W. Bartley, III (Eds.), *Evolutionary Epistemiology, Rationality, and the Sociology of Knowledge.* (pp. 47-89). La Salle, IL: Open Court.

Campbell, D.T. (1990). The Meehlian Corroboration-Versimilitude theory of science. *Psychological Inquiry, 1*(2), 142-147.

Campbell, D.T., and Fiske, D.W. (1959) Convergent and discriminant validation by the multitrait-multimethod matrix. *Psychological Bulletin, 56,* 81-105.

Copeland, A. L., and Brandon, T.H. (2002). Do desirability ratings moderate the validity of probability ratings on the Smoking Consequences Questionnaires. *Psychological Assessment, 14,* 353-359.

Cronbach, L.J., and Meehl, P.E. (1955). Construct validity in psychological tests. *Psychological Bulletin, 52*(4), 281-302.

Darkes, J., and Goldman, M.S. (1993). Expectancy challenge and drinking reduction: Experimental evidence for a mediational process. *Journal of Consulting and Clinical Psychology, 61,* 344-353.

Duhem, P. (1991). *The Aim and Structure of Physical Theory* (P. Weiner, translator). Princeton, NJ: Princeton University Press. First published in 1914 as *La Theorie physique: Son objet, sa structure.*

Dunn, M. E., and Goldman, M. S. (1996). Empirical modeling of an alcohol expectancy memory network in elementary school children as a function of grade. *Experimental and Clinical Psychopharmacology, 4, 209-217.*

Feyerabend, P. (1970). Against method. In M. Radner and S. Winokur (Eds.), *Minnesota Studies on the Philosophy of Science: Vol. IV. Analyses of theories and methods of physics and psychology* (pp. 17-130). Minneapolis, MN: University of Minnesota Press.

Fischer, S., and Smith, G. T. (2006). Binge eating, problem drinking, and pathological gambling: Linking behavior to shared traits and social learning. Manuscript submitted for publication.

Fister, S.M., and Smith, G.T. (2004). Media effects on expectancies: Exposure to realistic female images as a protective factor. *Psychology of Addictive Behaviors,* 18(4), 394-397.

Franko, D. L., and Omori, M. (1999). Subclinical eating disorders in adolescent women: A test of the continuity hypothesis and its psychological correlates. *Journal of Adolescence, 22,* 389-396.

Fromme, K., and D'Amico, E.J. (2000). Measuring adolescent alcohol outcome expectancies. *Psychology of Addictive Behavior, 74,* 206-212.

Goldman, M. S. (1999). Risk for substance abuse: Memory as a common etiological pathway. *Psychological Science,* 10 (3), 196-198.

Goldman, M. S., Brown, S. A., Christiansen, B. A., and Smith, G.T. (1991). Alcoholism and memory: Broadening the scope of alcohol expectancy research. *Psychological Bulletin, 110,* 137-146.

Heinberg, L. J., Thompson, K. L., and Stormer, S. (1995). Development and validation of the Sociocultural Attitudes Towards Appearance Questionnaire. *International Journal of Eating Disorders, 17,* 81-89.

Herrnstein, R.J. (1961). Relative and absolute strength of response as a function of frequency of reinforcement. *Journal of the Experimental Analysis of Behvior, 4,* 267-272.

Hohlstein, L. A., Smith, G. T., and Atlas, J. G. (1998). An application of expectancy theory to eating disorders: Development and validation of measures of eating and dieting expectancies. *Psychological Assessment, 10,* 49-58.

Keel, P. K., and Klump, K. L. (2003). Are eating disorders culture-bound syndromes? Implications for conceptualizing their etiology. *Psychological Bulletin, 129,* 747-769.

Kuhn, T.S. (1970). *The Structure of Scientific Revolutions.* Chicago, IL: University of Chicago Press.

Laessle, R.G., Beumont, P.J.V., Butow, P., Lennerts, W., O'Connor, M., Pirke, K.M., Touyz, S.W., et al. (1991). A comparison of nutritional management and stress management in the treatment of bulimia nervosa. *British Journal of Psychiatry, 159,* 250-261.

Lakatos, I. (1968). Criticism and the methodology of scientific research programs. *Proceedings of the Aristotelian Society, 69,* 149-186.

Lakatos, I. (1999). Lectures on scientific method. In I. Lakatos and P. Feyerabend (Eds.), *For and Against Method* (pp. 19-112). Chicago, IL: The University of Chicago Press.

Landy, F.J. (1986). Stamp collecting versus science: Validation as hypothesis testing. *American Psychologist, 41*(11), 1183-1192.

MacBrayer, E.K., Smith, G.T., McCarthy, D.M., Demos, S., Simmons, J. (2001). The Role of Family of Origin Food-Related Experiences in Bulimic Symptomatology. *The International Journal of Eating Disorders,* 30, 149-160.

MacCorquodale, K. and Meehl, P. E. (1953). Preliminary suggestions as to the formulation of expectancy theory. *Psychological Review,* 60(1), 55-63.

Meehl, P.E. (1978). Theoretical risks and tabular asterisks-Karl. Ronald, and slow progress of soft psychology. *Journal of Consulting and Clinical Psychology, 46,* 806-834.

Meehl, P.E. (1990). Appraising and amending theories: The strategy of Lakatosian defense and two principles that warrant it. *Psychological Inquiry, 1*(2), 108-141.

Messick, S. (1981). Constructs and their vicissitudes in educational and psychological measurement. *Psychological Bulletin, 89,* 575-588.

Miller, P. M., Smith, G. T., and Goldman, M. S. (1990). Emergence of alcohol expectancies in childhood: A possible critical period. *Journal of Studies on Alcohol, 51(4),* 343-349.

Mitchell, J. E., and Eckert, E. D. (1987). Scope and significance of eating disorders. *Journal of Consulting and Clinical Psychology, 55,* 628-634.

Olmsted, M.P., Davis, R., Garner, D.M., Rockert, W., Irvine, M.J., and Eagle, M. (1991). Efficacy of a brief group psychoeducational intervention for bulimia nervosa. *Behavious Research and Therapy, 29,* 71-83.

Ordman, A.M., and Kirschenbaum, D.S. (1986). Bulimia: Assessment of eating, psychological adjustment, and familial characteristics. *International Journal of Eating Disorders, 5,* 865-878.

Rachlin, H., Logue, A.W., Gibbon, J., and Frankel, M. (1986). Cognition and behavior in studies of choice. *Psychological Review, 93,* 33-45.

Schifter, D.E., and Ajzen, I. (1985). Intention, perceived control, and weight loss: An application of the theory of planned behavior. *Journal of Personality and Social Psychology, 49,* 843-851.

Simmons, J. R., Smith, G. T., Hill, K. K. (2002). Validation of Eating and Dieting Expectancy Measures in Two Adolescent Samples. *The International Journal of Eating Disorders, 31,* 461-473.

Smith, G. T. (2005). On construct validity: Issues of method and measurement. *Psychological Assessment, 17,* 396-408.

Smith, G. T., Goldman, M.S., Greenbaum, P.E., and Christiansen, B.A. (1995a). The divergent paths of high-expectancy and low-expectancy adolescents. *Journal of Abnormal Psychology, 104,* 32-40.

Smith, G. T., Simmons, J. R., Flory, K., Annus, A. M., and Hill, K. K. (in press). Thinness and eating expectancies predict subsequent binge eating and purging behavior among adolescent girls. *Journal of Abnormal Psychology.*

Smith, G. T., Spillane, N. S., and Annus, A. M. (2006). Implications of an emerging integration of universal and culturally-specific psychologies. *Perspectives on Psychological Science, 1,* 211-233.

Stice, E. (2002). Risk and maintenance factors for eating pathology: A meta-analytic review. *Psychological Bulletin, 128,* 825-848.

Stice, E. and Whitenton, K. (2002). Risk factors for body dissatisfaction in adolescent girls: a longitudinal investigation. *Developmental Psychology,* 38(5), 669-678.

Striegel-Moore, R.H. and Smolak, L. (2000). The influence of ethnicity on eating disorders in women. In R. M. Eisler and M. Hersen (Eds.), *Handbook of Gender, Culture, and Health* (pp. 227-254). Mahwah, NJ: Lawrence Erlbaum Associates.

Teachman, B. A. (2006). Aging and negative affect: The rise and fall of anxiety and depression symptoms. *Psychology and Aging, 21,* 201-207.

Tolman, E.C. (1932). *Purposive behavior in animals and men.* New York: Century Company.

Weimer, W.B. (1979). *Notes on the Methodology of Scientific Research.* Hillsdale, NJ: Lawrence Erlbaum Associates.

In: Leading-Edge Psychological Tests and Testing Research   ISBN: 978-1-60021-571-1
Editor: Marta A. Lange, pp. 71-88   © 2007 Nova Science Publishers, Inc.

Chapter 4

A PSYCHOMETRIC APPROACH TO HEALTH RELATED QUALITY OF LIFE MEASUREMENT: A BRIEF GUIDE FOR USERS

Penney Upton and Dominic Upton

Child and Family Research Group CR UK, Department of Psychology,
University of Sheffield, UK

ABSTRACT

In the past 20 years, health related quality of life (HRQL) has gained increasing recognition as a health outcome measure. Although no consensus exists about the precise definition of HRQL, a plethora of instruments have been developed to assess it. However, measurement standards and approaches to development may also differ between instruments, which can make choosing an appropriate instrument complex for would be users. The aim of this chapter is to reduce this barrier to HRQL application by providing a guide to the psychometrics of HRQL measurement. The chapter begins with a general overview of the current approaches to measuring HRQL, with the emphasis on quantitative methods. The psychometric approach is then compared to other approaches (e.g. the clinimetric method) and the advantages and disadvantages of each considered. Psychometrically based methods of instrument development are discussed and the main psychometric properties of a good HRQL instrument are outlined. Finally, some of the specific measurement problems of HRQL assessment (e.g. the need for and use of proxy reports) are also discussed. Points are illustrated through out with examples of instrument development.

BACKGROUND

In the past 20 years the measurement of health related quality of life (HRQL) has increased in importance in clinical and other health care settings. Whilst HRQL measurement has clear clinical applicability, the measurement of HRQL remains almost exclusively in the research setting. For this reason, this chapter is mainly concerned with the use of HRQL as an outcome measure applied to research. Although no consensus exists about the precise definition of HRQL, a plethora of instruments have been developed to assess it. However, measurement standards and approaches to development may differ between instruments, which can make choosing an appropriate instrument complex for would be users. The aim of this chapter is to reduce this barrier to HRQL application by providing a basic guide to the psychometrics of HRQL measurement.

DEFINING HRQL

Quality of life (QOL) is a difficult concept to define. It is a complex phenomenon which concerns an individual's satisfaction with life and incorporates satisfaction with all facets of life including physical, social, economic and psychological wellbeing. Health related quality of life (HRQL) is a distinct component of this construct, focusing specifically on the impact of health on an individual's wellbeing. Measures of health status and functional status should not be confused with HRQL. Although these terms are sometimes used interchangeably, this is conceptually inaccurate. Measures of health status or functional status take a single aspect of health, namely physical functioning, as their focus. HRQL is a more broad-based concept that includes psychosocial dimensions of functioning such as emotional, social, and role functioning as well as physical functioning. Indeed a recent meta-analysis has confirmed the appropriateness of this distinction and its application across most of the literature (Smith, Avis, and Assmann, 1999).

Despite the interest in and support for HRQL measurement within healthcare in recent years, it remains a relatively new research paradigm and there is as yet no consensus over how it should be defined. Thus many different ways of conceptualizing HRQL can be found within the literature. There are however, two central aspects of HRQL that are inherent in most definitions (Eiser and Morse 2001, Wallander et al 2001). Firstly, HRQL is subjective and should therefore be assessed from the individuals own perspective whenever possible. Secondly, it is a multidimensional construct that integrates a number of features including physical, social and psychological functioning. In practice, many definitions take the World Health Organization's (WHO's) statement that health is "a state of complete physical, mental, and social well-being; not merely the absence of disease" (WHO, 1948) as their conceptual foundation and often focus specifically on the impact of illness and treatment on these aspects of well-being. Divergence in definition is not the only area of difference in this area of research; there are also a range of approaches to measuring HRQL.

APPROACHES TO THE MEASUREMENT OF HRQL

Approaches to HRQL measurement may be either *qualitative*, with the aim of achieving a complete, detailed description of HRQL, or *quantitative*, in which the features of HRQL are classified, counted, and subjected to statistical analysis in an attempt to explain what is observed. In the former case data collection is often, though not exclusively based on focus groups, interviews or other individualized approaches, whilst the quantification of HRQL is mainly questionnaire based. In practice, most work in this area uses the latter approach and so will be the focus of most of this chapter. The benefits of this approach, especially in the case of patient completed measures include the comparatively low costs of administration in terms of time and money, the ease with which data can be gathered from a large number of people and the flexibility of mode of administration – for example postal administration of questionnaires may be useful in some circumstances. There are of course limitations to this approach – for instance they are not always adequate for more vulnerable groups including those with cognitive impairment or limited literacy skills. In this instance a qualitative approach may be more useful. Likewise if the aim of the study is to explore hidden aspects of HRQL in a particular group, then a qualitative approach will be more useful. Indeed, such exploratory qualitative work often provides the basis for development of quantitative measures.

Two broad types of quantitative instrument – generic and disease-specific – have been developed but there is some debate about their relative merits. Disease-specific measures evaluate domains relevant to a particular disease or health condition. The advantage of this method is that these measures are sensitive to even subtle changes in functioning. This makes them powerful at detecting intervention effects. The disadvantage is that disease-specific measures cannot be applied outside of the specified population. Thus they cannot be used to compare the quality of life of patients with a chronic health problem and those without. An assessment of this type needs a generic measure which can be applied to the general population as well as those with health problems. The advantage of a generic instrument lies therefore in its ability to measure broad aspects of HRQL and to provide a general sense of the effects of health on well-being and function. The disadvantage is that they are likely to be less powerful at detecting intervention effects. Generic and disease specific approaches are not therefore mutually exclusive. Each approach has advantages and disadvantages and so may be suitable for different circumstances; it has even been suggested that on occasions both generic and disease specific should be administered together (Varni, Burwinkle and Lane 2005). The choice of whether to use a generic or specific measure, or both will therefore depend on issues such as the purpose of the assessment and the target population.

Which ever method or type of instrument is chosen, the value of HRQL measurement remains the same; it allows the assessment of health outcomes from the perspective of the patient. Indeed there are many situations in which feedback from patients on their disease and/or treatment maybe useful as the following section shows.

THE VALUE OF HRQL MEASUREMENT

In the past, traditional medical models of illness concentrated on diagnosis and intervention with the intention of cure: what is known as the 'find it and fix it' approach (Kaplan 2003). Health outcomes were therefore most commonly measured in terms of disease related mortality. However, medical and social advances such as development of effective immunisation and better sanitation have ensured the virtual elimination of acute disease as the main threat to survival in western society. This has necessitated a change in the emphasis in healthcare from diagnosis and management of infectious disease, to the prevention and monitoring of chronic health conditions. The treatment of health problems that may endure over an lifetime has inevitably led to a change in emphasis in treatment, with a shift form cure to control. At the same time, there has been a progression from measuring treatment outcomes purely in terms of survival, to one that also takes into account the value, or quality of the resulting life. Thus HRQL is increasingly being recognised as an important outcome measure in many areas of healthcare. In addition, while there has been major progress in treatment of previously life threatening conditions such as cancer, treatments can be aggressive and are often associated with both acute, and long-term morbidity. Thus modern medicine must recognize that treatment may not always succeed in making people feel better; finding and fixing one disease does not necessarily lead to the best patient outcomes. The value of HRQL in these contexts is that by widening the clinical outcomes focus from the physical to the social and psychological HRQL measurement provides a more comprehensive account of patient based experience than that which is typically conveyed by traditional measures of health outcomes such as mortality, morbidity and functional status (Eiser et al. 1999). Indeed, modern medical models recognise the importance of a systems approach to healthcare, in which the body is recognised as a complete system in which 'the functioning of each part (including the psychological) cannot be understood independently of the functioning of other parts' (Kaplan, 2003).

Furthermore, whilst physiological measures provide objective information to clinicians about physical functioning, this may not correlate with an individual's everyday functioning and ability to carry out day to day tasks (Guyatt 1993). Furthermore, two patients with the same diagnosis and comparable clinical features may have noticeably different responses. For example, two children with a diagnosis of asthma may report the same symptoms, yet there may be differences between them in terms of school absences, participation in sport and other activities and so on. Likewise responses to medication have been noted to be different between individuals and this is likely to impact on HRQL as well as physical symptoms. Thus HRQL measures also allow greater patient participation in evaluation of healthcare outcomes, an area identified as important by health services across western Europe and north America (Crawford et al 2002).

HRQL measurement is also becoming an important focus in randomised control trials (RCTs) world wide (Naito et al 2002). Although RCTs highlight the effectiveness and safety of new interventions, there is growing consensus that assessment of HRQL is also useful as it provides a more complete picture of patient responses to new treatments (eg Matza et al 2004, Naito et al 2002), so leading to a greater understanding of the clinical impact of new interventions. Measuring HRQL assesses a broader range of the impact of new regimes on day-to-day functioning than can be achieved with clinical measures alone, which are often concerned primarily with physical symptoms.

However, the systematic use of HRQL measures in RCTs is not yet established – references to HRQL outcome measures in clinical trials increased from none in the early 1970s to 4.4% of trails at the start of the 21st century. Thus it is perhaps not surprising that recent reviews of HRQL measurement in RCTs have noted a lack of uniformity in the approach to HRQL assessment along with poor quality reporting of HRQL RCTs (Naito 2004, Efficace and Bottomley 2002). For example, some trials give only limited, if any, information about the properties of the measure used, or the criteria upon which it was chosen, whilst others have produced their own measures without providing details about the process of instrument development. While the CONSORT statement (Begg 1996, Moher et al 2001) establishes methods of RCT reporting, this guideline does not address the problems of selecting HRQL instruments, or reporting findings adequately. Although a call has been made for the standardisation of the conduct and reporting of studies incorporating HRQL measurement (Efficace and Bottomley 2002, Buchanan 2005), this seems no nearer resolution and choosing an appropriate measure can seem like a daunting task. The aim of the rest of this chapter is to reduce this barrier to HRQL application by providing a straightforward guide to the basics of HRQL instrument development and testing, ultimately addressing the issue of how to choose a clinically useful measure.

QUESTIONNAIRE DESIGN AND DEVELOPMENT

HRQL questionnaires are usually made up of a number of items (questions), organised into several domains, or dimensions. A domain or dimension refers to the area of functioning or experience that is being evaluated. As noted earlier, many definitions of HRQL are based on the World Health Organisation (WHO) recommendation that health is seen as a state of complete physical, mental, and social well-being and questionnaire domains frequently follow the same criteria. HRQL questionnaires should therefore include a measure of both physical and psychosocial wellbeing. Most HRQL questionnaires are designed for paper and pen self completion by the patient, although as new technologies for automated computer administration become more readily available, touch screen computer administration is likely to become more common. Some measures are already available in this format (eg Quality of Life in Reflux and Dyspepsia (HRQLRAD) Questionnaire (Kleinman et al 2001), Functional Assessment of Cancer Therapy – General (FACT-G) (Gil et al 2005)) and early evidence suggests this mode of administration does not compromise the psychometric properties of the questionnaire (Kleinman et al 2001, Gil et al 2005). However in some cases, for example when assessing the HRQL of certain groups such as very young children, the elderly or those with reading difficulties it maybe more appropriate that the administration is interviewer led in order to facilitate completion and many questionnaires are available in both formats (eg. SF36, PedsQL™). Clearly this method is more resource intensive, as it requires a trained interviewer, but it ensures compliance and decreases errors and missing items (Guyatt 1993).

Clinimetric and psychometric methods provide the techniques predominantly used for the development of multi-item health measurement scales such as HRQL questionnaires (Wright and Feinstein 1992). According to Feinstein (1999) clinimetric strategies rely principally on the opinions of patients and clinicians and aim to develop measures with good face validity, which make 'clinical common sense'. Thus this approach is concerned less with the homogeneity of scale items and more with their clinical relevance to a phenomenon. It is not uncommon therefore to develop a scale which includes heterogeneous items; Feinstein provides the Apgar scale as a prime example of an heterogeneous measure developed on the basis of clinimetric criteria. Psychometric strategies, it is argued (eg Marx et al 1999) rely more on statistical techniques and generally aim to develop a measure which is mathematically valid and reliable, which usually means a degree of homogeneity is valued. However, whilst much is made in the literature of the differences between the two methods (eg Feinstein 1999), there is rarely any evidence provided to suggest the superiority of one or other method. As Feinstein noted 'each has its own merits …… sometimes the best approach is to use both methods.'

Furthermore, despite the claimed difference in aims and strategy, in practice there is some overlap between the two techniques and it is easy to see how they might be complementary. Indeed, Striener (2003) goes one step further cogently arguing that clinimetrics is a misnomer – the strategies referred to as clinimetric practices are simply a subset of psychometry. Item generation for instance is similar for both measures and usually includes the derivation of an initial item pool based on a combination of literature review and focus groups or interviews with the target population, and relevant professionals. For example, during the initial developmental stage of constructing an HRQL measure for children in local authority care, Upton, Maddocks, Eiser et al (2005) carried out interviews with children in care, foster carers, community paediatricians and other relevant professionals such as social workers. The divergence in methods lies in deciding which items to keep. The clinimetric strategy relies on the ratings of patients and clinicians to determine which items to include in the final scale. Typically patients may be asked to rate the importance of each of the items in the initial pool on a five-point scale from 'not at all important' to 'extremely important' so that a mean importance score can be determined for each item. The items with the highest scores will then be selected for the scale. Item selection using the psychometric approach usually relies on factor analysis, a statistical method which organises items into factors according to their relationships with one another. Items selected for each scale therefore tend to have good homogeneity. Selection of items has been found to differ for the two methods, even when starting with the same item pool (Juniper et al 1997, Marx et al 1999) – that is the items patients perceive as important are not necessarily the same as those which show statistical importance. However, it should be noted that it is not uncommon for a scale to be modified by a clinician in order to improve content validity, which ever initial method of item section has been used (Marx et al 1999). Furthermore, it is also possible to combine both patient and statistical judgments in the choice of final items: Hutchings, Up[ton, Cheung et al (personal communication, May 2006) successfully used both psychometric analysis and patient ratings of items during the development of a generic measure of HRQL for children. The combined use of statistical analysis and human intuition, is according to Striener (2003) a common combination in psychometrics. Finally the methods used to confirm the reliability and validity of the newly minted measure are the same for both psychometrically and clinimetrically derived measures. For Striener 'The conclusion is that clinimetrics is not describing a new family of techniques that should be used with a unique type of scale, but is simply another word for a portion of what is done in psychometrics.' (Streiner, 2003, p 1144). Even ardent supporters of clinimetrics as a distinct method of questionnaire development, accept that there is much overlap with psychometrics. Indeed, the distinction between the terms psychometrics and clinimetrics is often hazy as both disciplines at times make use of the same methodological and statistical approaches (De vet et al 2003). The main difference it seems is in the emphasis given to patient and clinical opinion during item selection – in all other ways the practices of clinimetricians and psychometricians can be viewed as interchangeable.

What Makes a Good HRQL Measure?

Validity and reliability and are the most frequently cited requirements of an acceptable measure of HRQL. Validity is a way of measuring accuracy – ie does this questionnaire measure HRQL or some other concept? Reliability on the other hand is a measure of consistency – this can be either consistency (or homogeneity) within the scaling or in people's responses at different moments in time. There are different types of both validity and reliability and it is important to recognize the value of each test for a given measurement purpose; HRQL instruments are generally used either to discriminate between people who have a better HRQL and those who have a worse HRQL or to evaluate how much a person's HRQL has changed following a new intervention. The former studies tend to be cross-sectional in design as they rely on a between groups comparison, whilst the latter are inevitably longitudinal as they are concerned with changes in HRQL over time. The relative importance of different measures of validity and reliability will depend upon the purpose – evaluation or discrimination – for which the measure is to be employed (Guyatt 1993). In the next sections the key measurement properties for HRQL measures are described in turn and the relevance of each for discriminative and evaluative measurement is flagged.

Validity

Face and Content Validity

These are the most basic type of validation strategies and require no statistical techniques. This type of validity should be available for all HRQL measures. *Face validity* refers to subjective assessments of whether an instrument appears to be measuring what it is intended to measure. Determination of *content validity* is more systematic than for face validity and refers to judgments made by experts about the extent to which the content of the instrument comprehensively covers the characteristics or domains it is intended to measure. Face and content validity should answer the following question: Is the measure logically and sensibly designed – are the questions clear and the response categories easy to follow? Is there any bias in the question content? Are all relevant issues covered? Have any redundant items been included? During the development of the HRQL questionnaire for children in care already referred to earlier for instance, content validity was established by a panel of experts including community paediatricians, foster carers and social workers (Upton, Maddocks, Eiser et al 2005).

Construct Validity

A more rigorous approach to establishing validity is *construct validity*. A construct is a theoretically derived notion of the domain(s) it is hoped to measure. Construct validity refers then to the extent to which an instrument is a good representation of the construct being evaluated and is central in the appraisal of any measure whatever its purpose; it represents the key distinction of behavioural measurement as a science from non-scientific approaches. According to classical measurement theory (Cronbach and Meehl 1955), the first step in establishing construct validity is to formulate a model, or a set of theoretical concepts that represent an understanding of what is going to be measured. This then provides a basis for hypothesising or predicting the performance of the construct being studied, its relationship to other patient features and so on.

Classical measurement theory has advocated factor analysis as the ideal method for establishing construct validity (Cronbach and Meehl 1955, Guildford 1948). In summary it is proposed that the grouping of items which emerge from a factor analysis is taken as a working reference frame, for a measure's domains. Human interpretation is also important here as the choice of which set of factors from a given matrix is most useful will depend partly on the investigators preference and therefore his knowledge and understanding of the construct under investigation. In essence then, the preferred construct will be the one which best fits with the initial theoretical model. This is however one of the major disadvantages of using factor analysis. There may be many possible ways of subdividing the covariance matrix to produce groups of highly inter-correlated items, and thus to produce alternative, very different factorial solutions. Although many studies do use factor analysis, factors may be difficult to interpret and/or inconsistent across studies. Thus a second, confirmatory, sample should always be recruited in order to validate the model suggested by the factor analysis and good practice dictates that other methods of establishing construct validity should be employed alongside factor analysis if the robustness of a measure is to be confirmed.

Measures which are going to be used to discriminate between patient groups, or between patients and a healthy sample should be shown to have a very specific type of construct validity, known simply as *discriminant validity*. This may be validated by comparing two groups of patients with different levels of disease severity, or for a generic measure (but never a disease specific) a comparison of healthy and ill samples. For example Cheung et al (2000) in reporting the development of an HRQL measure for inflammatory bowel disease (the UK-IBDQ) established discriminant validity by comparing patients' scores on the UKIBDQ and their scores on an empirical index of disease activity; as predicted, they found that the group with the higher disease activity achieved lower scores on all dimensions of HRQL. In the same way Upton, Eiser, Cheung et al (2005) established the discriminant validity of the UK version of PedsQL™, by comparing the HRQL scores of healthy school children with those of children diagnosed with chronic disease; the children with a known chronic illness rated their HRQL as significantly lower than did the healthy children. Thus the measure was able to differentiate between the target group and the general population.

Criterion Validity

Criterion validity can be viewed as a special case of construct validity in which stronger hypotheses are made possible by the availability of a criterion or gold standard by which to evaluate the validity of a newly developed measure. Typically, when a new measure is developed, validity is established in relation to a previously accepted measure of the same concept. For example, any new measure of IQ has typically been validated against traditional measures (this assumes that traditional measures really measure IQ, but this is a separate problem).[1] This is possible because IQ is a long established concept, with a strong measurement history. With a newer concept such as HRQL, there is often an absence of appropriate traditional measures or gold standards against which new measures can be compared and this is especially true for disease specific measures. This can therefore be a limiting factor in establishing criterion validity in a conventional sense.

Although no accepted gold standard for HRQL exists, there are examples of occasions where another instrument can be treated as a criterion or gold standard for a specific HRQL

---

[1] This is also sometimes also referred to as *concurrent validity*, as typically the gold standard measure and the new measure are administered at the same time – ie concurrently. The alternative to this is known as *predictive*

domain. For example Williams et al (2003) hypothesised that there would be a correlation between scores on the emotional functioning subscale of a newly developed HRQL measure for children and an established measure of anxiety, the state-trait anxiety inventory for children or STAIC (Speilberger 1973); they found that children with higher trait anxiety scores showed significantly poorer emotional HRQL as anticipated. Criterion validity is also applicable when a shorter version of an instrument is used to predict the results of the full-length measure as exemplified by the development of the SF12 (Ware, Kosinski, Keller 1996). Furthermore, it is not uncommon to use an established generic measure to test the criterion validity of a newly developed disease-specific measure. Criterion validity for the UK IBDQ for example, was assessed by comparing it with the SF-36 health survey, with the expectation that correlations between the two measures would be greater for the subscales assessing the areas of health most affected by inflammatory bowel disease ie mental health, vitality, and pain (Cheung et al 2000). Likewise, validity for the HRQL measure developed for children in care was established in part by the correlation between this new measure and a generic HRQL questionnaire, the PedsQL (Upton, Maddocks, Eiser et al 2005).

Responsiveness

Responsiveness refers to an instrument's ability to detect changes over time – ie does a measure identify any improvement or deterioration in group or individual HRQL. Responsiveness is an important validity test for instruments, that are to be used for evaluative purposes; if a treatment results in an important change in HRQL, investigators want to be confident that they will detect any difference, even if it is only small. Hays and Hadorn (ref) argue that responsiveness is one aspect of validity rather than a separate entity. If an instrument is responsive to a clinical intervention, this fact provides some support for the validity of the instrument. A measure can be reliable, but unresponsive. Common methods for evaluating responsiveness include comparing scale scores before and after an intervention using the responsiveness ration (Deyo et al 1991), or comparing changes in scale scores with changes in other related measures that would be expected to move in the same direction as the target measure. For example Hutchings, Upton, Cheung et al (Personal communication, May 2006) evaluated the relationship between changes in health status and changes in HRQL. They found that when an improvement in physical health was reported over time, children's HRQL scores also improved, highlighting the responsiveness of the measure to changes in health.

As noted earlier, the more specifically relevant the measure is to the treatment being evaluated, the more sensitive to change it is likely to be – hence the enhanced sensitivity of disease specific measures in comparison to generic measures. While sensitivity to change is a valued characteristic of HRQL measures, it is also important that the measure can produce stable results when there is no reason to expect change – this flip side to responsiveness is test-re-test reliability or reproducibility and will be addressed in the next section.

---

validity and refers to a study in which the scores from the new measure are collected first; then at some later time the criterion measure is collected. This has had limited use in HRQL studies to date.

Reliability

Reliability of HRQL measures can be measured in two ways: internal reliability, sometimes also referred to as internal consistency and test retest-reliability. These two types of reliability function independently.

Internal Reliability

Single item measures of HRQL (eg 'How are you?) may not be satisfactory to the extent that individuals can respond generally (I'm OK) without giving details about different aspects of their lives that are far from OK. Therefore it is hoped that greater reliability can be achieved by using multiple items to measure the same concept. For example, we might ask children how things are in school, with their friends, and in their relationships with their families. The question then arises as to how far these multiple items really reflect the same underlying concept. *Internal consistency* refers to the extent to which the items of a domain or scale assess the same dimension (their homogeneity) and is normally measured using Cronbach's alpha (Cronbach 1951). This is a statistical assessment of the correlation between items within a dimension and tests whether items within a scale correlate positively, i.e. measure the same thing. An internal consistency of 0.70 has been recommended for measures used to detect between-group differences in clinical trials or outcomes research, and greater than 0.90 for interpreting individual scores (Nunally and Bernstein 1994).

Test Retest Reliability

Test retest-reliability refers to a measure's consistency over time. It is assumed that a measure is reliable over time where individuals whose illness and treatment status have not changed, complete a measure on two separate occasions, and the two sets of scores are positively correlated. In practice a measure can have high test-retest reliability even when the scores of individuals change over time, provided that individuals broadly retain their relative positions within the group. However, the assumption behind assessing reliability in this way is that individuals have not been differentially affected by anything that has happened to them between the two testing occasions. Measures of test-retest reliability in a clinical trial would provide reassuring evidence that changes in scores in the treatment group are reliable and not due to the chance result of an unstable measure that produces fluctuating scores under unchanging conditions. However, it has been argued that test-retest reliability may be less useful than internal consistency reliability in HRQL instrument development (Varni et al 2003). Internal consistency is suggested to be a more valuable assessment of the reliability of a measure because of the likelihood of short-term fluctuations in chronic health conditions, in which external factors such as disease and treatment variables are known to influence functioning. Whilst this may be acceptable when an instrument is to be used for discriminant purposes only, for an instrument to be applied evaluatively, the reproducibility of the measure must be given the same importance as its sensitivity to change.

Floor and Ceiling Effects

Floor and ceiling effects refer to the extent to which scores cluster around the top (ceiling) or the bottom (floor) of the scoring system. In theory a measure in which the full range of scoring options is used, without any clustering at either end would be ideal (the classic bell curve). In practice those scales which do report floor and ceiling effects may fall short of this ideal. For example a number of studies which have looked at the measurement properties of the PedsQL (eg Varni et al 2003, Upton, Eiser, Cheung et al 2005) report the use of the full range of scoring options on this measure, although responses tend to be skewed towards the top end of the scale for all subscales, showing some ceiling effects. SF36, another generic measure has also been shown to be susceptible to ceiling and floor effects and it has been suggested that ceiling and floor effects are to be expected in generic HRQL instruments, simply because they aim to be applicable to a wide range of populations (Wann-Hansson et al 2004). Furthermore, such ceiling effects tend to be more marked for healthy respondents, which is perhaps not so unexpected. Whilst this may not be too problematic in discriminatory studies (though it is still useful to be aware of any such issues), this has greater implications for evaluative studies; the responsiveness of evaluative instruments may be compromised by ceiling effects in which patients with the best score may have substantial improvement in their HRQL which can not be detected, whilst floor effects may mask the deterioration of patients who started off with the worst possible scores.

ISSUES IN HRQL MEASUREMENT

Cross-Cultural Use Of Measures

It is quite common for successful HRQL questionnaires to be translated into a number of languages (eg SF36; PedsQL™). However it is important that anyone undertaking a questionnaire translation recognises that as culture is one of the factors which influence HRQL, any new translation will require further psychometric testing. A full translation should include forward and backward translation to check the original meaning has been retained (ie the questionnaire should be translated into the new language then back into its original language), then the final translation should be tested for validity and reliability. If such translations can be shown to have kept functional equivalence, then they may be useful in cross-cultural studies such as epidemiological studies or international RCTs (Bullinger 2004). More recently new measures have been developed through cross-cultural collaboration for example the WHOQOL-100 and the WHOQOL-BREF for adults (http://depts.washington. edu/yqol/docs/WHOQOL_Info.pdf) and the DISABKIDS Project for children (http://www.disabkids.org). Guidelines have been developed to address the issues of cross-cultural instrument development and the interested reader is referred to these sources for further information (Spilker 1996, Bullinger et al 1006, Power et al 1999).

Issues in Paediatrics

The development and use of HRQL measures to assess children's health lag behind those of adults (Bradlyn and Pollock 1996, Brojkson 2001). Applying measures of HRQL developed for adults to this population, even those with good psychometric properties such as SF-36, has been shown to be invalid (Vitale MG, Levy DE et al. 2001)and the increasing recognition that children are able to use rating scales and assess their own HRQL (Cremeens, Eiser and Blades 2006) has resulted in a number of child friendly measures of HRQL being developed. There have been fewer attempts to develop generic compared with disease-specific measures for children, partly because the need to collect more psychometric data from children with different conditions, adds further burden to an already challenging task. Thus in paediatrics reliable, well-validated child specific measures designed specifically to assess the problems experienced by children are required. There are however, important methodological problems to address when developing child-specific measures.

First of all, children's concerns change with maturity and their concerns about illness can also change. A scale that was appropriate for 3-year old children for example, was shown to be inadequate for 5-year olds (Cadman and Goldsmith 1986). It is essential therefore, that any outcome measure for children is sensitive to changing developmental tasks and goals, whilst still allowing comparisons to be made across the age span.

Indeed childhood, adolescence and adulthood provide very different contexts within which disease and treatment are experienced, which is why measures developed for adults are usually inappropriate for the paediatric setting. Young children, for example, generally have a lower baseline of independence, although this will change over time and for individuals. However, it does mean that requiring assistance with certain aspects of physical functioning such as dressing may be less of a marker of severity than for adolescents and adults. Thus any items on a physical functioning domain which refer to the need for assistance will be irrelevant for this group. Likewise domains referring to social functioning will have to take into account differences in social groups, activities and interests across the life span. Thus although the fundamental domains of functioning that are tested for both adults and children may be the same, the relevance of each is different. Questions that bear little or no consequence to a respondent's life will serve no purpose, resulting in questionnaire items that are either left blank or answered randomly, making the resultant scores meaningless.

Furthermore, children have very different ideas about the meaning of health compared with adults. Younger children tend to describe good health as the ability to run faster than anyone else or to be an Olympic champion. With age, individuals increasingly describe good health as the ability to perform everyday functions, with the elderly describing themselves as healthy as long as they perform basic self-care activities (Millstein and Irwin 1987).

Limitations in cognitive or linguistic skills also raise unique methodological issues and have often been used as an argument against child-completed measures. For example, children have been considered less able to locate or identify common symptoms like pain and as a result, children's distress has often gone unrecognised. Indeed, children do not always use the same language as adults. The most fundamental requirement of HRQL measure development, finding questions meaningful to subjects, is especially critical when developing a child-completed measure. Extensive pilot work with children is needed to do this satisfactorily. Furthermore, great care must be taken with questionnaire administration and interpretation of findings, particularly with younger children. These requirements make heavy demands on resources.

The mode of administration used in paediatric HRQL measurement has also been the subject of discussion. The suitability of self completed measures for children has been the subject of much controversy, primarily because of uncertainty surrounding the age at which children are cognitively capable of understanding both the questionnaire items and the self completion instructions. This has led to the development of questionnaires with simpler response formats and the use of pictorial representations of responses. For example, the self-report version of PedsQl for use with ages 5-7 includes only three response categories rather than five, and this are illustrated by pictures of smiley, neutral and sad faces. Furthermore, in order to relieve the cognitive burden still further for children measures for younger children may either be interviewer led; it is recommended that the PedsQL is interviewer led for ages 5-7 years and for any other child who has literacy problems). Clearly if an interviewer is to be used this increases the administration burden. It is also good practice to ensure that all interviewers are fully trained in order to reduce administrator bias and improve inter-administrator reliability, which may incur training costs.

Using a Proxy Reporter to Estimate HRQL

Given this set of problems, it is perhaps unsurprising that it has previously been assumed that parents or health care professionals provide the most reliable sources of information about a child's well being. Thus the use of a parent proxy report has frequently been used as an alternative to interviewer based HRQL reporting for children. The idea of using a surrogate respondent is not however, unique to paediatrics; proxy reports can be provided, usually by a significant other, in any situation where the patient is either unable or unwilling to give their own rating of HRQL. According to Sneew et al (2002), proxy reports are most important for certain patient groups including children, the elderly, stroke survivors and others with neurological deficits. The use of proxies can be an advantage -for example, in studies which use HRQL as an outcome measure, bias maybe introduced by exclusion of subgroups of patients who are either unable or unwilling to complete a self-report measure and inclusion of a proxy report may well help rectify this imbalance (Sneew et al 2002). However, relying on proxy ratings of HRQL can only be acceptable if it can be established that the quality of such information is high (Sneeuw et al 2002). This means that reliability and validity for both proxy and patient reports should be estimated separately as limited reliability on one or both measures may lead to low levels of agreement.

Examining the extent to which proxy and patient reports concur can be assessed by examining agreement at either the level of the individual, or at the group level. Agreement at the individual level is measured by correlation statistics, whilst group level comparison involves testing the difference between proxy and patient mean scores, using a t-test. The former method provides a direct indication of the extent to which proxy ratings correspond with those of the patient themselves, whilst the latter method considers the direction and extent of any differences and therefore any systematic bias that might be introduced to a study when using proxy respondents alone. Studies often report only one of these statistics. However, a full assessment of concordance should report both group and individual level statistics. In addition, it has been suggested that since the significance of mean differences is partly dependent on sample size, standardized differences (effect sizes) should also be calculated (Sneeuw et al 2002).

Nevertheless, the use of proxy reports has its own methodological problems and it is essential that researchers know what the possible bias is to the study due to imperfections in proxy ratings, in order to make an informed decision about whether or not to include proxy reports in the absence of a patient self-report. This may well differ depending on the measure being used and it is therefore important to be aware of differences ion proxy-patient agreement for a specific measure. However, there are a few consistent differences that have been noted by some studies as follows.

It has been observed that for functional limitations, proxy respondents tend to consider patients as more impaired; that is, they rate patients as having greater dysfunction than do the patients themselves. This is particularly true for proxies who have the most contact with the patient whose HRQL is being rated (eg Rothman 1991). For other sorts of morbidity, patients tend to report the most problems, followed by close relatives, and clinicians report the least. Parents have also been found to report more problems than the children themselves (Eiser and Morse 2001). It has also been demonstrated that parent-child agreement is often better for externalising or acting out problems than for internalising problems such as anxiety or sadness (Elderbrock et al 1996; Loonen et al. 2002). This is likely to be because parents are not always aware of children's worries or concerns and there is evidence that even form a young age children are able to dissemble their true feelings in order to influence social interactions with others (Zeman and Garber 1996). Parents may also lack the direct information necessary to make competent ratings about difficulties experienced at school or with friends. Furthermore, it is likely that parent reports often reflect parental anxiety about child health or behaviour over and above more objective indicators. Thus parent reports provide a different perception of the impact of childhood chronic ill health, to that provided by the child (Ennett et al. 1991). These findings have important clinical implications because they suggest that wherever possible clinicians should collect patient reported assessment of HRQL. Furthermore, in situations when the patient is unable or unwilling to complete a self-report, using a proxy-report to estimate HRQL may be better than missing data, the knowledge that this estimate maybe inaccurate should be considered.

SUMMARY AND CONCLUSION

This chapter has outlined some of the main issues facing users of HRQL measures. When choosing an HRQL instrument as a research outcomes measure it is important to take the psychometric properties of the measure into consideration. However, it should also be recognised there are a number of other more pragmatic factors that will influence the choice of measure. Firstly the relative merits of generic and disease specific instruments should be considered. Which is most appropriate for the intended population and measurement aims? Or would measuring both generic and specific HRQL be valuable? The age range, cognitive abilities and cultural background of the population should also be deliberated and the appropriateness of the instrument items weighed up. Are questions relevant to the likely experiences of this group of participants? Furthermore, the expediency of administering a proxy measure should also be taken into account. If this will be necessary, what is the reliability and validity of available proxy reports for the intended population? What is known about the agreement between self reports and proxy reports on this measure? Once these questions have been answered satisfactorily the psychometric aspects of potential instruments can be given full consideration and table 1 provides a summary the key issues to consider. It is hoped that this may provide a useful guide to reviewing the psychometric properties of HRQL instruments and so go some way to reducing the complexity of choosing an appropriate HRQL measure.

Table 1. Summary of the Key issues to consider when reviewing the psychometric properties of HRQL instruments

Property	Definition	Relevance
Face Validity	Subjective assessment of whether an instrument is measuring HRQL	All measures should have face validity
Content validity	A more systematic assessment of whether an instrument is measuring HRQL usually made by experts	All measures should have content validity
Construct validity	Statistically testing that the instrument is measuring HRQL. Most commonly involves factor analysis, or testing the performance of the instrument in relation to known patient characteristics.	All measures should have some form of construct validity
Discriminant validity	Statistically testing the ability of the instrument to differentiate between groups of patients with different characteristics (eg disease severity), or patients and healthy individuals	Essential for any measure used for discriminant purposes
Criterion validity	Measuring construct validity by comparing a new HRQL instrument to an accepted gold standard of HRQL measurement (usually an established instrument)	Useful for any measure, though currently maybe difficult to establish in HRQL
Responsiveness	An instrument's ability to detect any improvement or deterioration in group or individual HRQL over time. Measured by the responsiveness ratio.	Important for measures used for evaluative purposes
Internal reliability	The extent to which the items of a domain or scale assess the same dimension. Assessed by Cronbach's Alpha.	Useful for all instruments
Test retest reliability	The extent to which responses to a measure remain stable across time.	Important for measures used for evaluative purposes
Floor and ceiling effects	The extent to which scores cluster around the top (ceiling) or the bottom (floor) of the scoring system.	May have implications for evaluative studies

REFERENCES

Begg C, Cho M, Eastwood S, Horton R, Moher D, Olkin I, Pitkin R, Rennie D, Schulz KF, Simel D, Stroup DF (1996) Improving the quality of reporting of randomized controlled trials. The CONSORT statement. *JAMA* 276:637-9.

Bjornson KF, McLaughlin JF. (2001) The measurement of health-related quality of life (HRQL) in children with cerebral palsy. *Eur. J. Neurol. Suppl.* 5:183-93.

Bradlyn AS and Pollock BH (1996). Assessment of quality of life [letter]. *New Eng. J. Med.* 521.

Buchanan DR, O'Mara AM, Kelaghan JW, and Minasian LM (2005) Quality-of-Life Assessment in the Symptom Management Trials of the National Cancer Institute – Supported Community Clinical Oncology Program. *J. Clin. Oncol.* 23:591-598.

Bullinger M, Power MJ, Aaronson NK, Cella DF, Anderson RT. (1996) Creating and evaluating cross-cultural instruments. In: Spilker B, ed. *Quality of Life and Pharmacoeconomics in Clinical Trials*. Philadelphia: Lippincott-Raven: 659–68.

Bullinger M, Von Mackensen S (2004) Quality of life assessment in haemophilia. *Haemophilia* 10 (Suppl. 1): 9–16.

Cheung WY, Garratt AM, Russell IT, Williams JG (2000) The UK IBDQ—A British version of the inflammatory bowel disease questionnaire: development and validation. Journal of Clinical Epidemiology 53 : 297–306.

Crawford MJ, Rutter D, Manley C, Weaver T, Bhui K, Fulop N, Tyrer P. (2002) Systematic review of involving patients in the planning and development of health care. *BMJ* 325(7375): 1263. PMCID: 136920.

Creemens J, Eiser C, Blades M (2006) Characteristics of Health-related Self-report Measures for Children Aged Three to Eight Years: A Review of the Literature. *Quality of Life Research* 15 (4): 575-766.

Cronbach LJ, Meehl PE (1955) Construct Validity In Psychological Tests. *Psychological Bulletin* 52: 281-302.

Cronbach, L.J. (1951) Coefficient alpha and the internal structure of tests. *Psychometrika* 16: 297-334.

de Vet HCW, Terwee CB, Bouter LM (2003) Clinimetrics and psychometrics: two sides of the same coin. *Journal of Clinical Epidemiology* 56: 1146–1147.

Deyo RA, Diehr P, et al. (1991). "Reproducibility and responsiveness of health status measures. Statistics and strategies for evaluation." *Control Clin Trials* 12(4 Suppl): 142S-158S

Edelbrock C, Costello AJ, Dulcan MK et al. (1996) Parent-child agreement on child psychiatric symptoms assessed via structured interview. *Journal of Child Psychology and Psychiatry and Allied Disciplines* 27(2):181-90.

Efficace F and Bottomley A 2002. *Do Quality-of-Life Randomized Clinical TrialsSupport Clinicians in Their Decision-Making?* 20 (19): 4126. (2002) downloaded from www.jco.org on October 18, 2006

Eiser C, Cotter I, et al. (1999). "Health-related quality-of-life measures for children." *Int. J. Cancer Suppl.* 12: 87-90.

Eiser,C and Morse, R. (2001)Quality-of-life measures in chronic diseases in childhood. *Health Technology Assessment*, 5(4), 1-147.

Ennett ST, DeVellis BM, et al. (1991). "Disease experience and psychosocial adjustment in children with juvenile rheumatoid arthritis: children's versus mothers' reports." *J. Pediatr. Psychol.* 16(5): 557-68.

Feinstein AR. (1987) *Clinimetrics Westford*, MA: Murray Printing Company.

Feinstein, AR (1999) Multi-item "Instruments" vs Virginia Apgar's Principles of Clinimetrics. *JOURNAL* 159(2): 125-128.

Gil K, Frasure HE, Hopkins MP, Jenison EL von Gruenigen VE (2005) Effect of method of administration on longitudinal assessment of quality of life in gynecologic cancer: An exploratory study *Health and Quality of Life Outcomes* 3:6 The electronic version of this article is the complete one and can be found online at: http://www.hqlo.com/content/3/1/6

Goldsmith C, Cadman D (1986) Construction of social value or utility-based health indices: the usefulness of factorial experimental design plans. *J. Chronic. Dis.* 39(8):643-51.

Guilford JP (1948) Factor analysis in a test-development program. *Psychol. Rev.* 55: 79-94.

Guyatt GH, Feeny DH, Patrick DL (1993) Measuring health-related quality of life. *Ann. Intern. Med.* 118:622-9.

Hays RD, Hadorn D. (1992) Responsiveness to change: an aspect of validity, not a separate dimension. *Qual. Life Res.* 1: 73-5. http://www.disabkids.org

Juniper EF, Guyatt G, Streiner DL, King DR. (1997) Clinical impact versus factor analysis for quality of life questionnaire construction. *J. Clin. Epidemiol.* 50:233–8.

Kaplan, R.M. (2003). "The significance of quality of life in health care." (AHRQ grant HS09170). *Quality of Life Research* 12(Suppl. 1), pp. 3-16.

Kleinman L, Leidy NK, Crawley J, Bonomi A, Schoenfeld P (2001) A Comparative Trial of Paper-and-Pencil Versus Computer Administration of the Quality of Life in Reflux and Dyspepsia (QOLRAD) *Questionnaire. Medical Care.* 39(2):181-189.

Loonen HJ, Grootenhuis MA, et al. (2002). "Measuring quality of life in children with inflammatory bowel disease: the impact-II (NL)." *Quality of Life Research* 11(1): 47-56.

Marx RG, Bombardier C, Hogg-Johnson S, Wright JG. (1999) Clinimetric and psychometric strategies for development of a health measurement scale. *J. Clin. Epidemiol.* ;52:105–11.

Matza LA, Swensen R, Flood EM, Secnik K, Leidy NK (2004) Assessment of Health-Related Quality of Life in Children: *A Review of Conceptual, Methodological, and Regulatory Value in health* 7 :79–92.

Millstein SG Irwin CE (1987) Concepts of health and illness: different constructs or variations on a theme? *Health Psychol.* 6(6):515-24.

Moher D, Schulz KF, Altman DG (2001) The CONSORT statement: revised recommendations for improving the quality of reports of parallel group randomized trials *BMC Medical Research Methodology.*

Naito M, Nakayama T, Fukuhara S (2004) Quality of life assessment and reporting in randomized controlled trials: a study of literature published from Japan. *Health and Quality of Life Outcomes* 2:31 doi:10.1186/1477-7525-2-31.

Nunally JC, Bernstein IH. (1994) *Psychometric Theory.* New York: McGraw-Hill.

Power M, Harper A, Bullinger M and the World Health Organization. (1999) WHOQoL-100 tests of the universality of quality of life in 15 different cultural groups worldwide. *Health Psychol.* 18: 495–505.

Rothman ML, Hedrick SC, Bulcroft KA, Hickam DH, Rubenstein LZ. (1991)The validity of proxy-generated scores as measures of patient health status. *Med. Care* 29:115-24.

Smith KW, Avis NE, Assmann SF. Distinguishing between quality of life and health status in quality of life research: a meta-analysis. *Qual. Life Res.* 1999;8: 447–459.Wallander et al 2001).

Sneeuw KC, Sprangers MAG, Aaronson NK (2002) The role of health care providers and significant others in evaluating the quality of life of patients with chronic disease. *Journal of Clinical Epidemiology* 55: 1130–1143.

Spielberger CD, Edwards CD, Lushene RE et al. State Triat *Anxiety Inventory Manual* (1973). Palo Alto Ca Consult Psy Press.

Spilker B. (1996) *Quality of Life Assessment in Clinical Trails.* New York: Raven Press.

Streiner DL (2003) Clinimetrics vs. psychometrics: an unnecessary distinction. *Journal of Clinical Epidemiology* 56 : 1142–1145.

Upton P, Maddocks A, Eiser C, Barnes PM, Williams JG (2005) Development of a measure of the health-related quality of life of children in public care Child: *Care, Health and Development* 31: 409–415.

Upton P, Eiser C, Cheung I et al. (2005) Measurement properties of the UK-English version of the Pediatric Quality of Life Inventory™ 4.0 (PedsQL™) generic core scales. *Health and Quality of Life Outcomes* 3:22 Available from Biomed Central at: http://www.hqlo.com/content/3/1/22.

Varni JW Burwinkle TM Lane MM. (2005) Health-related quality of life measurement in pediatric clinical practice: An appraisal and precept for future research and application. *Health Qual. Life Outcomes* [electronic resource] 3:34 Available from Biomed Central http ://www.hqlo.com/content/3/1/34

Varni JW, Burwinkle TM, Jacobs JR, Gottschalk M, Kaufman F, Jones KL (2003) The PedsQL in Type 1 and Type 2 diabetes: Reliability and validity of the Pediatric Quality of Life Inventory Generic Core Scales and Type 1 Diabetes Module. Diabetes Care 26:631-663.

Vitale MG, Levy DE, et al. (2001). Capturing quality of life in pediatric orthopaedics: two recent measures compared. *J. Pediatr. Orthop.* 21(5): 629-35.

Ware JE, Kosinski MM and Keller SD (1996) a 12-item short form health survey: Construction of scales and preliminary tests of reliability and validity. *Medical Care* 34 (3): 220 – 233.

Wann-Hansson C, Hallberg IR, Risberg B, Klevsgård R (2004) Comparison of the Nottingham Health Profile and Short Form 36 Health Survey in patients with chronic lower limb ischaemia in a longitudinal perspective. *Health Qual. Life Outcomes* 2:9.

WHO. Preamble to the Constitution of the World Health Organization as adopted by the International Health Conference, New York, 19-22 June, 1946; signed on 22 July 1946 by the representatives of 61 States *(Official Records of the World Health Organization, no. 2, p. 100)* and entered into force on 7 April 1948.

Williams JG, Russell IT, Upton P et al (2003) *Development and comparison of two quality of life measures for use with UK children.* Unpublished report to the Welsh Assembly Government.

Wright JG, Feinstein AR (1992). A comparative contrast of clinimetric and psychometric methods for constructing indexes and rating scales. *J. Clin. Epidemiol.* 42: 1201–1218.

Zeman J, Garber J. (1996) Display Rules for Anger, Sadness, and Pain: It Depends on Who Is Watching. *Child Development* 67: 957-973 doi:10.2307/1131873.

In: Leading-Edge Psychological Tests and Testing Research   ISBN: 978-1-60021-571-1
Editor: Marta A. Lange, pp. 89-108   © 2007 Nova Science Publishers, Inc.

Chapter 5

VALIDITY AND RELIABILITY OF THE STANDARDIZED ASTHMA QUALITY OF LIFE QUESTIONNAIRE – AQLQ(S) IN GREECE

E. Grammatopoulou, E. K. Skordilis and D. Koutsouki

Laboratory of Adapted Physical Activity/Developmental and Physical Disabilities
Department of Physical Education and Sport Sciences
National and Kapodistrian University of Athens, Greece

ABSTRACT

The study examined the validity and reliability of the Standardized Asthma Quality of Life Questionnaire-AQLQ(S) (Juniper, 1999a) in Greece. The AQLQ(S) incorporates 32 items, presented in a 7 point Likert scale, with four factors: 'Activity Limitations', 'Symptoms', 'Emotional Function' and 'Exposure to Environmental Stimuli'. Following translation validity evidence, 60 Greek adults were examined. The participants were divided to 30 patients and 30 non patients, from Athens, Greece. The group of asthmatics was tested during their visits at private clinics. The non asthmatic group was recruited from the general population and assimilated the asthmatic group according to age, gender and socioeconomic status. Construct validity was tested through the following comparisons: a) patients vs non patients with asthma, b) atopic vs non atopic patients, c) younger vs older patients with asthma and d) patients with mild, moderate and severe asthma. Statistical analyses, based on multivariate and univariate tests, supported our research hypotheses. Specifically, non patients scored significantly higher than patients in AQLQ(S), indicating, therefore, higher Quality of Life (QoL). Further, atopics scored higher than non atopics, younger scored higher than older patients and finally, patients with mild and moderate asthma scored higher than patients with severe asthma. Reliability was tested with the test retest method: a) for the total sample and b) for the asthmatic group. For the total sample, r was .911 for the total AQLQ(S) score, and ranged from .834 to .946 for the four AQLQ(S) factors. For the asthmatic group, overal r was .957, while test retest correlation coefficients, for the four separate factors, ranged from .915 to .966. At this point, the first validity and reliability evidence of the Greek AQLQ(S) are reported. The construct validity of the Greek AQLQ(S) must be re examined in the near future, through exploratory and confirmatory factor analysis, to strengthen the present findings. Further, Cronbach alpha reliability coefficients will provide internal consistency evidence for the four separate AQLQ(S) factors.

INTRODUCTION

Asthma is a chronic inflammatory disease of the lower airways, characterized by hyper responsiveness to various stimuli and therefore excessive narrowing (West, 2004). The chronic inflammation causes an associated increase in airway hyper responsiveness that leads to recurrent episodes of wheezing, breathlessness, chest tightness and coughing, particularly at night or in the early morning. These episodes are usually associated with widespread but variable airflow obstruction that is often reversible either spontaneously or with treatment (Global Initiative for Asthma, 2004). In general, patients with asthma experience a variety of symptoms, which differ according to severity (mild, moderate, severe and intermittent) (Sawyer et al., 1998; Global Initiative for Asthma, 2004), atopy (atopic and non atopic), age, etc. (West, 2004).

Asthma affects the quality of life (QoL) in adult populations (Juniper et al., 1992; Erickson, Cristian & Kirking, 2000; Ford et al., 2003; Thoonen et al., 2003; Juniper, 2005). Health related quality of life (HRQoL) has been defined by Schipper, Clinch, & Powell (1996) as 'the functional effects of an illness and its consequent treatment on a patient's life as perceived by him' (Schipper et al., 1996). Restrictions to asthmatic patient's quality of life (QoL) often lead to decrement of their physical and occupational function, psychological state, social interaction, etc. (Schipper et al., 1996).

Assessing QoL of adult patients with asthma is essential since it provides guidance for the design and implementation of therapeutic programs (Juniper, Guyatt, Ferrie, & Griffith, 1993; Bousquet et al., 1994). Quality of life, however, cannot be inferred from general clinical measurements (Juniper et al., 2004), since it has, for example, a weak relationship with lung function. It is a distinct component of asthma health status and therefore it must be measured by suitable questionnaires (Marks, Dunn, & Woolcock, 1992; Juniper, Gordon, Streiner, & King, 1997b).

Health related QoL questionnaires are suggested for use by various researchers (Juniper et al., 1992; Guyatt et al., 1997; Hyland, 2003; Juniper et al., 2004). Specifically, two types of questionnaires are used for that purpose: generic and specified questionnaires. The most commonly used generic questionnaires in adult patients with asthma are: The Medical Outcomes Survey Short Form (SF-36), (Ware & Sherbourne, 1992), the Sickness Impact Profile (SIP) (Bergner, Bobbitt, Carter, & Gilson, 1981), and the Nottingham Health Profile (Jans, Schellevis, & van Eijik, 1991). They assess, in general, the overall health related QoL, allowing comparisons between patients and healthy people, between patients with different diseases, but they have limited use in clinical practice (Juniper, 1997a; Ware & Sherbourne, 1992; Bousquet et al., 1994).

The specific questionnaires are used in patients with specific disease or functional impairment. They are suitable in detecting differences between patients with the same disease and changes as a function of time or treatment (Patrick & Deyo, 1989). The most commonly used specific questionnaires are the: a) St George Respiratory Questionnaire (SGRQ) (Jones, 1991), b) Asthma Quality of Life Questionnaire (AQLQ) (Juniper et al., 1992), c) Standardised Asthma Quality of Life Questionnaire AQLQ(S) (Juniper, Buist, Cox, Ferrie, &

King, 1999a), d) Mini Asthma Quality of Life Questionnaire (Mini AQLQ) (Juniper, Guyatt, Cox, Ferrie, & King, 1999b), e) Living With Asthma Questionnaire-LWAQ (LWAQ) (Hyland, 1991; Hyland, Finnis, & Irvine, 1991), etc.

Specifically, the AQLQ (Juniper et al., 1992) was developed to assess the health related impairment of QoL that adult asthmatic patients experience in their everyday life. During completion, patients recall their health status during the last two weeks. The AQLQ contains 32 items in four general factors: activity limitations (11 items); symptoms (12 items); emotional functioning (5 items) and exposure to environmental stimuli (4 items). Finally, Juniper et al., (1999a) reported that the AQLQ had appropriate validity and reliability indexes (ICC=.95) and is capable for clinical trials and particularly for measuring changes in QoL over time.

Leroyer et al., (1998) examined the cross-sectional validity of the French AQLQ version. The researchers found cross-sectional correlations of the French AQLQ with functional assessments and asthma severity similar to those observed with the original English version (Juniper et al., 1992). Leroyer et al., (1998) stated that the instrument had sufficient validity evidence and there may be a positive association between quality of life and patient's knowledge concerning asthma.

Sanjuas et al., (2001) developed the Spanish AQLQ version and presented sufficient evidence of internal consistency (Cronbach's alpha = .78 to .96) and reproducibility (ICC = .82 to .92). The cross-sectional and longitudinal correlations between AQLQ and the overall St. George's Respiratory Questionnaire were strong. Further, they were moderate to strong between AQLQ and dyspnea and weak to moderate between AQLQ and FEV1 (% predicted). Further, the changes in AQLQ scores were significantly different in patients whose asthma either improved or deteriorated, compared to patients whose asthma remained stable.

Spiric et al., (2004) developed the Serbian AQLQ version and presented high reliability evidence (Cronbach's alpha .72 – .93). The researchers stated that overall disease, severity, place of residence, weather conditions, age, and FEV1 (% predicted), were significantly related to the participant's QoL.

Juniper et al., (1999a) developed the standardized AQLQ(S), by formulating 5 generic activities (strenuous exercise, moderate exercise, work related activities, social activities, and sleep), to replace the 5 individualized activity limitations of the AQLQ. The researchers stated that the AQLQ(S) was developed to: a) facilitate the long term studies and clinical trials were individual features are less important, b) solve the reliability problems due to the 5 different individualized activity limitations that patients complete during retest, and c) limit the construction problems of the individualized questionnaires and data selection (Juniper et al., 1999a). Juniper et al., (1999a) found interclass correlation coefficient (ICC) of .96 for the AQLQ(S). Further, the responsiveness and construct validity (correlation with other measures of health status and clinical asthma) were at the appropriate range.

Tan et al., (2004) developed the English AQLQ(S) version in a multy-ethnic Asian population. The Cronbach's alpha coefficient for internal consistency ranged from .80 to .95. The interclass correlation coefficient (ICC) was .97 (95% CI: .94-.99) for the total AQLQ(S) score and ranged from .88 to .95 for the four AQLQ(S) factors . The responsiveness index was found 1.25 for the total AQLQ(S) score, and ranged from 1.06 to 1.60 for the four AQLQ(S) factors.

The development of the AQLQ (Juniper et al., 1992) and AQLQ(S) (Juniper et al., 1999a), has allowed researchers to examine a variety of populations and provide validity evidence for these measures in different countries, such as France, Spain, and Serbia (Leroyer et al., 1998; Sanjuas et al., 2001; Spiric et al., 2004). There is lack, however, of validated instruments measuring the QoL of adults with asthma in Greece. According to the aforementioned, the present study was designed to provide validity and reliability evidence for the AQLQ(S), in Greece. For that reason, we attempted to provide discriminant validity evidence by examining the differences between Greek asthmatics and non asthmatics on the total score and the 4 factors of the AQLQ(S) (activity limitations, symptoms, emotional function and exposure to environmental stimuli). Specifically, we examined the differences of Greek asthmatic patients who differed according to severity (mild, moderate, severe and intermittent asthma), atopy (atopic and non atopic asthma), age and smoking, on the AQLQ(S). Finally, the test retest method was utilized to provide reliability evidence. We anticipated, based on previous research findings, that: a) the asthmatics would score lower than the non asthmatics (Leynaert et al., 2000; Ford et al., 2003), b) the group of asthmatics would differ according to severity (Huss et al., 2001; Juniper et al., 1992, Spiric et al., 2004; and Moy et al., 2001), atopy (Ehrs et al., 2006), age (Hyland, 1991; Spiric et al., 2004; Ehrs et al., 2006) and smoking (Gallefoss & Bakke, 2001; Laforest et al., 2005; Ehrs et al., 2006), and c) the test retest reliability indexes of the total score and the 4 factors of the AQLQ(S) would be at the appropriate range.

METHOD

Researchers have reported the importance for providing validity and reliability evidence when measuring specific populations (Sherrill & O'Connor, 1999; Yun & Ulrich, 2002). Based on the above theory, the validity and reliability of AQLQ(S) for Greek asthmatics were examined, through the following steps: a) translation validity (Guillemin, Bombardier, & Beaton, 1993; Herdman, Fox-Rushby, & Badia, 1997), b) discriminant validity (Yun & Ulrich, 2002) and c) test retest reliability (Thomas & Nelson, 2003).

Participants

A total of 60 adults were examined. The participants, recruited through purposive sampling selection (Thomas and Nelson, 2003), were divided in two equal numbered groups of: a) asthmatics (n_1 = 30) and b) non asthmatics (n_2 = 30). The group of asthmatics varied according to the severity (mild, moderate and severe), atopy (atopic and non atopic), age, socioeconomic status, etc. The second group, of non asthmatics, assimilated the first group, according to their respective demographic characteristics. Overall, the demographics of our total sample may be found in Table 1.

Measuring Instrument

The AQLQ(S) (Juniper et al., 1999a) constitutes an extension of the initial AQLQ (Juniper et al., 1992). The difference between the two measures lies in the fact that the

AQLQ(S) does not include the 5 individualized activities found into the AQLQ. For the AQLQ(S), the aforementioned 5 individualized activities have been replaced with 5 general activities (vigorous activity, moderate activity, activities related to occupation, social interaction and sleep).

Table 1. General characteristics of the participants

Variable	Mean	SD	min	max	N
Asthmatics					
Age (years)	42.90	15.84	18.00	73.00	30
Health status					
In the last 2 weeks	3.67	.93	2.00	5.00	30
Gender					
Man					10
Woman					20
Atopy					
Atopics					24
non atopics					6
Severity					
Mild					9
Moderate					15
Severe					6
Duration	16.20	12.95	1.00	48.00	30
Smoking					
Smokers					8
non smokers					22
Participation in athletics					
Yes					11
No					19
Education status					
elementary scool					3
high school					9
College					3
technological educational institution					1
University					10
graduate studies					4
Residence					
City					14
Suburban					13
Rural					3
Annual income (euro)					
0-15.000					6
15.001-30.000					10
30.001 and above					14

Table 1. (Continued)

Variable	Mean	SD	min	max	N
Insurance					
Public					19
Private					5
Combined					5
no insurance					1
Visits in hospital	.13	.34	.00	1.00	30
Non asthmatics					
Age (years)	37.40	9.51	19.00	55.00	30
Health status					
In the last 2 weeks	5.00	.00	5.00	5.00	30
Gender					
Man					15
Woman					15
Smoking					
Smokers					13
non smokers					17
Participation in athletics					
Yes					13
No					17
Education status					
elementary school					1
high school					7
College					3
technological educational institution					3
University					13
graduate studies					3
Residence					
City					4
Suburban					26
Annual income (euro)					
0-15.000					2
15.001-30.000					16
30.001 and above					12
Insurance					
Public					13
Private					7
Combined					10
no insurance					0

The AQLQ(S), examining the functional (physical, emotional, occupational and social) difficulties of adults with asthma, incorporates 32 items, classified in 4 separate factors: a) 'activity limitations' (11 items), b) 'symptoms' (12 items), c) 'emotional functioning' (5 items) and d) 'exposure to environmental stimuli' (4 items). Individuals who respond to the questionnaire, recall the frequency, intension and severity of the health difficulties they have had, due to asthma, during the last two weeks. The responses in all 32 items are provided in a

7-point Likert scale, varying from 1: minimum score to 7: maximum score. The lower the score, the higher the restriction in the QoL (low QoL). The total score is the average emerging from the responses in all 32 items. The score for each factor separate, is emerging from the average of it's respective items. Juniper et al. (1999a) stated that the AQLQ(S) had sufficient construct validity, concurrent validity, intraclass reliability (ICC=0.96) and responsiveness (p<0.0001).

Table 2. Responces in the total score and the four AQLQ factors

Variable	Mean	SD	min	max	N
Asthmatics					
Activity limitations	5.17	1.16	2.73	6.64	30
Symptoms	5.09	1.26	2.33	6.92	30
Emotional function	5.09	1.47	2.40	7.00	30
Exposure to Environmental stimuli	4.79	1.24	2.25	7.00	30
Total score AQLQ(S)	5.03	1.19	2.64	6.78	30
Non asthmatics					
Activity limitations	7.00	.02	6.91	7.00	30
Symptoms	6.96	.09	6.67	7.00	30
Emotional function	6.93	.19	6.00	7.00	30
Exposure to Environmental stimuli	6.79	.21	6.25	7.00	30
Total score AQLQ(S)	6.92	.09	6.67	7.00	30
Mild asthma					
Activity limitations	5.94	.57	5.27	6.64	9
Symptoms	5.99	.64	4.58	6.83	9
Emotional function	5.98	.81	4.80	7.00	9
Exposure to Environmental stimuli	5.25	.98	4.00	6.75	9
Total score AQLQ(S)	5.79	.64	4.87	6.78	9
Moderate					
Activity limitations	5.94	.57	5.27	6.64	15
Symptoms	5.99	.64	2.53	6.92	15
Emotional function	5.98	.81	2.80	7.00	15
Exposure to Environmental stimuli	4.88	1.11	4.00	6.75	15
Total score AQLQ(S)	5.79	.64	2.64	6.74	15
Severe					
Activity limitations	4.11	1.27	2.73	5.55	6
Symptoms	3.93	.76	2.83	4.67	6
Emotional function	4.10	1.72	2.40	6.40	6
Exposure to Environmental stimuli	3.87	1.57	2.25	6.50	6
Total score AQLQ(S)	4.00	1.19	2.76	5.76	6
18-30 years old					
Activity limitations	5.52	1.06	3.36	6.64	7
Symptoms	5.40	1.22	3.42	6.92	7
Emotional function	5.54	1.42	3.00	7.00	7
Exposure to Environmental stimuli	5.21	1.03	3.75	6.50	7
Total score AQLQ(S)	5.42	1.12	3.38	6.58	7

Table 2. (Continued)

Variable	Mean	SD	min	max	N
31-50 years old					
Activity limitations	5.58	.91	3.82	6.64	15
Symptoms	5.37	1.04	3.67	6.83	15
Emotional function	5.45	1.32	2.80	7.00	15
Exposure to Environmental stimuli	5.08	1.25	2.25	7.00	15
Total score AQLQ(S)	5.37	.98	3.65	6.78	15
51 years old and above					
Activity limitations	4.12	1.12	2.73	5.27	8
Symptoms	4.28	1.46	2.33	6.63	8
Emotional function	3.97	1.36	2.40	6.20	8
Exposure to Environmental stimuli	3.87	.98	2.50	5.00	8
Total score AQLQ(S)	4.06	1.19	2.64	5.56	8
Atopics					
Activity limitations	5.46	.98	2.73	6.64	24
Symptoms	5.39	1.08	3.17	6.92	24
Emotional function	5.40	1.34	2.40	7.00	24
Exposure to Environmental stimuli	4.99	1.19	2.25	7.00	24
Total score AQLQ(S)	5.31	1.03	2.76	6.78	24
Non atopics					
Activity limitations	4.04	1.23	2.73	5.82	6
Symptoms	3.89	1.31	2.33	5.83	6
Emotional function	3.80	.36	2.60	6.20	6
Exposure to Environmental stimuli	4.00	1.17	2.50	5.75	6
Total score AQLQ(S)	3.93	1.25	2.64	5.90	6
Smokers					
Activity limitations	4.87	1.09	2.91	6.64	8
Symptoms	4.33	1.14	2.33	6.42	8
Emotional function	4.32	1.11	2.80	6.40	8
Exposure to Environmental stimuli	4.56	1.10	2.50	6.50	8
Total score AQLQ(S)	4.52	1.02	2.64	5.81	8
Non smokers					
Activity limitations	5.29	1.19	2.73	6.64	22
Symptoms	5.36	1.21	2.83	6.92	22
Emotional function	5.35	1.51	2.40	7.00	22
Exposure to Environmental stimuli	4.87	1.29	2.25	7.00	22
Total score AQLQ(S)	5.22	1.22	2.76	6.78	22

Procedure

Translation validity of the AQLQ(S) was established through the following steps:

a)   Translation from English to Greek. The questionnaire was translated from a first group of 2 medical doctors and 2 physical therapists, all with expertise in English and/ or holding a Ph.D from Universities using English as their primary language.

The above group worked together and concluded for the Greek version of the AQLQ(S).

b) The translated in Greek AQLQ(S) was back translated in English from a second group of 2 medical doctors and 2 physical therapists, all, again, with expertise in English and/ or holding a Ph.D from English spoken Universities. Again, the second group worked together and concluded for the re translated in English AQLQ(S). Further, the second group compared the re translated AQLQ(S) with the original AQLQ(S) of Juniper et al., (1999a) and found linguistic and content agreement above 80% (Thomas & Nelson, 2003).

c) Cultural adaptation. Five asthmatics and five non asthmatics were asked to complete the Greek AQLQ(S) and identify unclear items requiring modification. These individuals indicated that all 32 items were accurate and the questionnaire was easy for completion. Overall, no adaptations were required and the Greek AQLQ(S) was ready for administration.

d) b) The discriminant validity of the Greek AQLQ(S) was examined through the following steps: differences i) between asthmatics and non asthmatics, ii) among asthmatics with mild, mediate and severe asthma, iii) between atopic and non atopic asthmatics, iv) among asthmatics who differed according to age (18-30, 31-50 and above 51) and v) between smokers and non smokers, all patients with asthma. According to previous research studies, we expected: i) the asthmatic group to score lower than the non asthmatic (Leynaert et al., 2000; Ford, 2003), ii) patients with severe asthma to score lower than patients with mild and moderate asthma, (Juniper et al., 1992; Moy et al., 2001; Huss et al., 2001; Spiric et al., 2004), iii) young patients to score higher than older patients with asthma (Hyland, 1991; Spiric et al., 2004; Ehrs et al., 2006), iv) atopics to score higher than non atopics (Ehrs et al., 2006), and v) smokers with asthma to score lower than non smokers with asthma (Ehrs et al., 2006; Laforest et al., 2005; Gallefoss & Bakke, 2001).

e) The reliability of the Greek AQLQ(S) was tested with the test retest method (Thomas and Nelson, 2003). Specifically, the questionnaire was administered twice, to all 60 individuals, in January, with a time interval between the two measures of 10-15 days. The 10-15 days distance was considered appropriate for patients to respond for second time without learning, practice or motivation effect, (Beaton, Bombadier, Guillemin, & Ferraz, 2000; Guilford & Fruchter, 1978; Hopkins, 1998; Thomas & Nelson, 2003).

The Greek AQLQ(S) was self administered to 30 patients with asthma, in private respiratory clinics, in Athens, Greece. The primary researcher visited the above clinics, explained the purposes of the study to all patients and administered the questionnaires. All patients responded to a demographic data sheet, signed the informed consent form and responded to the AQLQ(S). Severity and atopy of the asthmatic group was obtained from their physicians (i.e. through spirometry norms). Age and smoking habits was obtained through the demographic data sheet. Finally, the participants from the non asthmatic sample were examined at their respective residence, from the primary researcher.

Statistical Analysis

The Statistical Package for the Social Sciences (SPSS) (Norusis, 1993), with MANOVA (Tabachnick & Fidell, 1998), ANOVA, t-test and Pearson correlation coefficient (Grimm, 1993) was used for data analyses. Specifically, the Pearson r examined the test retest reliability. The MANOVA, ANOVA and t-test examined the discriminant validity of the AQLQ(S). The .05 level of significance was selected to test the above statistical hypotheses.

RESULTS

The differences: i) between asthmatics and non asthmatics, ii) among asthmatics with mild, mediate and severe asthma, iii) between atopic and non atopic asthmatics, iv) among asthmatics who differed according to age (18-30, 31-50 and above 51) and v) between smoking and non smoking patients with asthma, were examined. The results were as follows:

i) Differences between Asthmatics and Non Asthmatics

According to the MANOVA results, there were significant differences in the mean vector of scores with the four factors of 'activity limitations', 'symptoms', 'emotional functioning' and 'exposure to environmental stimuli', between asthmatics and non asthmatics (Wilks' Lambda = .396, p=.000). Accordingly, post hoc discriminant function analysis revealed that the 'environmental stimuli' factor significantly separated the two groups. The regression equation predicting group membership ($Y = -6.529 + 1.127\ X_{envstim}$) could accurate classify 88.3% of the participants. Examination of the group membership table revealed that the 88.3% prediction rate was attributed to 7 asthmatics who were misclassified to the asthmatic group. Contrary to the above, all non asthmatic patients were classified correctly.

Independent sample t-test revealed significant differences, between the two groups, for the total AQLQ(S) score. Specifically, the non asthmatic group scored higher than the asthmatic group, indicating better QoL. Further, four independent sample t-tests revealed significant differences between the two groups, in the four AQLQ(S) factors. In the above comparisons, the non asthmatics scored higher than the asthmatics, indicating better QoL. The overall findings may be found in Table 3 and 4.

ii) Differences among Patients with Mild, Mediate and Severe Asthma (Severity)

The MANOVA revealed no significant differences, in the mean vector of scores with the four AQLQ(S) factors, between asthmatics with mild, moderate and severe asthma. The Wilks' Lambda value ($\Lambda = .581$) however, approached the significance level (p = .087) and the post hoc discriminant analysis was administered therefore. According to the discriminant function findings, the 'symptoms' factor significantly separated the three groups. The regression equation predicting group membership ($Y = -4.780 + .939\ X_{symptoms}$) accurately classified 53.3% of the participants. Examination of the group membership table revealed that the 53.3% prediction rate was mainly attributed to patients with moderate asthma. Specifically, among the 15 individuals with moderate asthma, 6 were classified as having mild, 5 were classified as having severe and only 4 were correctly classified as having moderate asthma (26.7%). Contrary to that, patients with mild asthma were 88.9% correctly classified while patients with severe asthma were 66.7% correctly classified accordingly.

Table 3. MANOVA findings

Effect	Wilks Lamda	F	P
Asthma vs non asthma	.396	21.010	.000
Age	.645	1.469	.087
Severity	.581	1.872	.087
Smoking	.743	2.160	.103
Atopy	.719	2.437	.074

Table 4. T- test for independed samples, in the total score and the four AQLQ factors

Effect	MO	Mean Diff	SE Diff	T	p
Asthmatics		- 1.89	.22	-8.65	.000*
Yes	5.03				
No	6.92				
Classification		1.38	.49	2.82	.009*
Atopics	5.31				
Non atopics	3.93				
Smoking		-.70	.48	-1.44	.160
Yes	4.52				
No	5.22				

Independent groups ANOVA revealed significant differences between the three groups in the total AQLQ(S) score. Post hoc Least Significant Difference-LSD test revealed that the differences were evident between the group of patients with mild and severe asthma. Specifically, the mild group scored higher than the severe group, indicating, therefore, higher QoL. The overall findings are presented in Tables 3 and 5.

Four independent groups ANOVAs were administered afterwards, to test for significant differences among asthmatics with mild, moderate and severe asthma, for the four AQLQ(S) factors. Significant differences were found separate for the three factors of 'symptoms', 'activity limitations' and 'emotional functioning'. No significant differences among groups were evident for 'exposure to environmental stimuli'. Post hoc Least Significant Difference-LSD analyses revealed that: a) The three groups differed significantly from each other in the 'symptoms' factor. Specifically, patients with mild asthma had significantly higher score than patients with moderate and severe asthma. Further, patients with moderate asthma had significantly higher score than patients with severe asthma. b) Regarding 'activity limitations', significant differences were found between patients with mild and severe asthma. Again, mild asthmatics scored higher than severe asthmatics. c) Finally, regarding 'emotional functioning', patients with mild asthma had significantly higher scores than patients with severe asthma.

iii) Differences between Atopic and Non Atopic Patients with Asthma

The MANOVA revealed no significant differences, in the mean vector of scores with the four AQLQ(S) factors, between atopic and non atopic patients with asthma. Again, since the Wilks' Lambda value ($\Lambda = .719$) approached the significance level ($p = .074$), post hoc discriminant analysis was administered. According to the discriminant function findings, the 'activity limitations' factor significantly separated the atopic and non atopic groups. The regression equation predicting group membership ($Y = -5.029 + .971 \ X_{act \ limitation}$) could accurate classify 80.0% of the participants. Examination of the group membership table revealed that 20 out of the 24 atopics were classified correctly (83.3%), while 4 out of 6 non atopics were classified correctly as well (66.7%).

Independent sample t-test revealed significant differences, between the two groups of atopic and non atopic patients, for the total AQLQ(S) score. Specifically, the atopics scored higher than the non atopics, indicating better QoL. Further, the independent sample t-tests revealed significant differences between the two groups, in the 'symptoms', 'activity limitations' and 'emotional functioning' factors. No significant differences between groups were found for the 'exposure to environmental stimuli' factor. In the above comparisons, the atopics scored higher than the non atopics, indicating better QoL. The overall findings may be found in Tables 3 and 4.

Table 5. Independent groups ANOVA examining differences across age and severity levels of asthmatics, in the total AQLQ(S) score

Effect	SS	Df	MS	F	p
Age[1]					
BG	10.29	2	5.15	4.51*	.021
WG	30.84	27	1.14		
Total	41.13	29			
Severity[2]					
BG	11.54	2	5.77	5.26*	.021
WG	29.60	27			
Total	41.14	29			

1: 18 > 51 and above, 31 > 51 and above
2: Mild > Severe

iv) Differences among Asthmatics Who Differed According to Age (18-30, 31-50 and above 51)

The MANOVA revealed no significant differences, in the mean vector of scores with the four AQLQ(S) factors, among the three age groups. Once again, the Wilks' Lambda value (Λ

= .645) approached the significance level (p = .087) and the post hoc discriminant analysis revealed that the 'activity limitations' factor significantly separated the three groups. The regression equation predicting group membership ($Y = -5.160 + .996\ X_{actlimitations}$) accurately classified 50% of the participants. Examination of the group membership table revealed that the 50% prediction rate was mainly attributed to patients whose age ranged from 18 to 30 years old. Specifically, among the 7 individuals in the 18-30 years age group, only 3 were classified correctly (42.3%). Percentage of correct classification for the 31-50 and above 51 age groups were 53.3% and 50% respectively.

Independent groups ANOVA revealed significant differences between the three age groups in the total AQLQ(S) score. Post hoc Least Significant Difference-LSD test revealed significant differences between: a) 18-30 and above 51, and b) 31-50 and above 51 age groups. In both findings, the younger asthmatics scored significantly higher than the older asthmatics, indicating, therefore, higher QoL. The overall findings are presented in Tables 3 and 5.

The independent groups ANOVA revealed significant differences among the different age group in the three AQLQ(S) factors ('activity limitations', 'emotional functioning', and 'exposure to environmental stimuli'). No significant differences among groups were found for 'symptoms'. Post hoc Least Significant Difference-LSD analyses revealed that patients 51 years old and above had significantly lower scores than patients 18-30 and 31-50 years old in 'activity limitations', 'emotional functioning' and 'exposure to environmental stimuli'.

v) Differences between Smoking and Non Smoking Patients with Asthma

The MANOVA revealed no significant differences, in the mean vector of scores with the four AQLQ(S) factors, between smoking and non smoking patients with asthma. Once again, the Wilks' Lambda value ($\Lambda = .743$) approached the significance level (p = .103) and the post hoc discriminant analysis was administered therefore. According to the discriminant function findings, the 'symptoms' factor significantly separated the smoking and non smoking groups. The regression equation predicting group membership ($Y = -4.266 + .838\ X_{symptoms}$) could accurate classify 73.3% of the participants. The above findings may be found in Tables 3 and 4.

Independent sample t-test revealed no significant differences, between the two groups, for the total AQLQ(S) score. Further, the independent sample t-tests revealed significant differences between the two groups, in the 'symptoms' factor only. Specifically, the non smoking group scored significantly higher than the smoking group.

vi) Reliability

The AQLQ(S) was administered twice to the sample of asthmatics and non asthmatics (test retest method), with a time interval of 10-15 days between the two testing sessions. Specifically, Pearson correlation coefficients were used in the total sample, to calculate the test-retest reliability of the: a) total AQLQ(S) and b) four separate factors. For the total AQLQ(S), a coefficient r = .957 (p < .05) was found. For the separate AQLQ(S) factors, the following coefficients were found: a) r = .951 (p < .05) for 'activity limitations' b) r = .915 (p

< .05) for 'symptoms', c) r = .966 (p < .05) for 'emotional functioning' and d) r = .949 (p < .05) for 'exposure to environmental stimuli', respectively.

Further, the Pearson tesr retesr reliability coefficients were calculated for the sample of asthmatic patients only. The results were: a) .911 for the total AQLQ(S) score, b) .910 for the 'activity limitations',c) .834 for 'symptoms', d) .946 for 'emotional functioning', and c) .900 for 'environmental stimuli' respectively.

DISCUSSION

The Greek version of AQLQ(S) could separate individuals with and without asthma, providing therefore initial construct validity evidence. More specifically, the univariate analyses indicated that asthmatics scored lower in the total AQLQ(S), as well as in the separate four factors ('symptoms', 'exposure to environmental stimuli', 'activity limitations' and 'emotional functioning'), compared to non-asthmatics. The above differences were confirmed through multivariate analysis which, in addition, showed that the 'exposure to environmental stimuli' factor significantly separated the two groups. The above finding is in agreement with Leynaert et al., (2000), and Ford et al., (2003). Leynaert et al., (2000) used the SF-36 to examine the QoL in adults with allergic rhinitis, either with or without asthma. Leynaert et al., (2000) found that individuals with asthma scored lower in the SF-36, thus having lower QoL than individuals without asthma. Ford et al., (2003) examined how self–reported asthma is associated with general self-reported health and four separate health-reported QoL measures. The participants with asthma reported significantly lower general self-reported health and health-reported QoL than participants who never had asthma.

Accordingly, the differences of asthmatic patients who differed on severity (mild, moderate, severe), atopy (atopic and non-atopic), age and smoking were assessed. Regarding severity of the disease, univariate analysis revealed differences in the total AQLQ(S) score as well as in the 'symptoms', 'activity limitations' and 'emotional functioning' factors. For the 'symptoms' factor, mild asthmatics indicated higher QoL than moderate asthmatics who, in turn, indicated higher QoL than severe asthmatics. The 'symptoms' therefore, could separate the three categories of asthmatics, according to severity. Regarding the 'activity limitations' and 'emotional functioning' factors, patients with mild asthma indicated a higher QoL than patients with severe asthma. No differences were evident between mild and moderate, or moderate with severe asthmatics.

Conclusively, the Greek AQLQ(S) could distinguish patients with mild and severe asthma. Patients with moderate asthma, however, could not be distinguished from the mild and severe groups. Explanation may be due to the fact that the distinction of patients' severity was obtained from their physicians, mainly through spirometry norms. Possibly, this separation was not the most effective to detect the differences of patient's subjective evaluation of their QoL.

Our findings are in agreement with Sawyer et al. (1998) who demonstrated inconsistency between the expected FEV1% and PEF% scores for the assessment of severity of asthmatic patients. According to Sawyer et al. (1998), it was common for practitioners to believe that the expected FEV1% and PEF% scores ranged at specific intervals within separate categories of severity. Further, the Global Initiative for Asthma (2004) uses, for severity classification, the FEV1% and PEF% scores. Overall, based on the present findings, additional examination of physiological parameters, like FEV1, describing severity of the disease, may be necessary for a valid distinction of patient's severity.

Our findings are in agreement with previous published research examining severity of asthmatic patients (Huss et al., 2001; Juniper et al., 1992; Spiric et al., 2004; Moy et al., 2001). In particular, Huss et al., (2001) examined the severity of asthma, skin allergies, exposure to environmental allergens and their impact on the QoL and the state of health of adult patients. Huss et al., (2001) found that patients with severe asthma had lower scores in the: a) total and b) four separate AQLQ factors, indicating that severity had a significant impact on QoL. Spiric et al., (2001) found significant differences in the: a) total and b) four separate AQLQ factors, according to severity. Juniper et al. (1992) evaluated the QoL and found that the total impact was greater for patients with severe asthma. Finally, Moy et al., (2001) studied the relationship between clinical indicators and severity of asthma. Moy et al., (2001) found that participants with moderate to severe asthma had lower QoL compared to those with mild asthma.

The Greek AQLQ(S) could separate asthmatics according to atopy (atopics and non atopics). In particular, the atopic group scored higher than the non atopic in the total as well as in three AQLQ(S) factors ('activity limitations', 'symptoms' and 'emotional functioning'). No differences between groups were evident in the 'exposure to environmental stimuli' factor only. Further, the differences between the two groups were confirmed through the multivariate analyses, demonstrating that the 'activity limitations' factor distinguished the groups of atopic and non atopic patients. Overal, the non atopic had lower QoL than the atopic patients, confirming this way our research hypothesis.

Regarding QoL and atopy our finding is in agreement with Ehrs et al., (2006), who studied the relationship between QoL and inflammation indicators. Ehrs et al., (2006) found that atopics scored higher than the non atopics and their differences were significant in the 'activity limitations' and 'exposure to environmental stimuli' factors. Further, our findings are partially in agreement with Spiric et al., (2004), who found that the two groups differed significantly in the 'symptoms' factor, with the atopics scoring higher than the non atopics. Spiric et al., (2004), however, found no differences, overall, between the two groups, which is not in agreement with the present findings.

Regarding age, univariate findings revealed significant differences between the following age groups: 18-30, 31-50, and 51 and above, in total AQLQ(S) score, as well as the 'activity limitations', 'emotional functioning' and 'exposure to environmental stimuli' factors. No significant differences were evident in the 'symptoms' factor. In any case, the younger asthmatics scored higher, indicating therefore better QoL, than the older asthmatics. Further, multivariate findings revealed that the 'activity limitations" factor separated significantly the three age groups, with a correct classification rate of 50%. This finding was attributed to the young group (18-30 years), which: a) did not differ from those aging from 31-50 years, and b) had the lower correct classification rate (42.9%). In the future, therefore, it may be more useful to separate patients with asthma in only two age categories (18-50 and 51 and above), which were consistently found to differ in their respective QoL.

Our findings, regarding age, agree with Hyland (1991), Ehrs et al., (2006), and Spiric et al., (2004). Hyland (1991) found that the QoL recedes as patients grow older. Spiric et al., (2004) found that old patients scored lower in the 'activity limitations' factor compared to young. Furthermore, Ehrs et al., (2006) found that elderly patients with asthma had low QoL scores, compared to younger patients. Spiric et al., (2004) stated that the higher QoL exhibited by young patients may be attributed to the fact that they adapt more easily to the disease by choosing less limiting every activities. Our findings, however, disagree with Juniper et al., (1992) and Wijnhoven, et al., (2001). Juniper et al., (1992) found that younger patients with asthma had lower QoL than older patients, while Wijnhoven et al., (2001) found that the younger the patients were, the lower their respective QoL. The findings of Juniper et al., (1992) and Wijnhoven, et al., (2001) suggest that the higher QoL of older patients may be due to temporal adaptation or acceptance of limitations they exhibit with increasing age. Overal, it appears that the effect of age in the QoL of patients with asthma needs to be re examined in the future. Possibly, a number of factors may influence the QoL exhibited by various age groups, such as severity (Bousquet et al., 1994).

Regarding smoking and QoL, the Greek AQLQ(S) could partially separate smokers and non smokers. In particular, the univariate analyses showed no significant differences in the total AQLQ(S) score. Significant differences were found only in the 'symptoms' factor, which were confirmed by the discriminant function analysis. Specifically, smokers had lower QoL than non smokers. These finding are in accordance with Gallefoss and Bakke (2001), Laforest et al., (2005) and Ehrs et al., (2006).

Gallefoss and Bakke (2001) found that smokers with asthma scored lower in the SGRQ and respectively had lower QoL compared to non smokers. Further, Laforest et al., (2005) found that smokers with asthma had lower QoL than non smokers, based on their scores in the 'exposure to environmental stimuli' factor. Ehrs et al., (2006) found that smokers with asthma had lower QoL than non smokers, based on their scores in the AQLQ.

Conclusively, the present findings provide initial construct validity evidence for the Greek AQLQ(S) (Thomas & Nelson, 2003). Specifically, the questionnaire successfully separated asthmatics and non asthmatics, as well as asthmatics who differed according to: a) severity of the disease b) atopy (atopic non atopic), c) age and d) smoking (smokers non smokers). Moreover, the responses on the questionnaire provided appropriate test-retest reliability evidence.

Certain limitations may have influenced the present findings. These limitations are referred to: a) the purposive sampling selection, b) the total number of participants (N=60), c) absence of relevant valid instruments measuring QoL in Greece, and d) absence of clinical indicators, like the predicted FEV1% and PEF%, to strengthen our findings. Future researchers may overcome the above limitations and provide further validity and reliability evidence, through factor analysis and Cronbach alpha reliability indexes, examine a more representative sample of asthmatic patients, correlate the Greek AQLQ(S) with clinical indicators, like the expected FEV1% , examine whether the AQLQ(S) can detect improvement or deterioration of the patient's QoL, etc.

REFERENCES

Beaton, E. D., Bombadier, C., Guillemin, F., & Ferraz, M. B. (2000). Guidelines for the process of cross cultural adaptation of self-report measures. *Spine, 25*(24), 3186-3191.

Bergner, M., Bobbitt, R.A., Carter, W. B., & Gilson, B. S. (1981). The Sickness impact profile: Development and final revision of a heart statues measure. *Medical Care, 19,* 787-805.

Bousquet, J., Knani, J., Dhivert, H., Richard, A., Chicoye, A., Ware, J. E., & Michel, F. B. (1994). Quality of life in asthma. Internal consistency and validity of the SF-36 questionnaire. *American Journal of Respiratory Critical Care Medicine, 149,* 371-375.

Erickson, S. R., Cristian, R. D., & Kirking, D. M. (2002). Relationship between patient and disease characteristics, and health-related quality of life in adylts with asthma. *Respiratory Medicine, 96,* 450-460.

Ehrs, P. O., Sundblad, B.M., & Larsson, K. (2006). Quality of life and markers of inflamation. *Chest,129,* 624-631.

Ford, E.S., Mannino, D. M., Homa, D. M., Gwynn, C., Redd, S. C., & Moriarty, D. G. (2003). Self- reported asthma and health–related quality of life. Findings from the behavioral risk factor surveillance system. *Chest, 123,* 119-127.

Gallefoss, F., & Bakke, P. S. (2003). Does smoking affect the outcome of patient education and self- management in asthmatics? *Patient Education and Counseling, 49,* 91-97.

Global initiative for asthma. (2004). Global strategy for asthma management and prevention NHLB/WHO. Work report. Available at: http: // www. ginasthma.org.

Grimm, G. L. (1993). *Statistical applications for the behavioral sciences.* New York, NY: John Wiley and Sons, Inc.

Guilford, J., & Fructer, B. (1978). *Fundamental statistics in psychology and education* (6th ed.). New York: McGraw-Hill.

Guillemin, F., Bombardier, C., & Beaton, D. (1993). Cross- cultural adaptation of health–related quality of life measures : Literature review and proposed guidelines. *Journal of Clinical Epidemiology, 46,* 1417-1432.

Guyatt, G. H., Naylor, C. D., Juniper, E., Hyland, D. K., Jaeschke, R., & Cook, D. J.(1997). Users' guides to the medical literature XII. How to use article about health-related quality of life. *The Medical Literature, 277*(15), 1232-1237.

Herdman, M., Fox- Rushby, J., & Badia, X. (1997). 'Equivalence' and the translation and adaptation of health- related quality of life questionnaires. *Quality of Life Research, 6,* 237-247.

Hopkins, K. D. (1998). *Educational and psychological measurement and evaluation* (8th ed.). Boston: Allyn and Bacon.

Huss, K., Naumann, P. L., Mason, P. J., Nanda, J. P., Huss, R. W., & Smith, C. M. (2001). Asthma severity, atopic status, allergen exposure and quality of life in elderly persons. *Annals of Allergy, Asthma, and Immunology, 86*(5), 524-530.

Hyland, M. E. (1991). The living with asthma questionnaire. *Respiratory Medicine, 85,* 13-16.

Hyland, M. E., (2003). A Brief guide to the selection of quality of life instrument. *Health and Quality of Life Outcomes, 1*(24), 1-5.

Hyland, M. E., Finnis, S., & Irvine, S. H. (1991). A scale for assessing of life in adult asthma sufferers. *Journal of Psychosomatic Research, 35*(1), 99-110.

Jans, M. P., Schellevis, F. G., & van Eijik, J. T. M. (1991). The Nottingham health profile: score distribution, internal consistency, and validity in asthma and COPD patients. *Quality of Life Rresearch, 8*(8), 501-7.

Jones, P. W. (1991). The St George's respiratory questionnaire. *Respiratory Medicine, 85*, 25-31.

Juniper, E. F. (1997a). Quality of life in adults and children with asthma and rhinitis. *Allergy, 52*, 971-977.

Juniper, E. F. (2005). Assessing asthma quality of life: It's role in clinical practice. *Breath, 1*(3), 193-204.

Juniper, E. F., Buist, S., Cox, F. M., Ferrie, P. J., & King, D. R. (1999a). Validation of a standardized version of the asthma quality of life questionnaire. *Chest, 115*, 1265-1270.

Juniper, E.F., Gordon, H. G., Streiner, D. L., & King, D. R. (1997b). Clinical impact versus factor analysis for quality of life questionnaire construction. *Journal of Clinical Epidemiology, 50*(3), 233-238.

Juniper, E. F., Guyatt, G. H., Cox, F. M., Ferrie, P. J., & King, D. R. (1999b). Development and validation of the mini asthma quality of life questionnaire. *European Respiratory Journal, 14*, 32-38.

Juniper, E. F., Guyatt, G. H., Epstein, R. S., Ferrie, P. J., Jaeschke, R., & Hiller, T. K. (1992). Evaluation of impairment of health related quality of life in asthma: Development of a questionnaire for use in clinical trials. *Thorax, 47*, 76-83.

Juniper, E. F., Guyatt, G. H., Ferrie, P. J., & Griffith, L. E. (1993). Measuring quality of life in asthma. *American Review of Respiratory Disorders, 147*, 832-838.

Juniper, E. F., Wisniewski, M. E., Cox, F. M., Emmett, A. H., Nielsen, K. E., & O'Byrne, P. M. (2004). Relationship between quality of life and clinical status in asthma: A factor analysis. *European Respiratory Journal, 23*, 287-291.

Laforest, L., Pacheco, Y., Bartsch, P., Vincken, W., Pietri, G., Ernst, P., Bèrard, A., & van Ganse, E. (2005). Correlates of quality of life in patients with asthma. *Annals of Allergy, Asthma, & Immunology, 94*, 473-479.

Leroyer, C., Lebrun, T., Proust, A., Lenne, X., Lucaw, E., & Rio, G. (1998). Knowledge, self-management and quality of life in asthma: A cross- sectional study of the French version of the asthma quality oflLife questionnaire. *Quality of Life Research, 7*, 267-272.

Leynaert, B., Neukirch, C., Liard, R., Bousquet, J., & Neukirch, F. (2000). Quality of life in allergic rhinitis and asthma. *American Journal of Respiratory and Critical Care Medicine, 162*, 1391-1396.

Marks, G. B., Dunn, S. M., & Woolcock, A. J. (1992). A scale for the measurement of quality of life in adult with asthma. *Journal of Clinical Epidemiology, 45*(5), 461-472.

Moy, M. L., Israel, E., Weiss, S. T., Juniper, E. F., Dube, L., & Drazen, J. M. (2001). Clinical predictors of health-related quality of life depend on asthma severity. *American Journal of Respiratory Critical Care Medicine, 163*, 924-929.

Patrick, D. L., & Deyo, R. A. (1989). Generic and disease specific measures in assessing health status and quality of life. *Medical Care, 27*(3), S217-32.

Sanjuas, C., Alonso, J., Ferre, M., Curull, V., Broquetas, J. M., & Anto, J. M. (2001). Adaptation of the asthma quality of life questionnaire to a second language preserves its critical proporties: The Spanish Version. *Journal of Clinical Epidemiology, 54*, 182-189.

Sawyer, G., Miles, J., Lewis, S., Fitzharris, P., Pearce, N., & Beasley, R. (1998). Classification of asthma severity: should the international guidelines be changed? *Clinical and Experimental Allergy, 28*, 1565-1570.

Schipper, H., Clinch, J., & Powell, V. (1996). Definitions and conceptual issues. In B. Spilker (Ed), *Quality of life and pharmacoeconomics in clinical trials.* (pp. 11-23). Philadelphia: Lippincott-Raven.

Sherrill, C., & O' Connor, J. (1999). Guidelines for improving adapted physical activity research. *Adapted Physical Activity Quarterly, 16,* 1-8.

Spirić, V. T., Bogić, S. M., Janković, S., Maksimović, N., Miljanović, S. M., Popadić, A. P., Rasković, S., & Milić, N. (2004). Assessment of the asthma quality of life questionnaire (AQLQ): Serbian translation. *Croatian Medical Journal, 45,* 188-194.

Tabachnick, B. G., & Fidell, L. S. (1998). *Using multivariate statistics.* (4th ed.) New York, NY: Harper Collins.

Tan, W.C., Tan, J.W.L., Wee, E.W.L., Niti, M., & Ng, T.P. (2004). Validation of the English version of the asthma quality of life questionnaire in a multi-ethnic Asian population. *Quality of life Research, 13,* 551-556.

Thomas, J., & Nelson, J. (2003). *Research methods in physical activity.(3rd ed.)* (Editor of translation: Karteroliotis, K.). Athens: Medical Publications Pashalidis.

Thoonen, B. P., Schermer, T. R., and van den Boom, G., Molema, J., Folgering, H., Akkermans, R. P., Grol, R., van Weel, C., & van Schayck, C. P. (2003). Self-management of asthma in general practice, asthma control and quality of life: a randomised controlled trial. *Thorax, 58,* 30-36.

Ware, J. E. J., & Sherbourne, C. D. (1992).The MOS 36- items short- form health survey (SF-36). I. Conceptual framework and item selection. *Medical Care, 30,* 473-483.

West, J.B. (2004). *Pulmonary Physiology, the basics.* (6th ed.). New York, NY: Lippincott, Williams and Wilkins.

Wijnhoven, H., Kriegsman, D., Hesselink, A., Pennix, B., & de Haan, M. (2001). Determinants of different dimensions of disease severity in asthma and COPD. *Chest, 119,* 1034-1042.

Yun, J., & Ulrich, D. (2002). Estimating measurements validity: a tutorial. *Adapted Physical Activity Quarterly, 19,* 32-47.

In: Leading-Edge Psychological Tests and Testing Research ISBN: 978-1-60021-571-1
Editor: Marta A. Lange, pp. 109-127 © 2007 Nova Science Publishers, Inc.

Chapter 6

MEASUREMENT OF MORAL DEVELOPMENT IN SPANISH-SPEAKING ADULTS AND CHILDREN. ERASMO AND DM-NJ TESTS

Cristina Villegas de Posada[*]

Department of Psychology, University of Los Andes
Cra. 1E No. 18 A 10, Bogotá, Colombia S. A.

ABSTRACT

This article describes the steps of construction, standardization and validation of two tests for measuring moral development (MD) in Spanish-speaking children and adults. Both tests were developed on the basis of a moral development notion that includes moral feelings and several differentiated aspects of moral reasoning. The test for adults was standardized with 623 subjects, employees or candidates for employments in various companies in Bogotá. The test for children was standardized with 1166 children and youths in ages of 9 to 18 years. Additionally, there are data from university students. Results with different samples show that both test have an adequate reliability and that the test for adults discriminates between normal individuals and criminals.

Morality is referred to notions of wrong, good, bad, just and unjust. Moral development can be described as the changes in reasoning, feelings and action that arise when one is faced with issues that require moral judgment. These three aspects are not covered by most of the instruments designed to measure moral development; hence, this notion has been restricted to one aspect of moral reasoning. In this paper I discuss at length the shortcomings of such a limited notion and what this implies for the measurement of moral development. I also present two tests for the assessment of morality in Spanish-speaking adults and children.

Traditionally, moral development has been associated with the development of moral reasoning. Piaget (1932/1977), a pioneer studious of the subject, maintained that morality consisted of a series of rules. Thus, his study centered on the emergence of rules and

---

[*] Fax (57)1-3324365. E-mail: cvillega@uniandes.edu.co

regulations and their subsequent evolution; and children's notions of distributive and retributive justice and punishment, from early childhood through to adolescence.

Years later, Kohlberg began his research on the subject, and under the influence of Rawls (1971), considered that what is moral is also just and that, therefore, any psychological investigation about morality must be centered on topics related to justice (Kohlberg, 1976; 1984).

According to Kohlberg, the "most" essential structure referring to morality is that relating to justice as it allows for the resolution of conflictive situations, and it encompasses all the other orientations: "Moral situations imply conflicts of interest or perspective; justice principles are concepts for resolving these conflicts, for giving each his due" (Kohlberg, 1976, p. 40). The justice orientation encompasses all the other perspectives because defending law and order can be seen as justice, as can the maximizing of utility (understood as welfare). However, the nucleus of justice is about the distribution of rights and duties, regulated by concepts of equality and reciprocity. Thus, according to Kohlberg, justice represents a balance or equilibrium similar to that found in other areas of logical thought.

To support his theory that morality corresponds to justice, Kohlberg adds that one can be moral and at the same time disagree with all rules and norms as well as the highest good, but it is impossible to be moral if one questions the need for justice. This clear position defines the object of study for Kohlberg and numerous subsequent psychologists as relating to the way in which notions of justice are manifested in different ages and how these notions change throughout life. Through his analysis of moral reasoning he established six stages of development, ranging from childhood up to adulthood. These stages can be grouped into three levels: pre-conventional, conventional, and post-conventional. The stages represent forms of justification, and the unifying aspect of the various levels and stages represents the socio-moral perspective, which includes both moral judgments and the taking of a perspective. Taking a perspective refers to the point of view the individual adopts when defining social facts and socio-moral values or duties (Kohlberg, 1976).

At pre-conventional level the social perspective is individual and concrete; others' interests are not considered nor are they recognized as being different to one's own. Or, it can be considered that each individual has his or her own interests, but that this leads to conflict, and so what is *correct* is relative. At this level law has to be imposed.

At conventional level there is a social perspective, or a point of view that is shared by all members of a relationship or group. In the early stages of this level shared feelings and interests take precedence over individual ones and different points of view are discussed by putting oneself in the place of others; but, society in general is not, as yet, taken into consideration. The later stage of this level differentiates between interpersonal motives and agreements, and the point of view of society, which takes precedence. The conventional individual subordinates individual necessities, to social ones. Social approval is an important issue, as is loyalty to people, groups, authorities, and to keeping within the law in order to promote the wellbeing of society at large. This individual believes that law is for everyone, and it exists because it contributes to everyone's wellbeing.

At post-conventional level, we go back to an individualistic point of view. Not as member of society, but rather as a person whose point of view can be made universal; in other words, the point of view of any moral and rational individual. Social obligations are justifiable for any rational person, and, in turn, they promote commitment to those same obligations. According to Kohlberg (1984), "...it is the perspective of an individual who is morally committed, or that upholds laws on which a just and good society is based. It is by this perspective that (1) a society in particular or a group of social practices must be judged, and (2) by which a person can, rationally, commit to society " (p. 191).

Another aspect by which we can define the socio-moral perspective is that of moral orientation; that is, the elements used when prescribing what is good and right.

McCabe (1992) points out that, despite the importance of reasoning, there has been little interest in defining it and separating it from other concepts. The author quotes Gibbs (McCabe, 1992), who considers that moral reasoning envelops the *prescription, evaluation,* and *justification* of that which is considered good and correct. Liebert (cit. in McCabe, 1992) on the other hand, differentiates between *moral judgment, moral expectations,* and *moral justifications.* The first of the three expresses the individual's evaluation as to what is correct or incorrect from various possible courses of action; the *moral expectations* refer to the individual's expressions of what might happen in a morally conflictive situation; and finally, *moral justifications* are explanations or reasons given by an individual to justify his or her moral judgment in a given situation.

Under the influence of Kohlberg, the study of moral development does not consider what the individual might believe is right or wrong – or his or her *moral judgment*; instead, the study centers on *moral justifications*, or, in other words, the reasons that an individual has for believing that something is either right or wrong. Judgment expresses an evaluation made using a moral standard. The reason for not considering the role of judgment is, in part, due to the fact that it does not reveal anything about an individual's thinking structure, as interested Kohlberg, but is simply part of the content, which, according to the author, does not deserve consideration. In this perspective, standards are not so important as justifications are. Although Piaget (1977) had an interest in moral standards, he never studied the rule or the moral standard in itself; but, rather, how rules were assumed in a game of Marbles (for example, as something unchangeable, from Divine origin, or as something that can be modified through consensus).

Moral expectations, which constitute another of the aspects of moral reasoning according to Liebert (cit. en McCabe, 1992), have been considered as part of the justifications and not as a separate element. An important aspect of moral expectation refers to consequences, which, in turn, reflect a moral perspective. Thus, depending on whether consequences are foreseen only for the agent, and not for others, the resulting perspective will be different. On the other hand, the ability to foresee consequences for oneself, for others, and for society at large is part of mature reasoning and therefore it should be part of moral reasoning.

The *prescriptive* aspect, i.e., the course of action that a person considers best when faced with a moral dilemma, is another area which has not enjoyed sufficient consideration. This could be due Kohlberg's initial position, stating that what is important is the type of reasoning or justification behind a given action, because the same action could be justified in different ways, and, in turn, the same justification could give way to different prescriptions. This position is reflected in the manner of evaluating moral reasoning by Kohlberg and other authors, whereby although the subject is asked what the person facing the dilemma should do, the answer is not taken into consideration in the scoring.

Kohlberg's position on the prescriptive, which received many criticisms, changed in his later writings (Kohlberg, 1984). He recognized that people in the higher stages of moral reasoning had a tendency to coincide in actions that were prescribed as correct. He also subdivided each of the stages into sub-stages A and B, and only in sub-stage B is judgment prescriptive and universal.

The above discussion shows that the notion of moral reasoning has been limited to only one aspect: That of moral justification. These justifications demonstrate the changes in the structure of reasoning, even though a similar change can be seen also in the consideration of the consequences and in other aspects of reasoning.

MORAL EMOTIONS

Despite the fact that Fridja, Mesquita, Sonnemans and van Goozen (1991) draw a series of distinctions among what they denominate as *emotive states*: emotions, feelings and passion, in this text no differentiation will be made between emotions and feelings.

Moral Emotions are a fundamental part of one's moral system as they regulate behavior, and because emotions such as guilt set aside a normal person from that of a psychopathic one. Thus, although our emotions play an important part in our moral development, due to the emphasis on moral reasoning, studies on the way in which they develop and their role on morality have not been very extensive.

Moral feelings, or moral emotions, are feelings elicited by a moral situation. Some only occur in the face of moral situations (guilt, shame, empathy or sympathy, indignation and resentment), while others, such as anger and pride can arise in moral situations, but also in non-moral instances. Guilt, shame and pride are self-evaluative or self-centered emotions, the first two of which are considered essential to moral development (Harter, 1999; Kagan, 1984, Lewis, 1995; Tangney, 1998). Moral emotions attest the importance given, by an individual, to moral norms or principles and are predictors of moral actions (Montada, 1993).

There are numerous perspectives about emotional development, perspectives, that according to Griffin and Mascolo (1998), differ, not in what constitutes emotion, but in what develops and the influencing factors of this development. Most perspectives consider that changes occur in physiological aspects, in corporal expressions or manifestations, and with respect to certain feelings and experiences.

The most important emotions related to morality are, besides empathy or sympathy, the emotions labeled self-conscious (Lewis, 1995): embarrassment, pride, shame and guilt, These emotions appear early in life. Although many authors use the term self-conscious to refer to these emotions, the term self-evaluative describes emotions that result from an evaluation where one is the agent, or as a person faced with a standard.

Lewis (1995) maintains that there are various stages in this self-evaluation. In the first stage the person has to decide whether an event is the result of his or her actions, or of external factors. Whether or not the person makes external attributions depends on the situation as well as on personal characteristics. If the person attributes the result to him or herself, then he or she passes to the next stage in which the individual can decide whether or not he or she has been successful. In the last stage the person decides whether the success or failure is global or specific, where global attributions are referred to the global person as "I am good". In this particular case not the action but the person is evaluated as both subject and object, whereas in other cases the contrary is true. Depending on whether the person or the action is evaluated, different emotions such as shame and guilt can arise, as we will look at in more detail later on. The likelihood of making global or specific attributions depends on personality traits.

Although the emotions that are most related with morality are empathy, sympathy, shame and guilt, it is also important to consider pride as a positive emotion that results from carrying out correct action.

Positive Self-Evaluative Emotions: Pride

Pride is a positive emotion that comes about as a result of an action that is in accordance or supersedes the standard one has set for oneself. This emotion has not enjoyed much attention in the field of morality and all the information we have about the emotion derives from investigations into achievement motivation. Lewis (1995) considers pride and arrogance as the two positive self-evaluative emotions. While pride is the satisfaction one feels due to a specific action, arrogance is an exaggerated and usually undesirable feeling of pride or self-confidence. Pride, results from a specific evaluation of an action or a result, whereas arrogance entails a global evaluation of the person. When we feel proud it is because we are pleased with the result of a particular action, thought or feeling - here the subject and the object are separate. Due to the positive state associated with pride, people are inclined to repeat actions which generate the feeling, and as it implies a sense of self-satisfaction, the subject has to perceive his or her responsibility in the action. Thus, no one can feel proud for something that they did not do, that they consider pure chance or that they put down to luck.

Pride, demonstrated by a smile and the head held high, for the accomplishment of a particular target has been observed in children of between three and four years of age. However, no analysis has yet been made of when a child can feel pride for resisting temptation or for helping others. According to Kagan (1984), in the west, adults find it increasingly difficult to feel good about themselves for resisting temptation because self-denial is not perceived as a positive trait. One would have to analyze whether or not Kagan is correct in his appreciation, but what does seem certain is that abstention when faced with a prohibited action or a permitted one (sacrifice) gives rise to feelings of pride and satisfaction. Nevertheless, the popular idea is that doing the right thing is natural and that we should, therefore, not feel proud. Consequently, we are losing one of the most important sentiments that play such an important role in the issue of moral behavior.

Negative Self-Evaluative Emotions: Shame and Guilt

Shame. As shame and guilt arise as a result of violating a set standard, for many years both were treated as one and the same. Nowadays, however, they are recognized as separate emotions, but there is much debate on what it is that makes them separate and different. Kagan (1984) differentiates them according to: a) whether others might know about the violation, and b) the existence of options and, therefore, personal responsibility. Thus, shame is felt when the agent believes that there were no other options to the choice he or she made (Harter, 1999), and that others know of the transgression. Guilt, on the other hand, is felt when the agent thinks that there were other options, but that no one necessarily knows about the transgression According to this criterion, shame implies public exposure, or what some authors refer to as audience, whereas guilt is more private. If the agent thinks that there were other options and that people know about the transgression he or she will feel a combination of guilt and shame. Other authors maintain that the presence or lack of an audience is not a criterion by which one can differentiate the two sentiments, seeing as the investigation has shown that adults feel shame even in the absence of an audience (Tagney, 1998). The problem may reside in the fact that adults use the terms as synonyms; however, this does not mean that the two emotions are the same, or that the presence of an audience is not important. Harter (1999), on the other hand, considers that shame manifests when we violate our own ideals, the ideals that others attribute to us, or when our action does not correspond to the standards we have set for ourselves, or to general social standards. Lewis (1995) links shame to the failure of an action in relation to the standards of the person, rules or targets, and makes global attributions such as, "I am bad". When we feel shame we want the ground to swallow us, to disappear off the face of the Earth; we shy away and avoid eye-contact. It is, therefore, an extremely painful and negative experience which disturbs our behavior, and causes confusion and inability to speak. The person in question will try to free themselves from this all-encompassing intense devaluation, but this is not easy. The author maintains that feelings of shame do not arise due to a specific situation, but rather the agent's interpretation of the event. Harter (1999) points out that shame is linked to an "I-Self" that judges negatively.

Guilt. For Lewis, guilt goes hand in hand with shame, appearing when there is a shortcoming with respect to a standard. However, the difference between them is that guilt does not imply that the person as a whole is a failure, but that the failure is to do with specific aspects or conditions that person may be in at a particular point in time. Guilt is, therefore, not as destructive as shame and there are possibilities of putting things right. In fact, Lewis (1995) considers that the physical manifestations of guilt are different in that when we feel guilt we are not overwhelmed with the desire to hide away, but we move in order to try to repair the damage done. Harter (1999) maintains that guilt is felt in response to a violation of standards that affects others, but at the same time she accepts Kagan's (1984) notion, that there must be a sense that the action in question was controllable, that is, there were options available and therefore there was also a possibility to act differently. For Harter, guilt includes a negative evaluation (by the agent) of actions against others for which one assumes responsibility.

Despite the aforementioned technicalities, it would seem that we feel shame when we are not able to achieve what we wanted to achieve. For example, we can feel ashamed of the grade we get in an exam, or for not finishing a project in time. But, we feel guilt for not doing what we should have done, so guilt is more tightly linked with moral standards than shame. Therefore, in the case of a bad grade, if this is due to the fact that we did not study enough, we would feel guilt at not having studied, but not shame. Guilt can manifest because there are moral standards and there is the possibility of self-evaluation when faced with these standards. The fact that guilt is linked with moral standards makes it the most genuine of moral emotions - the stronger the standard, the stronger the emotion tied to its violation (Montada, 1993).

Although children begin to have these self-evaluative emotions at around the age of four, people differ in the intensity and the manifestation of such emotions when faced with particular situations.

MORAL ACTION

Moral action is of utmost importance because if people were to exercise only moral reasoning and not moral action, then morality would be of little use. Bandura (2002) mentions that people suffer through the actions of others, irrespectively of whether their actions can be justified. Nevertheless the field of moral action has not enjoyed enough attention, primarily due to the fact that a) there can be several options for the justification of the same course of action; and b) because the same judgment can lead to different courses of action. Although the former is true: Two people can avoid a particular course of action, one of them for fear of punishment and the other because they know it is unjust, the latter fact seems somewhat unsustainable. So, there is little probability that two people that reason at similar levels and apply universal criteria could justify different actions. Kohlberg seems to have recognized this fact not as a necessity derived of the application of moral criteria, but as an empirical fact. He pointed out that people in the later stages tend to coincide in the type of action that should be carried out in moral situations (Kohlberg and Candee, 1984).

Moral action considered together with reasoning and emotions revels personal consistency. So, a person is consistent if he or she thinks something is bad, he or she feels bad about doing it, and, therefore, avoid doing it. On the contrary, a person is inconsistent if he or she thinks something is bad but performs the action. Consistency is a sign of maturity, in moral and other aspects.

Another differentiating factor with respect to action is whether people are only able to avoid immoral actions, or whether they are capable of carrying out prosocial actions that benefit others, but imply a personal sacrifice. Research in relation to this topic is sparse, although in a narrative analysis of studies about the relationship between moral reasoning and conduct, the prosocial aspect showed more correlation with reasoning (Blasi, 1980). The explanation is that we do not need a lot of reasoning to avoid negative conduct, given that following the moral standards that prohibit such conduct is usually enough. However, more reasoning is needed in order to carry out prosocial actions.

Finally, action can be subject to change considering a cost-benefit balance or neutralizing mechanisms such as those proposed by Bandura (1999, 2002). The role of action in the evaluation of morality and moral development is an important aspect that can not remain unconsidered.

Ways of Evaluating Morality

There are two existing trends in the study of moral evaluation: On the one hand, that of those interested in evaluating moral development according to what has been proposed by Kohlberg and exceptionally by Piaget; and, on the other, that of those who are more interested in behavior and evaluating what is called *moral integrity*.

Following Kohlberg, the evaluation of moral development has centered exclusively on *reasoning*, i.e., on moral justifications. He proposed as evaluation form an interview called the MJI. A series of aspects from this are scored in order to obtain a classification by stages and a global score for moral maturity.

The scoring of the interview was simplified in the last version of the instrument (Kohlberg, 1984), and although it shows a high grade of reliability and is the most widely-used method to measure moral development, it has several drawbacks. For example, it only evaluates reasoning; it is based on rather drawn out, time consuming interviews; it is impossible for it to be used massively; and, it is difficult to score without previous training. The MJI presents the interviewee with three dilemmas for which he or she has to give reasons for justifying or not particular courses of action. For example, stealing medicine in order to help a sick spouse, or breaking a promise to a child. In order to grade the answers each one is compared with a prototype answer representing one of the stages. This prototype response, called *criterion concept* (Kohlberg, 1976), "…is the reasoning pattern that is most distinctive of a given stage" (p. 45).

Another widely used instrument is the Defining Issues Test (DIT) by Rest (1979). This instrument is made up of six dilemmas, for each of which the subject has to indicate what the protagonist should do, and mark on a chart the importance that should be given to each of the twelve aspects related to the situation. These aspects represent arguments for Kohlberg's stages 2 to 6 and are noted in a chart that goes from 'very important' down to 'not important'. Finally, the person has to choose the four most important arguments and arrange them in order of importance, from the most important, which receives four points, to least important – one point. The grading takes into account the sum of the importance given to each argument, from each stage. The score obtained for the arguments for stages 5 and 6 is divided by the total points in the scale (60) in order to obtain the score (P), which represents the proportion of reasoning based on principles: "The P index then represents the sum of weighted ranks given to "Principled" items, and is interpreted as the relative importance given to Principled moral considerations in making a moral decision" (Rest, 1979, p. 101).

The advantages of the DIT, to which some adjustments have recently been made, are its easy application, correction and interpretation, as well as its psychometric analysis that prove its reliability and validity. According to Kohlberg (1976), the test is a continuous variable of moral maturity rather than qualitatively different stages, as is the case in his test.

The Socio-Moral-Reflection Test (SMR-T) by Gibbs, Wideman and Colby (1982) is more open than the DIT and has not been as widely diffused as the other two tests. The test is structured in the same way as the MJI, but it is a written test whereby the subject is required to circle the chosen option. The test, which has been standardized with adults and children, shows an index of internal consistency of .78 for university students and .53 for adults. Although the internal consistency for adults is low, the test shows an important correlation with the MJI and its power of discrimination in various validating studies.

Another widely used instrument is the Moral Judgment Test (MJT), developed by Lind (1985, 1998). According to its creator, the MJT measures moral competence, which includes not only reasoning, but also an emotional component; however, a detailed analysis shows us that the test measures consistence in the form of reasoning (Villegas de Posada, 2005; Lind, 2006). The MJT is made up of two dilemmas, each with twelve arguments, two of them corresponding to each stage. Half of the arguments are in favor of a particular course of action and the other half are against, and the job of the subject is to weigh up the importance of each argument. In order to score the answers the consistency in the weight given to the arguments for and against is considered, and expressed in index C, which shows the correlation between the weight given to the two types of argument (Villegas de Posada, 2005). The test has a number of limitations, among them the absence of psychometric studies and the fact that, according to Lind, it cannot be used for evaluating individuals. Concerning the aspect that it measures, one has to remember that consistency in argumentation is an aspect of reasoning, related also to the ability of putting emotions to one side and considering, with equal importance, arguments that are contrary, but part of the same stage. This dimension, however, is not the same as what has been understood as reasoning or moral judgment.

Moral development tests have been used mainly for investigative purposes. Integrity tests, on the other hand, have been developed for the organizational sphere. They evaluate the presence or absence of immoral behavior and are used when selecting new staff members. According to a meta-analysis carried out by Ones, Viswesvaren and Schmidt (1993), the tests are indicative of performance as well as the presence or lack of disruptive behavior. A subsequent meta-analysis by Schmidt and Hunter (1998) showed that integrity tests significantly increase prediction when they are used in conjunction with other instruments and interview. However, the theoretical bases of the tests are not clear, and it is not easy to scrutinize the tests hence the grading techniques and the manner of obtaining results are not very widely known.

THE ERASMO TEST

The name of the test comes from its Spanish acronym: *Evaluación del razonamiento, la acción y los sentimientos morales* (Evaluation of Reason, Action, and Moral Emotion), and it was developed to evaluate adults. It can be used either on an individual or group basis, with pencil and paper or on the computer, and it can be scored using specially designed software, which calculates the total points, and offers the possibility of obtaining a descriptive profile of the evaluated subject.

Structure

The test is made up of two parts. The first, includes four dilemmas, of which the first and last evaluate helping others in contraposition to one's own wellbeing. The second dilemma evaluates the responsibility or indifference towards decisions taken by others, and their wellbeing, as well as the role of friendship and confidentiality. The third dilemma evaluates respect for others' property over and above individual benefit. The first dilemma, which was similar to Kohlberg's Heinz dilemma, was changed given its low reliability and little discrimination between the subjects. In Kohlberg's version, a woman is seriously ill and her husband has not been able to raise enough money to buy her the drugs she needs. The pharmacist refuses to take payment in installments or to sell the drug at a discount, and so the husband has to decide whether he should steal the drug to save his wife's life. The ERASMO version featured a young man, Juan, who had to face the decision of whether to steal a piece of medical equipment that would save his father's life.

Each dilemma is followed by five questions:

1.   A definition or selection as to what the protagonist should do in the dilemma.

2. A judgment of how adequate or inadequate it would be for the protagonist to carry out the moral option (in both dilemmas) or the immoral option (in the other two dilemmas).
3. A justification of the above judgment (reason).
4. An expression of what the protagonist is likely to feel if he or she were to act according to the judgment made.
5. A judgment of the gravity (weight) if the protagonist were to choose the immoral option (in three of the dilemmas) or the moral option (in one of the dilemmas).

Examples of questions for Juan's dilemma (eliminated in the final version of the test) are as follows:

1. What should Juan do? Take the piece of equipment or not?
2. If he does take it, would his action be good or bad?
3. Why?_____
4. If he were to take it, would he feel good or bad?
5. Given the situation Juan is in, taking the equipment would be:

                    _____ not serious
                    _____ serious
                    _____ very serious

Four of the questions are closed questions with only two possible answers to choose from for the answers. The only open question evaluates the reasons or justification for the chosen action.

The second part of the test evaluates how much weight the subject gives to the cost-benefit balance of a moral action and how it affects the decision and the feelings generated.

In order to do this the person is asked to reconsider the situation of the protagonist in the fourth dilemma, and decide what he or she should do, taking into account that there is a 90% probabilities that the protagonist will suffer a certain number of problems (e.g. being taken to jail) and a 90% probabilities that the action will be beneficial to another person within the dilemma (e.g. improving health for the father). The person is also asked how much importance they would place on the costs and the benefits (maximum, average, minimum) and what the possibility of feeling good about their action would be (maximum, average, minimum). Following that, the questions are repeated but with only a 10% possibility of producing benefits for the other person.

The open questions, the ones requiring justification, are categorized as pragmatic, ethical or moral, according to the three uses of practical reason proposed by Habermas (1991). These three levels are closely linked to the pre-conventional, conventional and post-conventional levels proposed by Kohlberg (1976).These answers as well as the answers to the closed questions receive numerical scores, which render a global score. This score varies between 17 and 85. Although each dilemma has five questions, three of them are not included in the total score as they showed low reliability in the analysis of items.

The answers given in the second part of the test are not included in the total score for the test, but they are used in the software program in order to obtain a descriptive profile, together with the total ERASMO score and the sub-scores for the different aspects evaluated by the test (option, judgment, reasons, feelings, moral weight).

Standardization

The test was standardized using a total of 623 subjects, divided into 2 sample groups.[1] The first sample group was made up of 312 people, belonging to the health, financial, industrial and public services sector. The second was made up of 311 people, belonging to private and public companies in the same sectors (except health) as in sample one. Employees from all levels and positions participated; from shop floor workers to managerial level and within an age range of 18 to 55. For the second sample, the first dilemma was changed for one that would allow more discrimination among the subjects, whereas the remaining dilemmas were kept the same. As no sex differences were obtained, the results are presented including the whole samples. The descriptive statistics for the two samples can be seen in table 1, calculated for the parts in common to all the samples (dilemmas 2, 3 y 4). The data shows that the samples are very similar.

Table 1. Descriptive Statistics for the Total Sample in Dilemmas 2, 3 and 4

	N	Mean	Median	S. D.	S. E.	Range
Sample 1	312	44.38	45	8.08	.458	23 - 60
Sample 2	311	45.82	45	7.07	.437	25 - 63
Total	623	45.10	45	7.92	.317	23 - 63

The results for the second sample are shown in table 2, which shows the average and the standard deviation for the global score in the ERASMO test, made up of the four dilemmas.

Table 2. Descriptive Statistics for the Second Sample in Dilemmas 1, 2, 3 y 4

	N	Mean	Median	S. D.	S. E.	Range
Sample 2	311	52.86	51	9.56	.543	29 - 77

The data in table 2 are used to compare the results obtained with ERASMO.

Factorial Structure

In order to explore the underlying structure of the test an exploratory common factor analysis with varimax rotation was carried out. Data from the second sample was used for this analysis, which yielded six factors with eigenvalues higher than 1, which represent 61% of the variance. As shown by the results in table 3, the first two factors correspond to the responses to the dilemmas 4 and 1, that is, they represent the prosocial aspect.

The answers to the other two dilemmas are grouped into four factors. The results show that the content of the dilemmas plays an important role, insofar the first two factors correspond to prosocial dilemmas, whereas the other factors correspond to the dilemmas which relate to prohibition. These findings confirm what other authors have pointed out about the importance of content.

---

[1] There is also a standardization for university students

Table 3. Matrix of Rotated Factors with Varimax Rotation

	Factor					
	1	2	3	4	5	6
Option1		0.783				
Judgment1		0.834				
Reason1		0.664				
Feeling1		0.756				
Weight1		0.407				0.447
Option2			0.756			
Judgment2			0.658			
Reason2				0.236		
Feeling2			0.593			
Weight2						
Option3						
Judgment3				0.752		
Reason3				0.274		
Feeling3				0.429		
Weight3					0.786	
Option4	0.776					
Judgment4	0.822					
Reason4	0.626					
Feeling4	0.860					
Weight4	0.593					

Extraction method: common factor analysis. KMO = .77.

RELIABILITY AND VALIDITY

Reliability

Given the similarity of the two samples, only one sample was made up for the analysis of internal consistency of dilemmas 2, 3 and 4. The internal consistency of dilemma 1, was only evaluated with the data gathered from the second sample. Given the results of the internal consistency, the questions which negatively affected the reliability index (measured using Cronbach's Alpha) were eliminated.

Once the items were eliminated, two reliability indexes, the Cronbach's Alpha and Spearman-Brown's split-half index, were drawn up using the information from the second sample. The results are shown in table 3.

As we can observe, the reliability index for the split-half method is high. With respect to the internal consistency, the coefficient of .71 is an acceptable index for the personality tests.

Table 4. Reliability indexes for the sample 2

Index	
Spearman- Brown split-half	0.85
Cronbach's alfa for seventeen items	0.71

Validity

Construct Validity

Three samples were used for comparing: The first two groups, from which were expected low scores, were made up, one, of jailed policemen and the other of ex – guerillas members; the third group was formed by carefully selected subjects from the financial sector, whose scores were expected to be very high. The data to compare was obtained from dilemmas 2, 3 and 4, which were common to all the samples.

The first sample group included 47 policemen between the ages of 24 and 54, and jailed for crimes such as homicide, kidnapping, extortion, embezzlement, extortion, theft or falsity. The second, ex – guerilla, group was made up of 22 men and 3 women between the ages of 18 and 40.

The third sample, from the financial sector, included 8 men and 14 women, belonging to the same company. These individuals were responsible for authorizing credit and had access to all the clients' financial information. They were very carefully selected by the company and made to undergo an awareness raising process with respect to ethical issues.

For each sample the score corresponding to percentile 25, 50 and 75 was calculated, as can be seen in table 4. The table shows that the convicts and the ex – guerillas obtained a mean of 40 - a little lower that the standardization sample, but much lower than the financial sector sample, whose average was 48.65. We can also see the big difference in the minimum score which in the convict sample was 13 as opposed to 23 obtained by the standardization sample.

However, the most significant differences between the scores of the outlaws and the standardization sample can be seen in percentiles 25 and 50, which show the validity of the test as a exclusion test. We can see that in the standardization sample, the lowest 25% obtained a score equal to or inferior to 39, while for the convicts group the score for the same was 29.

Table 5. Scores for percentiles 25, 50 and 75 (dilemmas 2, 3, 4) in the standardization sample and in the comparison samples

Sample	n	Mean in ERASMO	Range	Percentiles		
				25	50	75
Standardization sample	623	45	23 - 63	39	45	52
Financial Sector	22	48	35 - 61	41	52	55
Convicted police	46	39	13 - 55	29	39	51
Ex guerrillas	25	40	20 - 57	35	39	46

In addition, 46.47% of the samples made up of convicted police and ex – guerilla scored below 39, while in the standardization sample only 25% of the group scored this. For the 50 percentile, we can see that the standardization sample scored 45, while the convicted police and ex – guerilla groups scored 39, and for the remaining percentiles the financial sector scores were the highest.

The construct validity can also be seen in a follow-up study with the ex – guerilla group. Fourteen of the members of this group participated in a series of moral development workshops for nine weeks, but it was only possible to obtain pre-test and post-test results from 10 of these members. The means were 60.8 and 66.4, U = .84, p = .10. Although the score in ERASMO increased from the pre-test to the post-test, the differences were not significant and it was not possible to have a control group.

Convergent Validity

For the police sample the ERASMO correlation was calculated using scale G of the 16PF. A value of r = .20, $p < .05$ was obtained.

DM-NJ TEST

The test takes its name from its initials in Spanish *desarrollo moral* (moral development) and from the group it is aimed at: *niños y jóvenes* (children and youths), with an age range of between 9 and 18 years. Similar to the ERASMO, it can be applied individually or collectively, but the grading can be calculated manually or using the specialized software.

Structure

The test includes four dilemmas and seven questions per dilemma. The first dilemma, similar to the Heinz dilemma, analyses the value given to life versus others' property. The second evaluates the importance of keeping a promise versus obedience and the implied personal cost. The third and fourth dilemmas are the same as the third and fourth of the ERASMO test.

Each dilemma is followed by the same six questions as in the ERASMO, plus an extra question about the consequences of acting morally (in two of the dilemmas) and those of acting immorally (in the remaining two dilemmas). Also, the beneficiary of the moral or immoral action is graded, and unlike the ERASMO test, this one contains more open questions. The ERASMO test was developed later, and designed to be graded, in its entirety, using the computer program.

The answers are scored in the same way as for the ERASMO test. The responses referring to the consequences were qualified as: Physical-economical, psychological and moral. The aspect referring to the beneficiary of the consequences is also graded depending on how egocentric or wide the perspective is. The score for 24 questions can vary between 28 and 100.

Standardization

The test was standardized in Bogotá, using 1166 children and adolescents, between the ages of 9 and 18, from all economic strata, and distributed as seen in table 6.

From a schooling point of view, the sample covered students from third grade to eleventh grade. Table 7 shows the average scores and the deviations for the various age groups.

Table 6. Sample´s Distribution by Age

Age	Frecuency	Percentage	Cumm. %
Non reported	2	0,2	0,2
8	3	0,3	0,4
9	71	6,1	6,6
10	139	11,9	18,6
11	146	12,5	31,3
12	168	14,4	45,8
13	122	10,5	56,4
14	136	11,7	68,2
15	127	10,9	79,2
16	119	10,2	89,5
17	86	7,4	97
18	35	3	100
>18	12	1	
Total	1166		

Table 7. Mean and Standard Deviation by Age

Age	Mean	S. D.	n
9	63.79	12.76	71
10	65.72	14.48	138
11	66.49	13.71	139
12	66.57	13.18	151
13	66.81	11.19	98
14	65.95	12.86	123
15	64.63	13.42	126
16	66.12	13.33	115
17	67.07	13.04	85
18	67.01	12.27	36
			1082

In table 7 we can observe that the scores for moral development remain similar between the ages of 12 and 16, and that in some ages they diminish. When comparing the averages obtained at 9 years and at 12 years of age the following was attained $t(222) = 2.77$, $p <.06$, for a one-tailed t-test, and comparing the averages obtained at 9 and 17 years of age gave $t(153) = 3.28$, $p <.05$. Thus, there are differences that hint at being significant between the end of childhood and the beginning of adolescence, and statistical significant differences between childhood and the end of adolescence.

The apparent halt in MD in adolescence and indeed the diminishing of scores in some ages can have a number of explanations. On the one hand, moral development is slow and gradual in Kohlberg's levels 5 and 6, and these levels are reached by very few individuals (Kohlberg, 1984), with the vast majority reaching only level 4. On the other, going through crises and difficulties with respect to norms and values is in itself part of adolescence, and this is reflected in the total scores for the test. Some authors point out that adolescence gives way to a moral relativism, with a tendency to see morality as very contextualized. In later stages of adult life one considers the context, not in a specific way, but as something that could be generalized and analyzed with a universal principle. While for adolescents the context and case are thought of as particular to a situation, for adults in stage 6 they can be made universal.

The trend towards relativism could explain the regressions that Kohlberg saw in some of the cases that he followed over a period of years. He saw these regressions as being due to problems with his instrument which he corrected in the final version. It is not known whether by making the correction he may have masked a problem inherent to adolescence.

If we were only to consider moral reasoning, it would be more probable that we would find an increase according to age. As Kohlberg explains moral reasoning is related to cognitive development and in adolescence, in as far as formal operations, this is not yet fully developed. In fact, when correlating the score of the DM-NJ test with age, the highest correlation is obtained for reason ($r = .15$, $p<.001$); there is no correlation, however, for judgment, choice and feeling.

No significant differences were found in relation to gender.

RELIABILITY AND VALIDITY

Reliability

Internal consistency and the split-half index were calculated for the standardization sample (sample 1). For a second sample used in a validation study (sample 2) the Alpha index was also calculated. After eliminating four questions, the reliability results appear in table eight.

The Alpha coefficients obtained are comparable to those by Gibbs, Widaman and Colby (1982) who reported Alpha coefficients of values between 75 for 7th grade and 63 for 10th grade. In sample 1 reliability was also obtained for dilemmas 1 to 4, with Alphas of .55, .51, .66 and .79 respectively.

With respect to the inter-rater reliability, two judges independently qualified 15 protocols. Their agreed average percentage for the open questions was 67%, but considering the total test, the agreed percentage was 89%.

Table 8. Reliability Indexes

Index	
Sample 1 Spearman- Brown split-half	0.70
Cronbach's alfa (24 ítems)	0.64
Sample 2 Cronbach's alfa (24 ítems)	0.74

Validity

Construct Validity

The validity of the DM-NJ as a development test was established in a study with a sub-sample of 26, 12 and 13 year old girls in eighth grade, which was part of the original standardization sample. They were evaluated again two years later. The average score in the pre-test was 61.03 and in the post-test it was 75.5, $t(26) = 4.79$, $p <.05$, so the results show a significant advance after the two year period. Of the 26 cases, 24 advanced morally, whereas 2 diminished. The two girls that had diminished scores had the highest scores in the initial test, and could be an example of the above-mentioned regressions.

The DM-NJ test predicts helpful behavior, as seen in a sample made up of 30 boys and 28 girls, belonging to two mid economic strata schools. The children's ages ranged from 9.0 to 11.11 years and they were in grades 4 to 6. The children were subjected to an experimental situations where help was required, and the correlation between the scores obtained and the DM-NJ was: $r(55) = .46$, $p <.05$.

Differences per socioeconomic strata are frequently reported in studies on moral development. In the standardization sample, differences were observed between schools, which can be attributed to differences in economical status. In a co-variance analysis, keeping the age range constant, the following was obtained: $F(10, 1160) = 3.097$, $p <.001$. The four schools with the highest average scores had students from mid to upper economical strata families, and the average of these schools presented significant differences with the three schools that obtained lower averages, with students from mid to low economical strata families.

The DM-NJ sensitivity to changes brought about by MD workshops was seen in a study carried out with a sample of 83 youths in 9th grade. The students were divided into three classes of which two were randomly chosen to participate in activities to promote moral development, while the other served as a control group. The DM-NJ post-test score was carried out blindly, with no previous knowledge of the types of activities that took place. The results can be seen in table 9.

As we can appreciate in table 9, the two experimental groups increased their scores in the post-tests. This increase was significant in group 1, whereby in the experimental group the score remained almost identical. Lind's MJT was applied simultaneously with the DM-NJ, but it did not register any significant changes in either of the groups (Villegas de Posada, 2002).

Table 9. Differences in MD between pre- and post-test, by experimental or control group

Group	Condition	Mean	S. D.	n	r	t	Sig.
Exp. 1	Pre-test	68.3	11.04	30	-.13	2.4	.01
	Post-test	76.14	12.40	30			
Exp. 2	Pre-test	63.20	10.83	28	.38	1.27	.10
	Post-test	66.29	12.16	28			
Control	Pre-test	69.95	15.08	25	.20	0.18	.42
	Post-test	70.36	15.78	25			

Other validity studies have been reported in Villegas de Posada (1996).

CONCLUDING REMARKS

The two test reported were a response to a more ample notion of moral development than the traditional one considered in much existing literature. Different elements are evaluated such as the different aspect of reasoning, moral emotions, action, and in the case of ERASMO, the circumstantial aspects linked to a cost-benefit balance.

Both scales are advantageous in that they allow for mass application as they are easily corrected using an almost totally automated software program. Their psychometric characteristics allow for both of them to be used for investigation or for diagnostic tests, and ERASMO is also used in the selection of new staff members. The two tests fulfill a necessity for moral development tests in general, and ones specially designed for Spanish-speakers.

It is hoped that the use of these two tests will help in obtaining more data on moral development.

REFERENCES

Bandura, A. (1999). Moral disengagement in the perpetration of inhumanities. *Personality and Social Psychology Review.* [Special Issue on Evil and Violence], *3*, 193-209.

Bandura, A. (2002). Selective moral disengagement in the exercise of moral agency. *Journal of moral education, 31(2)*, 101-119.

Blasi, A. (1980). Bridging moral cognition and moral action: A critical review of the literature. *Psychological Bulletin, 88*, 1-45.

Fridja, N., Mesquita, B., Sonnemans, J. and van Goozen, S. (1991). The duration of affective phenomena or emotions, sentiments and passions. In: K. T. Strongman (Ed.). *International review of studies on emotion (pp.*187-225). Chichster: John Wiley and sons.

Gibbs, J. C., Wideman, K. F., and Colby, A. (1982). Construction and validation of a simplified, group-adminsterable equivalent to the moral judgment interview. *Child Development, 53*, 895-910.

Griffin, Sh. and Mascolo, M. (1998). On the nature, development and functions of emotions. In: M. Mascolo and Sh. Griffin (Eds). *What develops in emotional development* (pp. 3-27). Nueva York: Plenum Press.

Habermas, J. (1992). *Erläterungen zur Diskursethik*.Frankfurt am Maim: Suhrkamp.

Harter, S. (1999). *The construction of the self*. New York: The Guilforfd Press.

Kagan, J. (1984). *The nature of the child*. New York: Basic Books.

Kohlberg, L (1976). Moral Stages and moralization: the cognitive-developmental approach. In: T. Likona (Ed.) *Moral development and behavior* (pp. 31-53). New York: Holt, Rinehart, and Winston.

Kohlberg, L. (1984). *The Psychology of moral development*. San Francisco: Harper and Row.

Kohlberg, L. and Candee, D. (1984).The relationship of moral judgment to moral action. In W. Kurtines, and J. Gewirtz (Eds). *Morality, moral behavior and moral development* (pp. 52-73). New York: John Wiley and Sons.

Lewis, M. (1995). Self-conscious emotions. *American Scientist, 83*, 68-78.

Lewis, M. (1998). The development and structure of emotions. In: M. Mascolo and Sh. Griffin (Eds). *What develops in emotional development* (pp. 29-50). New York: Plenum Press.

Lind, G. (1985). Inhalt und Struktur des moralischen Urteilens. Unpublished thesis, SFB 23, University of Konstanz.

Lind, G. (1998). Fostering democratic competencies in schools. Invited main lecture, September 24, Universidad de Los Andes, Bogotá, Colombia.

Lind. G. (2006). The Moral Judgment Test: Comments on Villegas de Posada's Critique. *Psychological Reports, 98*, 580-584.

McCabe, Sh. P. (1992). Moral reasoning. In: R. Knowles and G. McLean (Eds). *Psychological foundations of moral education and character development: An integrated theory of moral development* (2.nd. ed., Vol 2, pp. 45-62). Washington: the Council for Research in Values and Philosophy.

Piaget, J. (1977). *El criterio moral en el niño*. Barcelona: Fontanella (Orig. 1932).

Rawls, J. (1971). *A theory of justice*. Cambridge: the Belknap Press of Harvard University.

Rest, J. (1979). *Development in judging moral issues*. Minneapolis: University of Minnesota Press.

Tagney, J. (1998). How does guilt differ from shame. In: J. Bybee (Ed). *Guilt and children*. San Diego: Academic Press.

Ones, D. S., Viswesvaren, C. and Schmidt, F. L. (1993). Comprehensive meta-analysis of integrity tests validities. Findings and implications for personnel selection and theories of job performance. *Applied Psychology, 74(4)*, 679-703.

Schmidt, F. L., Hunter, J. E. (1998). The validity and utility of selection methods in personnel psychology: practical and theoretical implications of 85 years of research findings. *Psychological Bulletin, 124(2)*, 262-274.

Villegas de Posada, C (1996). Desarrollo moral y agentes socializadores. Construcción vs. socialización. *Revista Latinoamericana de Psicología, 28(3)*, 523-532.

Villegas de Posada, C. (2005). Some problems with the use of the moral judgment test. *Psychological Reports, 96*, 698-700.

In: Leading-Edge Psychological Tests and Testing Research   ISBN: 978-1-60021-571-1
Editor: Marta A. Lange, pp. 129-143   © 2007 Nova Science Publishers, Inc.

Chapter 7

THE EMERGING ROLE OF CLINIMETRICS IN PSYCHOLOGICAL ASSESSMENT

*Elena Tomba and Giovanni Andrea Fava**

Department of Psychology, University of Bologna, Bologna, Italy

ABSTRACT

Psychometric theory is the basis for the development of psychological assessment. However, the psychometric model appears to be inadequate in many clinical situations, because of the lack of sensitivity to change and its quest for homogeneous components. The term clinimetrics was introduced by Alvan R. Feinstein in 1982 to indicate a domain concerned with indexes, rating scales and other expressions that are used to describe or measure symptoms, physical signs, and other distinctly clinical phenomena in medicine. Clinimetrics offers a valuable alternative or integration to psychometrics, both from conceptual and methodological viewpoint. Current diagnostic entities in clinical psychology and psychiatry are based on clinimetric principles, but their use is still influenced by psychometric models. Clinical exemplifications of the clinimetric approach to psychological testing are illustrated, with particular reference to the concepts of macro-analysis and micro-analysis.

INTRODUCTION

For over a century and since its appearance as a medical discipline, assessment in psychiatry and clinical psychology did not include the quantification of psychopathological phenomena. Acute but irreproducible long descriptions were the way of communicating clinical observations among researchers [1]. In the late 50s and early 60s the need for more objective ways of assessment of the severity and the change in psychiatric facts emerged.

* Affective Disorders Program, Department of Psychology, University of Bologna, Bologna, Italy and Department of Psychiatry, State University of New York at Buffalo, Buffalo, New York. Address corrispondence to Dr. Fava, Dipartimento di Psicologia, Università di Bologna, viale Berti Pichat 5, 40127 Bologna, Italy. phone: 011-39-051-2091339; fax : 011-39-051-243086; e-mail: giovanniandrea.fava@unibo.it

There were two main reasons for such a pursuit: the concurrent expansion of psychopharmacology, with its need of an empirical, scientific evaluation of the new products, and the need for a reaction to the current of thought, prevalent at that time, that, inspired by phenomenology and psychoanalysis, maintained subjectivity and irreproducibility as the basic principles of psychopathology [1]. Since then, modern clinical psychology and psychiatry have therefore put all their emphasis on inter-clinician reliability and the assessment of clinical changes started to rely on instruments which have characteristics of validity and reliability [2]. In its quest for validity and reliability of assessment, research has rested on the clinically shaky grounds of psychometric theory [2] . The development of psychometrics, however, had taken place outside of the clinical field, mainly for measuring psychological phenomena or educational achievements in the educational and social areas [3]. Since the phenomena under observation in the development of psychometric principles were not clinical, it is not surprising that they could not be automatically adjusted to clinical psychology and psychiatry. [4].

We will discuss the inadequacies of the psychometric model in the clinical setting and the need of its supplementation with another conceptual framework, clinimetrics.

INADEQUACIES OF PSYCHOMETRIC MODEL

Psychometric theories have produced a number of variable methods for improving the validity and reliability of instruments used in psychological research. However the psychometric instruments appear to be built on criteria often of statistical but not of clinical significance [5].

The inadequacies of the results produced by psychometric instruments, their improper use, such as to promote and justify artificial findings in clinical setting were first pointed out by Shapiro [6], who outlined the methodological difficulties in applying psychometric principles to diagnostic psychological testing in 1951. Kellner [7,8], in the early seventies, described the psychometric problems related to assessment of changes in distress.

Sensitivity to change in distress is a requirement for the clinical validity of an outcome scale. Scales may be valid and reliable, but may lack sensitivity. The ability of a rating or self-rating scale to discriminate between different groups of patients suffering from the same illness (e.g., depressed inpatients and outpatients) and to reflect changes in experiments in therapeutics such as drug trials has been defined by Kellner as sensitivity [9]. This concept is particularly important when treatment effects are small and in the setting of sub-clinical symptoms [10].

The psychometric model appears also to be largely inadequate in clinical setting because of its search of homogeneity. Homogeneity of components, as measured by statistical tests such as Cronbach's alpha, is often seen as the most important requirement for a traditional rating scale. However, the same properties that give a scale a high score for homogeneity may obscure its ability to detect change [11]. The redundant nature of a scale's items may increase Cronbach's alpha, but decrease its sensitivity. In psychometrics, a high correlation is often regarded as evidence that the two scales measure the same factor. However, a high correlation does not indicate similar sensitivity [9]. Two scales may have common content which insures a high positive correlation, but the items they do not share may be important in determining sensitivity [12,13]. When a new scale is developed with "item analysis", some of the essential variables that are sensitive to change may be either removed or not included [14].

The Hamilton Depression Scale (HAM-D) [15] is an example of an instrument based on the classical psychometric model. The key flaw of such an instrument, developed on the basis of factor analysis or principle component analysis (in which correlation coefficients are operating, inter alia, by giving symptoms equal weights), is that the same score at the Hamilton Rating Scale for Depression [15] may be the product of few very severe core symptoms (e.g. a severely retarded depressed patient) or of several mild accessory symptoms (reflecting perhaps a subject affected by a mild form but with many symptoms and a complaining behaviour)[1]. Correspondingly, when in the research routine the total scores to quantify the clinical response are used, the greatest distance between 'scientific' assessment and clinical observation ensues [1].

The sensitivity of the HAM-D has been poor compared to subscale scores of the HAM-D based upon core symptoms of depression [16] or global indexes of change [17]. This is probably due to the fact that the HAM-D is a weak index of severity of depression [18].

Faravelli notes that, as to depression, the convention of using a 50% reduction in the total score at the HAMD as a measure of 'response' is perhaps the biggest falsity of psychiatric evaluation [1]. In point of fact, the decrease in the final score may be attributable to the improvement/disappearance of the typical depressive signs (e.g. mood, anhedonia, guilt, suicidal ideation, psychic signs and retardation), which is a good purpose on clinical grounds, or to the alleviation of accessory symptoms (e.g. anxiety, appetite, insomnia, sexual interest and somatic symptoms), which is of little worth both for the patient and for the clinician. Besides, adverse effects of treatments (e.g. sleepiness or sedation) may decrease the total score of the rating scale, producing an artificial improvement.

Yet, in the past decade there has been an increasing number of clinical trials failing to disclose significant differences between active treatment and placebo [19,20]. Lack of sensitivity of outcome measures such as the Hamilton Rating Scale for Depression has been one of the potential explanations. Moreover, two widely used and validated self-rating scales for depression, the Beck Depression Inventory and the Zung Self-Rating Depression Scale, however, were found to be even less sensitive than the HAM-D [14,21].

Wright and Feinstein [11] provide an explanation for the disappointing performance that multi-item scales such HAM-D may present. It is interesting to note that extremely simple and rough methods for assessing psychopathology, such as the global measures (e.g. the Clinical Global Impression, the Visual Analogue Scales, and the Social and Occupational Functioning Assessment Scale) are generally more sensitive than the fully structured and spelled out multi-item scales. They maintain, however, approximately the same level of reliability. In other words, asking a doctor to score a patient 'from zero to ten' (or similar), without any other explicit rule or reference, is as reproducible as using instruments that require long and specific training [1]. Not surprisingly, in clinical trials, simple one-item global scales, which offer a clinical synthesis of heterogeneous components, often discriminate better than complex multi-item tools [5,19].

Despite such conclusions the HAM-D in depression trials has been the gold standard instrument for establishing and comparing the efficacy of treatments [17] and is still used by the Food and Drug Administration or other analogous regulators as outcome measure for drug licensing of antidepressants [22].

Because of insufficient sensitivity and inability to detect small changes, instruments such as HAMD have caused investigators to fail to reject the null hypothesis (to accept that no difference exists), with the result that potentially effective antidepressants are kept out of the market [23].

Scales and instruments not weighting core items more than the many unspecific items in the enlarged HAM-D versions have delayed the progress of clinical psychiatry in pharmacology in the field of depression [20].

Psychometrics is the managed care of methods [23]; all variables have the same weight, just as all physicians have the same value, regardless of experience, expertise, or judgement. An alternative model, clinimetrics is proposed as the conceptual basis to assess clinical phenomena, diagnosis, prognosis, and therapeutics [1,4,5,23]

CLINIMETRICS

The term "clinimetrics" was introduced by Alvan R. Feinstein in 1982 [24] to indicate a domain concerned with indexes, rating scales and other expressions that are used to describe or measure symptoms, physical signs, and other distinctly clinical phenomena in medicine. The purpose of clinimetric science was to provide an intellectual home for a number of clinical phenomena, which do not find room in the customary clinical taxonomy. Such phenomena include the types, severity and sequence of symptoms; rate of progression of illness, severity of comorbidity; problems of functional capacity; reasons for medical decisions; and many other aspects of daily life, such as well-being and distress [4,25]. Examples of clinimetric indexes are Jones criteria for rheumatic fever [24], the New York Heart Association Functional Classification [26] and Apgar's method of scoring the newborn's condition [27]. Clinimetrics has a set of rules which govern the structure of indexes, the choice of component variables, the evaluation of consistency and validity [28].

The clinimetric model introduced by Feinstein [28] combines theories of measurement with theories of clinical phenomenology. In his monograph on clinimetrics, the Author describes the problem with statistical coherence of models such as the Cronbach coefficient alpha and factor analysis within clinical framework. Nierenberg and Sonino [23] remember how he reprimanded the field of clinical psychiatry research for always seeking the grail of a statistically significant *p value* without predetermining the size of a difference between groups that would be considered clinically important [29]. He criticized the 'abstruseness' of the statistics used to describe differences between two groups [30]. He insisted to defend the link between clinical phenomena and pathophysiology [31,32] and the importance of clinical investigators who studied clinical phenomena [33].

Within the clinical framework, Feinstein [28] observes that patients use the clinimetric form of assessment when they say they have severe pain, a slight headache or a great improvement in appetite. Psychiatrists and clinical psychologists, in particular, are very familiar with clinimetric indexes, since, they may weigh factors such as the progression of disease, the overall severity of the disorder, the patients'social support and their adaptation, resilience and reaction to stressful life circumstances, response to previous treatment [33]. For this reason Feinstein [28], quotes Molière's bourgeois gentleman who was astonished to discover that he spoke in prose as an example of clinicians who may discover that they constantly communicate with clinimetric indexes.

The differential aspects of clinimetrics and psychometrics have become the focus of a debate [34,35-38,39]. De Wet et al. [35,37] and Fava and Belaise [39] argued for the importance of clinimetrics as a methodological discipline which is concerned with measurement issues in clinical medicine and [35,37] emphasized the substantial overlap between clinimetrics, psychometrics and biometrics together with the need for a better integration of the fields. Streiner [36,38] however advocated the abolishment of clinimetrics, as a redundant addiction to the set of rules developed within the psychometric field. Emmelkamp [33] states that although clinimetrics may have a number of advantage over the more classical psychometrically based measures, such as being more sensitive to change, there are still a number of methodological issues that deserve to be studied before we may abandon the psychometrically based methods.

CLINIMETRIC IMPLICATIONS FOR ASSESSMENT IN CLINICAL PSYCHOLOGY AND PSYCHIATRY

Clinimetrics may offer a conceptual and methodological ground for a substantial revision of clinical assessment providing a number of methodological and clinical advantages over traditional psychometric measures.

Development of Rating Scales

Clinimetrics needs should be considered in the development of rating scales. As an example several versions of a shortened HAMD have been found more sensitive to change than the full HAMD just because they were found to be consistent with Item Response Theory [40-43], defined by Bech (5) as the combination between clinical coherence with statistical coherence. The item response theory, introduced by Rasch [41] is thus a modern psychometric theory of measurement that uses a sensible method to assess symptoms based on their prevalence in those with a disorder (clinical coherence) and the importance of those symptoms for clinicians to define severity (weighting of symptoms) [5].

The Choice of Instruments: Incremental Validity

The concept of incremental validity refers to the unique contribution or incremental increase in predictive power associated with the inclusion of a particular assessment procedure in the clinical decision process [44]. Each distinct aspect of psychological measurement should deliver a unique increase in information in order to qualify for inclusion. The concept is mainly applied to the selection of instruments in a psychometric battery. In clinical research, however, several highly redundant scales are often used under the misguided assumption that nothing will be missed [44]. On the contrary, violation of the concept of incremental validity only leads to conflicting results. The concept, however, should also be extended to inclusion of items in the construction of a scale, with particular reference to sensitivity to change. The customary psychometric goal is to achieve a unidimensional construct, in which the relatively homogeneous components all measure essentially the same phenomenon [22]. In this process, components that seem to be different and may be likely to detect change may be discarded.

Diagnostic Categorization

Despite current diagnostic entities are based on clinimetric principles and they are particularly helpful in setting a threshold for conditions worthy of clinical attention, their use is still influenced by psychometric models. Already Engel [45] warned about the inhibiting influence of nosology on the formulation of a general concept of disease. 'Diagnostic labels are ways of indicating categories of information about our patient. A diagnostic label rarely, if ever, fully defines the illness. Rather, it has statistical and predictive value' [45].

Take for example DSM-IV diagnosis of major depressive disorder, which requires at least 5 of a set of 9 symptoms to be present. However, according to the psychometric model, all items are weighed the same, unlike in clinical medicine, where major and minor symptoms are often differentiated (e.g., the Jones criteria for rheumatic fever). As a result, a patient with severe and pervasive anhedonia, incapacitating fatigue and difficulties in concentrating, which make him/her unable to work, would not be diagnosed as suffering from a major depressive disorder, despite the clinical intuition of potential benefit from pharmacotherapy. The diagnosis could be performed in a patient who barely meets the criteria for five symptoms.

As Emmelkamp highlights [34] in the realm of personality disorders this may also be troublesome. In borderline personality disorder, five criteria may reveal a very severe case in which hospitalization is necessary, while in another case five (different) criteria might indicate a rather mild disorder without a crucial need for treatment. In practice this means that totally different persons may fulfil the diagnostic requirements for borderline personality disorder, but this does not say anything about the severity of the disorder or treatment planning [34]

The hidden conceptual model is psychometric: severity is determined by the number of symptoms, not by their intensity or quality, to the same extent that a score on the depression rating scale depends on the number of symptoms that are scored as positive. As Faravelli [1] remarks, the effect of psychometric theory on psychiatric assessment is to consider an illness as the sum of its symptoms, which, in turn, are represented by the numbers associated with specific behavior.

A clinimetric, instead of psychometric, model should guide the assessment tools in psychiatry since this model is focused on the evaluation of the severity and sequence of symptoms, rate of progression of the illness, severity and type of comorbidity, problems of functional capacity together with many other aspects of daily life, such as well-being and distress [4,39].

Longitudinal Assessment

Clinimetrics suggests that a satisfactory assessment requires multiple points of observation during the course of illnesses by calling in fact for a substantial modification of the flat, cross-sectional approach based on DSM-IV criteria only. A longitudinal consideration of the development of disorders, may prove to be more fruitful for clinical decision making and treatment planning than a cross-sectional diagnosis [4,34,33,39]. This approach is also in accordance with the sequential model of treatment, which was found to be effective in clinical medicine and psychiatry [46].

In the past decade, in clinical psychiatry several investigations have suggested the usefulness of a sequential way of integrating pharmacotherapy and psychotherapy in affective disorders.

Residual symptoms, despite successful response to therapy, appear to be the rule after completion of drug or psychotherapeutic treatment in both mood and anxiety disorders [47,48]. The presence of residual symptoms has been correlated with poor long-term outcome [47,48]. There appears to be a relationship between residual and prodromal symptomatology: most of the residual symptoms occur in fact in the prodromal phase of illness. These findings have led to the hypothesis that residual symptoms upon recovery may progress to become prodromal symptoms of relapse and that treatment directed toward residual symptoms may yield long-term benefits [49]. Treatment which potentially aims to different effects (e.g., pharmacotherapy and psychotherapy) may thus be used in a sequential order. One type of treatment (e.g., psychotherapy) may be employed to improve symptoms which the other type of treatment (e.g., pharmacotherapy) was unable to affect. The aim of the sequential approach is to add therapeutic ingredients as long as they are needed. In this sense, it introduces a conceptual shift in clinical practice. Therapeutic targets are not predetermined, but depend on the response of patients to the first course of treatment.

Comorbidity

Another line of evidence potentially supporting the importance of the longitudinal observation of the disorder is the increasing awareness of the role of comorbidity [50-53]. In major depression, two-thirds of the patients meet the criteria for another Axis I disorder (particularly anxiety disorders) and one third has 2 or more disorders [54]. The presence of anxiety disorders appears to predict persistence and recurrence of depressive illness in major depression [55,56]. Some forms of comorbidity may be covered by the acute manifestations of the disorder and become evident only when the most severe symptoms have abated [47].

Recovery

Clinimetrics provides also relevant clinical implications in the definition of recovery. Commonly, the concept of recovery reflects that of "improvement" which refers to the clinical distance along which the current state of the patient is compared to the pre-treatment position [57]. In this sense, recovery can be expressed either as a categorical variable (present/absent) or as a comparative category (nonrecovered, slightly recovered, moderately recovered, greatly recovered). Both expressions require arbitrary cut-off points related to the amount of improvement.

Feinstein [28] differentiates between the monadic transition index (devoted exclusively to the rating of change during treatment), the dyadic component index (e.g., before and after treatment ratings) and polyadic component index (when more than two ratings, such as with the sequential model, have been performed). A depressed patient who is asked how he or she feels after 3 weeks of treatment with an antidepressant drug and replies "just fine" (instead of "better") uses a self-monadic component. The amount of change induced by treatment, however, may make him/her overlook the distance from an intended goal, such as the pre-episode state. The physician may collude with the patient in this illusion of wellness, since he/she may be gratified more by the amount of improvement induced in the patient, than by the current distance from an intended goal [10]. Clinicians may choose recovery as a target that is negotiated between the doctor and the patient. The doctor can insist that the target be reasonable (e.g., not asking to be better than before the illness). Nevertheless, the idea of successful recovery may differ from one patient to the next and should not be constrained too much by the doctor's ideas. We should accept the possibility that a treatment may determine abatement of symptoms in some patients, leave a substantial residual symptomatology in others, yield an unsatisfactory response in others, and provide no benefit or even cause harm in a few. The type of residual symptomatology varies widely from patient to patient and needs to be assessed individually [10].

In a survey on factors identified by depressed outpatients as important in determining remission, the most frequently judged as such were the presence of features of positive mental health, such as optimism and self-confidence, a return to one's usual, normal self; and a return to the usual level of functioning [58]. In 1958 Marie Jahoda outlined some tentative criteria for positive mental health, encompassing attitudes toward the self, growth, integration, autonomy, perception of reality and environmental mastery. Such criteria were refined and expanded in Carol Ryff's multidimensional model (1989), which was then applied in a variety of clinical settings [59]. Ryff's psychological dimensions may be instrumental in assessing both the process and the definition of recovery [see Table 1]. Table 2 provides a clinimetric definition of recovery applied to major depression.

Macro and Micro-Analysis

As a response to the current flat diagnostic evaluation, Emmelkamp et al. [60] and Fava et al.[4] distinguish, in the initial psychological assessment, two levels of functional analysis: macro-analysis (a relationship between cooccurring syndromes is established in order to enable the therapist to determine which problem should be targeted first) and micro-analysis (a detailed analysis of symptoms). Problems may be caused by different factors and may be maintained by different factors [33]. As reported above [50-53], very seldom these different diagnoses undergo hierarchical organization (e.g., generalized anxiety disorder and major depression), or attention is paid to the longitudinal development of disorders. There is comorbidity which wanes upon successful treatment of one disorder, e.g., recovery from panic disorder with agoraphobia may result in remission from co-occurring hypochondriasis, without any specific treatment for the latter [48].

Table 1. Modification of the six dimensions of Psychological Well-being according to Ryff's model (1989). At least A or B or C should be present for satisfying criteria for each dimension

Dimensions	Optimal level
Environmental mastery	A. The subject has a sense of mastery and competence in managing the environment; B. Makes effective use of surrounding opportunities; C. Is able to create or choose contexts suitable to personal needs and values.
Personal growth	A. The subject has a feeling of continued development; B. Has sense of realizing own potential; C. Sees improvement in self and behavior over time.
Purpose in life	A. The subject has goals in life and a sense of directedness; B. Feels there is meaning to present and past life; C. Holds beliefs that give life purpose.
Autonomy	A. The subject is self-determining and independent; B. Is able to resist to social pressures; C. Evaluates self by personal standards.
Self-acceptance	A. The subject has a positive attitude toward the self; B. Accepts his/her good and bad qualities; C. Feels positive about past life.
Positive relations with others	A. The subject has warm and trusting relationships with others; B. Capable of strong empathy affection, and intimacy; C. Understands give and take of human relationships.

Table 2. Definition of Recovery from a Major Depressive Episode

a) the patient remains in full remission despite discontinuation of treatment (whether pharmacological or psychotherapeutic);

b) if subclinical or subsyndromal symptoms are present, these are judged to be likely to improve spontaneously over time or not to affect the course of the illness. Residual symptoms which occurred also in the prodromal phase of illness are unlikely to be devoid of clinical implications;

c) the patient reports psychological well-being in at least one of the six areas outlined in Table 1;

d) normalization of altered biological markers in the acute phase of illness (if available) should have occurred.

Other times, treatment of one disorder does not result in disappearance of comorbidity.

Emmelkamp [33] provides an example of the surplus value of a macro-analysis. A substantial number of depressed patients presenting for treatment also experiences marital distress, whereas in approximately half of the couples that have marital problems at least one of the spouse is depressed. These data suggest that depression and marital distress are closely linked. Furthermore, marital distress is an important precursor of depressive symptoms. In addition, persons who, after being treated for depression, return to distressed marriages are more likely to experience relapse [61].

Although in depressed patients either antidepressant drugs or cognitive behavior therapy are the treatment of choice, clinimetric assessment including macro-analysis might reveal that behavioral marital therapy should be preferred in depressed maritally distressed couples. Taken the results of the studies in this area together, in maritally distressed depressed couples behavioral marital therapy seems to have an exclusive effect on the marital relationship, which is not found in individual cognitive-behavior therapy, while it is as effective as cognitive therapy in reducing depressed mood [62]. Not surprisingly, behavioral marital therapy was hardly effective in depressed patients who did not experience marital problems [63].

A patient may present with a major depressive disorder, obsessive-compulsive disorder and hypochondriasis. In terms of macroanalysis, the clinician may gives priority to the pharmacological treatment of depression, leaving to post-therapy assessment the determination of the relationship of depression to obsessive-compulsive disorder and hypochondriasis. Will they wane as depressive epiphenomena or will they persist, despite some degree of improvement? Should, in this latter case, further treatment be necessary? What type of relationship obsessive-compulsive symptoms and hypochondriasis entertain? On the basis of the type and longitudinal development of hypochondriacal fears and beliefs [64] the clinician may decide to tackle obsessive compulsive disorder, regarding hypochondriasis as an ensuing phenomenon. Or he/she may consider them as independent syndromes. If the clinical decision of tackling one syndrome may be taken during the initial assessment, the subsequent steps of macro-analysis require a re-assessment after the first line of treatment has terminated.

The Roll-Back Phenomena and the State-Trait Distinction

Detre and Jarecki [65] provided a model for relating prodromal and residual symptomatology in psychiatric illness, defined as the rollback phenomenon: as the illness remits, it progressively recapitulates (though in a reverse order) many of the stages and symptoms that were seen during the time it developed. "For example, if an illness begins with occasional anxiety attacks that are superseded some week later by depressive symptoms which become progressively more severe until, after several months, the patient develops total insomnia and confusion, the symptoms tend, as the condition improves, to remit in reverse order, the confusion and insomnia diminishing first, and the depressed mood next. After the depression the depression lifts, the patient may again experience anxiety attacks for several weeks, until finally these symptom, too, disappear" [65]. According with the rollback model, there is also a temporal relationship between the time of development of a disorder and the duration of the phase of recovery. This has several exemplifications in clinical medicine. For instance, herpes zoster (chickenpox) has a sudden onset and quick recovery in children, whereas it develops insidiously and tend to leave a long residual phase in adults.

The psychometric distinction between state and trait may also reflect the rollback phenomenon and it may hinder detection of change. There is evidence – reviewed in detail elsewhere [10]– that personality assessment is considerably influenced by state variables, i.e. the relationship of antidepressant treatment to personality measurements [10,66]. Psychological constructs traditionally conceived as trait dimensions may surprisingly display sensitivity to change in a specific clinical situation, whereas constructs viewed as state dimensions may display unexpected stability throughout the longitudinal development of the disorder [67].

CONCLUSION

Clinimetric theory offers the conceptual and methodological ground for a substantial revision of assessment parameters and for linking co-occurring syndromes. Such switch may produce substantial clinical and research advantages. By a clinical viewpoint, it may allow more flexibility and be more in tune with the clinician's reasoning, both in terms of diagnostic assessment and evaluation of comorbidity, once variables are no longer considered as equal. By a research viewpoint, it may pave the way for inclusion criteria and assessment tools which are more suitable for the purposes of clinical research. Rigid adherence to the psychometric model may only prevent such progress.

If clinical research uses the wrong measures to assess efficacy, if subjects included in clinical trials fail to represent the patients who are encountered in clinical practice, if diagnostic tests are not thought through so that clinicians can apply them properly then the results of 'hard science' become merely academic, without improving the lives of our patients [23,68].

The conceptual crisis of research in psychiatry results from a narrow concept of science which neglects clinical observation, the basic method of medicine [69] , and simply attempts to apply oversimplified neurobiological and psychometric models to the understanding and treatment of mental disorders. Enhancing the benefits of research where clinical need is greatest, and not only where commercial opportunity is perceived, is a current priority of medicine [70,71] . However, such priority could hardly be achieved in clinical psychology and psychiatry unless a critical examination and update of current paradigms is endorsed.

REFERENCES

[1]   Faravelli, C. Assessment of psychopathology. *Psychother. Psychosom.* 2004;73:139-141.

[2]   Bech, P. Rating Scales for Psychopathology, *Health status and Quality of Life*. Berlin: Springer-Verlag, 1993.

[3]   Rust, J; Golombok, S. Modern Psychometrics. *The science of psychological assessment*. London: Routledge, 1989.

[4]   Fava, GA; Ruini, C; Rafanelli, C. Psychometric theory is an obstacle to the progress of clinical research. *Psychother. Psychosom.* 2004;73:145-148.

[5]   Bech, P. Modern Psychometrics in Clinimetrics: Impact on Clinical Trials of Antidepressants. *Psychother. Psychosom.* 2004;73:134–138.

[6]   Shapiro, MB. An experimental approach to diagnostic psychological testing. *J. Ment. Sci.* 1951; 97: 748-764

[7]   Kellner, R. Part 1. Improvement criteria in drug trials with neurotic patients. *Psychol. Med.* 1971; 1: 416-425.

[8]   Kellner, R. Part 2. Improvement criteria in drug trials with neurotic patients. *Psychol. Med.* 1972; 2: 73-80.

[9]   Kellner, R. The development of sensitive scales for research in therapeutics. In: Fava M, Rosenbaum JF, eds. *Research Designs and Methods in Psychiatry*. Amsterdam: Elsevier, 1992: 213-222.

[10]   Fava, GA. The concept of recovery in affective disorders. *Psychother. Psychosom.* 1996; 65: 2-13.

[11]   Wright, JG; Feinstein, AR. A comparative contrast of clinimetric and psychometric methods for constructing indexes and rating scales. *J. Clin. Epidemiol.* 1992; 45: 1201-1218.

[12]   Fava, GA; Kellner, R; Lisansky, J; Park, S; Perini, GI; Zielezny, M. Rating depression in normals and depressives. *J. Affect. Disord.* 1986; 11: 29-33.

[13]   Ruini, C; Ottolini, F; Rafanelli, C; Tossani, E; Ryff, CD; Fava, GA. The relationship of psychological well-being to distress and personality. *Psychother. Psychosom.* 2003; 72:268-275.

[14]   Carroll, BJ; Fielding, JM; Blashki, TG. Depression rating scales. *Arch. Gen. Psychiatry.* 1973; 28: 361-366.

[15]   Hamilton, M. Development of a rating sale for primary depressive illness. *Br. J. Soc. Clin. Psychol.* 1967;6:278–296.

[16]   Faries, D; Herrera, J; Rayamajhi, J; De Brota, D; Demitrack, M; Potter, WZ. The responsiveness of the Hamilton Depression Rating Scale. *J. Psychiat. Res.* 2000; 34: 3-10.

[17]   Demyttenaere, K; De Fruyt, J. Getting what you ask for: on the selectivity of depression rating scales. *Psychother. Psychosom.* 2003; 72: 61-70.

[18]   Gibbons, RD; Clark, DC; Kupfer, DJ. Exactly what does the Hamilton Depression Rating Scale measure? *J. Psychiat. Res.* 1993; 27: 259-273.

[19]   Fava, M; Evins, AE; Dorer, DJ; Schoenfeld, DA. The problem of the placebo response in clinical trials for psychiatric disorders: culprits, possible remedies, and a novel study design approach. *Psychother. Psychosom.* 2003; 72: 115-127.

[20]   Grandi, S. The sequential parallel comparison model. *Psychother. Psychosom.* 2003; 72: 113-114.

[21]   Kearns, NP; Cruickshank, CA; McGuigan, KJ; Riley, SA; Shaw, SP; Snaith, RP. A comparison of depression rating scales. *Br. J. Psychiatry.* 1982; 141: 45-49.

[22]   Healy, D: *The Creation of Psychopharmacology*. Cambridge, Harvard University Press, 2002.

[23]   Nierenberg, AA; Sonino, N. From Clinical Observations to Clinimetrics: A Tribute to Alvan R. Feinstein. *Psychother. Psychosom.* 2004;73:131–133.

[24]   Feinstein, AR. The Jones criteria and the challenge of clinimetrics. *Circulation* 1982; 66: 1-5.

[25]   Feinstein, AR. An additional science for clinical medicine. IV. The development of clinimetrics. *Ann. Intern. Med.* 1983; 99: 843-848.

[26]   The Criteria Committee of the New York Heart Association. *Disease of the Heart and Blood Vessels.* 6th edn. Boston: Little Brown, 1964.

[27]   Feinstein, AR. Multi-item "instruments" versus Virginia Apgar's principles of clinimetrics. *Arch. Intern. Med.* 1999; 159: 125-128.

[28]   Feinstein, AR. *Clinimetrics*. New Haven, CT: Yale University Press, 1987.

[29] Feinstein, AR. The inadequacy of binary models for the clinical reality of three-zone diagnostic decisions. *J. Clin. Epidemiol.* 1990;43:109– 113.

[30] Yueh, B; Feinstein, AR. Abstruse comparisons: The problems of numerical contrasts of two groups. *J. Clin. Epidemiol.* 1999;52:13–18.

[31] Feinstein, AR. Basic biomedical science and the destruction of the pathophysiologic bridge from bench to bedside. *Am. J. Med.* 1999;107:461–467.

[32] Feinstein, AR. Clinical judgement revisited: The distraction of quantitative models. *Ann. Intern. Med.* 1994;120:799–805.

[33] Fava, GA; Kellner, R. Staging: a neglected dimension in psychiatric classification. *Acta. Psychiat. Scand.* 1993; 87: 225-230.

[34] Emmelkamp, PMG. The additional value of clinimetrics needs to be established rather than assumed. *Psychother. Psychosom.* 2004;73:142-144.

[35] de Wet, HCW; Terwee, CB; Bouter, LM. Current challenges in clinimetrics. *J. Clin. Epidemiol.* 2003;56:1137-1141.

[36] Streiner, DL. Clinimetrics vs psychometrics: an unnecessary distinction. *J. Clin. Epidemiol.* 2003;56:1143-1145.

[37] de Wet, HCW; Terwee, CB; Bouter, LM. Clinimetric versus psychometrics: two sides of the same coin. *J. Clin. Epidemiol.* 2003;56:1146-1147.

[38] Streiner, DL. Test development: two-sided coin or one-sided Mobins strip? *J. Clin. Epidemiol.* 2003;56:1148-1149.

[39] Fava, GA; Belaise, C. Clinical assessment: the role of clinimetrics and the misleading effects of psychometric theory. *Journal of Clinical Epidemiology* 2005;58:754-756.

[40] Gill, TM; Feinstein, AR. A critical appraisal of the quality-of-life measurements. *JAMA* 1994; 272:619–626.

[41] Rasch, G. *Probabilistic Models for Some Intelligence and Attainment Tests.* Chicago, University of Chicago Press, 1980.

[42] Bech, P; Cialdella, P; Haugh, M; Birkett, MA; Hours, A; Boissel, JP; Tollefson, GD. A metaanalysis of randomised controlled trials of fluoxetine versus placebo and tricyclic antidepressants in the short-term treatment of major depression. *Br. J. Psychiatry.* 2000;176:421– 428

[43] Bech, P. Meta-analysis of placebo-controlled trials with mirtazapine using the core items of the Hamilton Depression Scale as evidence of a pure antidepressive effect in the short-term treatment of major depression. *Int. J. Neuropsychopharmacol.* 2001;4:337–345.

[44] Derogatis, LR; The Derogatis Stress Profile (DSP): Quantification of psychological stress; in Fava GA, Wise TN (eds): *Research Paradigms in Psychosomatic Medicine.* Basel, Karger, 1987, pp 30-54.

[45] Engel, GL. A unified concept of health and disease. *Perspect. Biol. Med.* 1960; 3: 459–484.

[46] Fava, GA; Ruini, C; Rafanelli, C. Sequential treatment of mood and anxiety disorders. *J. Clin. Psychiatry.* 2005; 66: 1392–1400.

[47] Fava, GA. Subclinical symptoms in mood disorders. *Psychol. Med.* 1999; 29: 47-61.

[48] Fava, GA; Mangelli, L. Subclinical symptoms of panic disorder. *Psychother. Psychosom.* 1999; 68: 281-289.

[49] Fava, GA; Kellner, R. Prodromal symptoms in affective disorder. *Am. J. Psychiatry* .1991; 148: 823-830

[50] Maj, M. The aftermath of the concept of psychiatric comorbidity. *Psychother. Psychosom.* 2005; 74: 65-67.

[51] Pincus, HA; Tew, JD; First, MB. Psychiatric comorbidity: is more less? *World Psychiatry* 2004; 3: 18-23.

[52] Regier, DA. State-of-the-art psychiatric diagnosis. *World Psychiatry* 2004; 3: 25-26.

[53] Murthy, RS. Psychiatric comorbidity presents special challenges in developing countries. *World Psychiatry* 2004; 3: 28-30.

[54] Zimmerman, M; Chelminski, I; McDermut, W. Major depressive disorder and Axis 1 diagnostic comorbidity. *J. Clin. Psychiatry* 2002; 63: 187-193.

[55] Sherbourne, CD; Wells, KB. Course of depression in patients with comorbid anxiety disorders. *J. Affect. Disord.* 1997; 43: 245-250.

[56] Gaynes, BN; Magruder, KM; Burns, BJ; Wagner, HR; Yarnall, KSH; Broadhead, WE. Does a coexisting anxiety disorder predict persistence of depressive illness in primary care patients with major depression? *Gen. Hosp. Psychiatry* 1999; 21: 158-167.

[57] Bech, P. Measurement of psychological distress and well-being. *Psychother. Psychosom.* 1990; 54: 77-89

[58] Zimmerman, M; McGlinchey, JB; Posternak, MA; Friedman, M; Attiullah, N; Boerescu, D. How should remission from depression be defined? *Am. J. Psychiatry.* 2006; 163: 148-150.

[59] Fava, GA; Ruini, C. Development and characteristics of a well-being enhancing psychotherapeutic strategy: well-being therapy. *J. Behav. Ther. Exp. Psychiatry* 2003;34, 45-63.

[60] Emmelkamp, PMG; Bouman, TK; Scholing, A. *Anxiety Disorders.* Chichester, Wiley, 1992.

[61] Emmelkamp, PMG; Vedel, E. Spouse-aided therapy; in Hersen M, Sledge W (eds): *The Encyclopedia of Psychotherapy.* New York, Academic Press, 2002, vol II, pp 693–698.

[62] Emmelkamp. PMG. Behavior therapy with adults; in Lamberts L (ed): *Bergin and Garfield's Handbook of Psychotherapy and Behavior Change*, ed 5. New York, Wiley, 2003, pp 396–449.

[63] Emanuels-Zuurveen, L; Emmelkamp, PMG. Spouse-aided therapy with depressed patients: A comparative evaluation. *Behav. Modif.* 1997;21:62–77.

[64] Savron, G; Fava, GA; Grandi, S; Rafanelli, C; Raffi, AR; Belluardo, P; Hypochondriacal fears and beliefs in obsessive-compulsive disorder. *Acta. Psychiat. Scand.* 1996; 93: 345-348

[65] Detre, TP; Jarecki, HJ. *Modern Psychiatric Treatment.* Philadelphia, Lippincott, 1971

[66] Petersen, T; Hughes, M; Papakostas, GI, Kant, A; Fava, M; Rosenbaum, JF; Nierenberg, AA. Treatment-resistant depression and Axis II comorbidity. *Psychother. Psychosom.* 2002; 71: 269-274

[67] Rafanelli, C; Park, SK; Ruini, C; Ottolini, F; Cazzaro M; Fava, GA. Rating well-being and distress. *Stress. Med.* 2000; 16: 55-61.

[68] Fava, GA. The Intellectual Crisis of Psychiatric.*Research Psychother Psychosom* 2006;75:202–208.

[69] Engel, GL. Clinical observation. The neglected basic method of medicine. *JAMA* 1965; 192: 157–160.

[70] Moses, H; Dorsey, ER; Matheson, DHM; Their, SO. Financial anatomy of biomedical research. *JAMA* 2005; 294: 1333–1342.

[71]   Gannon, F. Is the system dumbing down research? *EMBO Reports* 2005; 6: 387.

In: Leading-Edge Psychological Tests and Testing Research   ISBN: 978-1-60021-571-1
Editor: Marta A. Lange, pp. 145-158   © 2007 Nova Science Publishers, Inc.

Chapter 8

PRACTICAL INTELLIGENCE (PI): TESTING OF DOING OR KNOWING HOW TO DO?

Shira Yalon-Chamovitz[*]

Ono Academic College
102 Zahal St, Kiryat Ono, Israel

ABSTRACT

The study of intelligence has been dominated for years by the study of abstract or academic intelligence. The emphasis on intelligence as it operates in a real world context led to the development of the study of practical intelligence (Stemberg, 1986). Practical intelligence (PI) refers to the cognitive underpinning of everyday function and has been variously defined either as an intellectual process or capacity (Mathias and Nettelback, 1992; Wagner and Kistner, 1990); as a product or outcome of behavior, mainly as manifested in adaptation (Luckasson et al, 1992; Stemberg et al. 1995); or as a set of intellectual abilities which contribute to adaptation (Gardner, 1993; Greenspan and Driscoll, 1997).

Preliminary studies exploring the construct of PI consisted mainly of anecdotal examples of specific tasks thought of as unique representations of PI (Carraher, Carraher, and Schliemann, 1985; Ceci, and Liker, 1988; Lave, Murtaugh, and de la Roche, 1984). Currently, the most comprehensive body of data stems from the exploration of the role of PI in the successful manifestation of various occupational pursuits (for review see Sternberg, et al. 2000; Wagner, 2000), with the accumulating data suggesting that PI is psychologically distinct from academic intelligence (Sternberg, et al. 2001).

Practical intelligence is not assessed in traditional intelligence (IQ) tests, and, while some claim it is easy to measure (Sternberg, et al. 1995) others question the reliability and validity of various PI measures developed (McDaniel, 2003) as well as their factor structure, methods, and item selection (Kyllonen, 2003). Measures of practical intelligence should attempt to tap the covert, underlying cognitive components that may contribute to competence, but are not synonymous with performance. Some of the obstacles encountered include (a) difficulty in devising stimulus materials (such as might be found in a test kit) that correspond to the nature and complexity of practical

---

[*] E-mail: shirayc@gmail.com; shirayc@ono.ac.il

intelligence tasks in the everyday world, and (b) the fact that performance in a simulation test (such as would be created if an individual were to be presented with practical tasks to solve) runs the risk of confounding competence with performance and bringing into the equation various motivational, affective and other potential sources of error variance (Chang, 2000). This chapter presents a broad review of current measures of practical intelligence as well as suggestions for further research and test development.

INTRODUCTION

Intelligence affects all aspects of human existence. The construct of intelligence had drawn many debates over the years (Sternberg, 1986a). Indeed, the challenge of defining intelligence falls under what Hofstadter (1999) describes as the almost impossible task of defining something that is intuitively understood. To date there is no single agreed upon definition of intelligence, nor is there consensus regarding its factor structure, which element of human experience it entails, or whether it represents a general intellectual ability (g) or multiple competences (for review see Thorndike, 1997). The study of intelligence has been dominated for years by the study of abstract or academic intelligence. This has been attributed to various factors but can be primarily related to the fact that intelligence tests, intended originally to screen for academic failure, were developed before there was a clear understanding and definition of what intelligence is (Greenspan, 1979).

Growing dissatisfaction with the predictive value of intelligence tests (e.g. IQ scores) beyond academic settings (Sternberg, et al. 1995), as well as the realization that intelligence can only be understood within a sociocultural context (Goodnow, 1986) has led to broadening the scope of intellectual behavior (Rogoff, 1984). This is manifested in the paradigm shift from dominantly viewing intelligence as a unitary construct to a multiple intelligence approach (Daniel, 1997), as well as the growing interest in the study of intelligence in real world settings (Sternberg, 1986; Sternberg, at al. 2000). Studies aimed at differentiating PI from academic intelligence were conducted with such diverse populations as high level executives (Wagner, and Sternberg, 1991), children with learning disabilities (Wagner, and Kistner, 1990), entrepreneurs (Baum, and Bird, 2005), adults with intellectual disabilities (Yalon-Chamovitz, and Greenspan, 2006), and military officers (Hedlund, et al. 2003) to name just a few. Several excellent papers cover the ongoing, heated debate regarding the essence of intelligence, in particular as it relates to asserting a general factor underlying mental ability (g) and its interrelationship with PI (Brody, 2000; Ceci, 1990; Gottfredson, 2003; Sternberg, 2003; Sternberg, and Wagner, 1993) and is beyond the scope of this chapter. Suffice it to say that the study of PI, as well as the tests and measurements presented below, should be seen, to a large extant, as a derivative of multiple intelligence approaches.

THEORETICAL UNDERPINNINGS OF PRACTICAL INTELLIGENCE

The emphasis on intelligence as it operates in a real world context led to the development of the study of PI (Sternberg, 2000). PI refers to the cognitive underpinning of everyday function and has been variously defined either as an intellectual process or capacity (Goodnow, 1986; Mathias, and Nettelback, 1992; Wagner, and Kistner, 1990); as a product or outcome of behavior, mainly as manifested in adaptation (Campione, Brown, and Ferrara, 1982; Luckasson et al. 1992; Stemberg, et al. 1995, Sternberg, et al. 2000); or as a set of intellectual abilities which contribute to adaptation (Gardner, 1993; Greenspan, 1981; Greenspan, and Driscoll, 1997; Guilford, 1967).

Preliminary studies exploring the construct of PI consisted mainly of anecdotal examples of specific tasks thought of as unique representations of PI, for example, grocery shopping (Lave, Murtaugh, and de la Roche, 1984; Murtaugh, 1985), horserace handicapping (Ceci, and Liker, 1986, 1988), packing expertise of milk plant workers (Scribner, 1984, 1986), or street peddling of Brazilian children (Carraher, Carraher, and Schliemann, 1985). While these studies all explored very different tasks, they all demonstrated that performance of these tasks was not predicted by IQ measures nor correlated with academic-type tests. These finding provided the support, and enthusiasm, for further studying the notion of PI as separate from academic intelligence. Currently, the most comprehensive body of data stems from the exploration of the role of PI in the successful manifestation of various occupational pursuits (for review see Sternberg, et al. 2000; Wagner, 2000), with the accumulating data indicating that PI is psychologically distinct from academic intelligence (Sternberg, et al. 2001), and can also be differentiated from experience (Yalon-Chamovitz, 2000).

In addition to the above mentioned research, PI emerged as a construct within two well-developed theoretical models: (a) The Triarchic Theory of Human Intelligence (Sternberg, 1985), and (b) The Model of Personal Competence (Greenspan, 1981).

The Triarchic Theory of Human Intelligence (Sternberg, 1985), later termed the Triarchic Theory of Successful Intelligence (Sternberg, 1997, 1999), describes the contribution of analytical (i.e. academic), creative, and practical intelligence to adaptation. PI is defined within as the ability to adapt to, shape, and select everyday environments, or what most people call "common sense" (Sternberg, et al. 2000). Preliminary studies by Sternberg and colleagues, within specific occupational pursuits, led to the introduction of *tacit knowledge* as the core element of PI (for review see Sternberg, and Wagner, 1993). Tacit knowledge refers to the practical know-how that is usually not directly taught, or even openly expressed. It is the type of knowledge that one is likely to acquire through experience on the job or in everyday situations, rather than through formal instruction (Sternberg, Wagner, and Okagaki, 1993). Tacit knowledge was further differentiated into knowledge about three kinds of content (i.e. managing self, managing tasks, managing others), as well as two orientations - local and global (Wagner, 1987). What followed was the introduction of a knowledge-based approach to PI, as manifested in the gradual development of various, occupation specific, tacit knowledge tests conceptualized as measures of PI (Sternberg, et al. 2000). Despite a number of tacit knowledge measures developed, a major critique of this theory relates to the justification of the relatively narrow representation of PI as measured by tests of tacit knowledge (Broody, 2003; Gottfredson, 2003). Indeed, Sternberg and colleges recently started developing a somewhat broader, skill-based or problem-solving-based approach to the measurement of PI within the Triarchic Theory of Successful Intelligence, where tacit knowledge is more broadly conceived as a function of the ability to learn from and to solve everyday problems in order to adapt to, select, and/or shape environment in the pursuit of personal goals (Hedlund, Wilt, Nebel, Ashford, and Sternberg, 2006; Stemler, and Sternberg, 2006).

The Model of Personal Competence. Greenspan (1981) portrays intelligence as the subset of skills that involves thinking and understanding within the context of human function.

Intelligence is viewed, within this broad model of personal competence, as incorporating all the skills that contribute to attaining goals or solving challenges (Greenspan, and Driscoll, 1997). PI is defined as the ability to think about and understand mechanical, technical or physical problems found in everyday settings (Greenspan, and Driscoll, 1997), and is a subcategory of everyday functioning along with social intelligence. PI is further differentiated into the underlying processes of problem identification, insight, and problem-solving. *Problem identification* refers to one's ability to recognize that a practical problem has occurred; *insight* or *problem explanation* refers to one's ability to reflect upon and understand the meaning of the problem and its underlying processes; and *problem solving* refers to one's ability to deal effectively with a practical problem (Yalon-Chamovitz, and Greenspan, 2005). Physical competence as well as practical intelligence contribute to problem solving in the practical domain, but the basic process involved in PI is a cognitive one (Greenspan, 1981). Several studies have aimed at establishing the construct validity of Greenspan's model, emphasizing mainly the interrelationships between practical intelligence and social intelligence as either separate factors or a single factor of everyday intelligence (Mathias, and Nettelbeck, 1992; McGrew, and Bruininks, 1989; McGrew, Bruininks, and Johnson, 1996; Widaman, and McGrew, 1996). Although generally supportive, some inconclusive findings were attributed mainly to methodological limitations of factor analysis studies given the nature of measurement instruments of these constructs (Greenspan, and McGrew, 1996). Elaboration of the model has concentrated primarily on the social domain (Greenspan, and Love, 1997). Recently, a PI measure developed based on The Model of Personal Competence presented a problem-solving based approach to the measurement of PI (Yalon-Chamovitz, and Greenspan, 2005).

MEASUREMENT AND TESTING OF PRACTICAL INTELLIGENCE

Intelligence testing was first introduced in the early twentieth century and has been the focus of extensive scientific inquiry ever since (reviewed in Flanagan, Genshaft, and Harrison, 1997). Measures of academic or abstract intelligence (e.g. IQ tests) evolved mainly within the scope of psychometric approaches and the study of individual differences (Sternberg, 2000). Practical intelligence is not assessed in traditional intelligence (IQ) tests (Psychology matters, 2006), and measures of PI were originally developed partly in an attempt to replace these tests as predictors of success beyond academic settings (Sternberg, et al. 1995). However, current PI measures often strive to complement rather than replace traditional intelligence tests, and it is acknowledged that traditional tests of intelligence can be useful, when carefully interpreted in conjunction with other measures (Sternberg, Grigorenko, and Bundy, 2001). For example, Hedlund at al (2003) developed a supplemental measure of PI and creative intelligence that was found to add on to the predictive validity of the GMAT in the process of MBA college admission.

While some claim facile and clear measuring of PI (Sternberg, et al. 1995), others question the reliability and validity of the various PI measures developed (McDaniel, 2003), as well as their factor structure, methods, and item selection (Kyllonen, 2003). Traditional intelligence tests evolved mainly within a linear, reductionist paradigm while PI measures represent, to a large extant, a paradigm shift towards dynamic, non-linear systems approaches, wherein intelligence is viewed as emerging through the dynamic interaction of individual and environment (Davidson, and Downing, 2000, Smith, 2005). Within this paradigm, PI is considered highly context specific (Sternberg, 2000).This contextual approach led to the development of occupation-specific, culture-specific or population-specific measures of PI and tacit knowledge.

Table 1. Overview of available measures of PI

Measure	Method	Target population	Ref.
Tacit knowledge in academic psychology	Paper and pencil, Situational Judgment Test	Academic psychologists	1, 2
TKIM Tacit Knowledge Inventory for Managers	Paper and pencil, Situational Judgment Test	Managers and Executive	3
TKML Tacit Knowledge for Military Leaders Inventory	Paper and pencil, Situational Judgment Test	Military leaders	4
TKS Tacit Knowledge Inventory for Sales: Written	Paper and pencil, Situational Judgment Test	Sales people	5
YSPI Yup'ik Scale of Practical Intelligence	Multiple choice interview	Alaskan Yup'ik Eskimos adolescent	6
Test of Natural herbal Medicine	Multiple choice interview	Rural adolescents in west Kenya	7
Practical intelligence test for entrepreneurs	Paper and pencil, Situational Judgment Test	Entrepreneurs	8
VMPI Video Measure of Practical Intelligence	Video based simulations	Adults with intellectual disabilities	9

The data presented in this table is a non-exhaustive list of currently available measures of PI.
(1) Sternberg and Wagner, 1985; (2) Wagner, 1987; (3) Wagner and Sternberg, 1991; (4) Hedlund, Forsythe, Horvath, Williams, Snook, and Sternberg, 2003; (4) Wagner and Sternberg, 1989; (5) Wagner et al. 1999; (6) Grigorenko, Meier, Lipka, Mohatt, Yanez, and Sternberg, 2004; (7) Sternberg, et al. 2001; (8) Baum and Bird, 2005; (9) Yalon-Chamovitz and Greenspan, 2005.

Measures of practical intelligence should attempt to tap the covert, underlying cognitive components that may contribute to competence and adaptation but are not synonymous with performance, thus differentiating between doing and knowing how to do (Yalon-Chamovitz, and Greenspan, 2005). However, several obstacles delay the development of such measures. The two major challenges encountered include (a) difficulty in devising stimulus materials (such as might be found in a test kit) that correspond to the nature and complexity of practical intelligence tasks in the everyday world, and (b) the fact that performance in a simulation test (such as would be created if an individual were to be presented with practical tasks to solve) runs the risk of confounding competence with performance and bringing into the equation various motivational, affective and other potential sources of error variance (Chang, 2000; Yalon-Chamovitz, and Greenspan, 2005). Therefore, tests of analytical abilities are seemingly easier to create than tests of practical abilities (Sternberg, 2003). Despite these challenges, and though the development of PI tests and measures is relatively young, they are gradually accumulating (see Table 1). These measures represent various methodological approaches (e.g. knowledge-based, skill-based, problem-based), as well as diverse methods of measuring (e.g. paper-and-pencil, in-basket tests, simulation or video-based measures). Below are some examples of current PI and tacit knowledge measures followed by recommendation for further study and development.

EXAMPLES OF PRACTICAL INTELLIGENCE MEASURES

As mentioned above, the most comprehensive body of PI measures are tests of tacit knowledge based on Sternberg's Triarchic Theory of Human Intelligence. This knowledge-based approach to PI led to several methods for measuring real-world competencies developed for the filed of personnel selection. These methods include mainly critical incident techniques, situational judgment tests (SJT), and simulations (McDaniel, and Whetzel, 2005; Sternberg, et al. 2000). Through an elaborate process of situational interviews and expert analysis, a set of detailed situation descriptions is developed (Sternberg, et al. 2000). The tacit knowledge measure usually includes seven to twelve such descriptions presented in a paper-and-pencil test. These descriptive scenarios are followed by a list of several possible responses which the respondents are asked to rate according to quality and/or appropriateness on a 7-9 point Likert scale (for review see Sternberg, et al. 2000).

Most tacit knowledge tests are scored not for their accuracy but for their similarity to expert responses. Scoring procedures may include correlation to index of group membership (i.e. expert, intermediate, novice), judgment by professional rule of thumb; or computing difference to expert prototypes (Sternberg, Wagner, Williams, and Horvath, 1995; Sternberg, Forsythe et al. 2000). Some tacit knowledge measures have been formally developed and extensively studied over the years (e.g. TKS, TKIM[TM], TKML), while others are based on anecdotal measures, usually developed through the above mentioned process of tacit knowledge measure development, for a specific study, task, or research population (Baum, and Bird, 2005; Sternberg, et al. 2001; Denney, and Palmer, 1981; Grigorenko, and Sternberg, 2001)

One of the first measures of tacit knowledge published was developed to measured tacit knowledge important for success in the field of academic psychology (Sternberg, and Wagner, 1985). A revised version of this occupation-specific paper-and-pencil measure included a series of 12 work-related situations, followed by 7-9 response items (Wagner, 1987).

Below is an example of a work-related situation and associated response items taken from Sternberg et al. (2000):

It is your second year as an assistant professor in a prestigious psychology department. This past year you published two unrelated empirical articles in established journals. You don't, however, believe there is yet a research area that can be identified as your own. You believe yourself to be about as productive as others. The feedback about your first year of teaching has been generally good. You have yet to serve on a university committee. There is one graduate student who has chosen to work with you. You have no external source of funding, nor have you applied for funding.

Your goals are to become one of the top people in your area of the field and to get tenure in your department. You believe yourself to be a hard worker but find that you do not have enough time to get the important things done. You believe that you have not given enough thought to the relative importance of the tasks you find yourself engaged in and therefore are developing an agenda of things to do in the next 2 months that will increase the chances of success in your career.

The descriptive scenario is followed by 7-9 responses. After reading the description, participants are asked to rate the responses provided on a 7 point Likert scale by their quality (how good a response) and level of importance within the academic world as they know it (actual) as well as in an ideal academic world. Below are examples of responses to the item above:

The following is a list of things you are considering doing in the next 2 months. You obviously cannot do them all. Rate the importance of each by its priority as a means of reaching your goal:

Actual Ideal

1. ___ ___   Improve the quality of your teaching.
2. ___ ___   Write a grant proposal. ...
9. ___ ___   Begin several short-term research projects, each of which may lead to an empirical article.

The Tacit Knowledge Inventory for Managers - TKIM^{TM} (Wagner, and Sternberg, 1989) is perhaps the most rigorously researched example of an occupation-specific tacit knowledge measure. The TKIM^{TM} was developed to measure experience-based knowledge of managers, as well as potential for successful performance in managerial or executive careers (Hedlund, et al. 2003). The formal version of the TKIM^{TM} includes a SJT type paper-and-pencil series of 9 work-related situations, each followed by 10 response items (Wagner, and Sternberg, 1991). Below is an example of a TKIM^{TM} item as provided in Practical Intelligence in Everyday Life (Sternberg, et al. 2000):

Your immediate supervisor has asked you for your opinion on a new promotional campaign that she has developed. You think the promotional campaign is terrible and that using it would be a big mistake. You have noticed previously that your supervisor does not take criticism well, and you suspect she is looking more for reassurance than for an honest opinion.

The descriptive scenario is followed by 10 responses. After reading the description, participants are asked to rate the quality of the responses provided on a 7 point Likert scale given their present situation. Below are two examples of responses to the item above:

a) Tell her you think the campaign is great.
b) Tell her you like the work but have some reservations about whether it is the right campaign for this client.

Tacit Knowledge Inventory for Sales (TKS) is yet another occupation-specific measure of tacit knowledge which was developed to assess tacit knowledge among insurance sales people (Wagner, et al. 1999). Unlike other measures of tacit knowledge in which participants responses are scored based on their similarity to expert responses, TKS responses are scored for their accuracy in comparison to professional rules of thumb (Sternberg, et al. 2000). TKS includes a SJT type paper-and-pencil series of 8 work-related situations, each followed by 8-11 response items.

Below is an example of a TKS item taken from Sternberg, et al. (2000):

> You have been in sales for four years. Your sales record is better than average, but not outstanding, and you wish to become the top sales-person in your area. You have decided to set goals for improving your sales performance. Goals you have been considering are listed below. Rate their quality as a means of improving your sales performance

This item is followed by 10 responses. After reading the description, participants are asked to rate the quality of the responses provided on a 9 point Likert scale. Below are some examples of responses to the item above:

> 1. Increase my sales volume in units sold by 30 percent per week for the next year.
> 6. Make 10 more sales presentations to potential costumers each month
> 9. Work 10 more hours a month than I currently do

The Tacit Knowledge for Military Leaders Inventory (TKML), was more recently developed (Hedlund, et al. 2003). Following the process for developing tacit knowledge measure, as portrayed by Sternberg et al (2000), inventories were developed to assess tacit knowledge for successful military leadership at various levels of command. Below is an example of a TKML item as provided by Hedlund, et al. (2003):

> You are a company commander, and your battalion commander is the type of person who seems always to "shoot the messenger" – he does not like to be surprised by bad news, and he tends to take his anger out on the person who brought him the bad news. You want to build a positive, professional relationship with your battalion commander. What should you do?

The brief description of a leadership problem is followed by a set of 5 to 15 possible options for handling the problem. After reading the description, participants are asked to rate the quality and appropriateness of the responses provided on a 9 point Likert scale. Below are examples of responses to the item above:

1. Speak to your battalion commander about his behavior and share your perception of it
2. Attempt to keep the battalion commander "over-informed" by telling him what is occurring in your unit on a regular basis (e.g., daily or every other day)

3. Keep the battalion commander informed only on important issues, but don't bring up issues you don't have to discuss with him

An example of an anecdotal, domain and population specific, tacit knowledge measure can be seen in the report of a measure developed to assess everyday-life knowledge in various content areas relevant to adaptation of Yup'ik people in Alaska (Grigorenko, et al. 2004). The test, named YSPI, included 36 multiple choice items depicting everyday tasks such as gathering and processing herbs and berries, fishing and fish preparation, knowledge of weather and indigenous tradition, and hunting. An example of "knowledge of weather" item on this test would be:

When Eddie runs to collect the ptarmigan that he's just shot, he notices that its front pouch (balloon) is full of ptarmigan food. This is a sign that:

(a) there's a storm on the way.* (b) winter is almost over.
(c) it's hard to find food this season. (d) it hasn't snowed in a long time

Examples of other tacit knowledge measures developed for specific occupations and target population include: A test of tacit knowledge for natural herbal medicines among youth in a rural village in Western Kenya (Sternberg, et al. 2001); A measure developed to assess tacit knowledge among entrepreneurs in the printing industry (Baum, and Bird, 2005); or a self reported measure of tacit knowledge with regard to the social and family domains as well as the ability to come up with effective resolution of sudden problems in the rapidly changing society of Russia (Grigorenko, and Sternberg, 2001).

All these measures use a similar structure and methodology. Sternberg and colleagues have acknowledged the low fidelity of paper-and pencil test for the measurement of practical tasks, but state that they are used for practical reasons (Sternberg, et al. 2000). Another major criticism of Sternberg and colleagues relates to the limited view of equating PI with tacit knowledge. Although tacit knowledge plays an important role in intelligent behavior and adaptation, reliance upon it as the sole source of individual difference in PI is restricted (Brody, 2000; Gottferdson, 2003). While maintaining a predominantly knowledge-based approach, Sternberg and colleagues are gradually exploring problem-based and skills-based measures of tacit knowledge and practical intelligence within the Triarchic Theory of Successful Intelligence (Hedlund, et al, 2006).

While the problem-solving-based approach to PI and its measurement represents a shift for Sternberg and colleagues, it has always been a central part of Greenspan's Model of Human Competence (Greenspan, and Driscoll, 1997). As mentioned above, developing test items that capture the complex nature of practical problems, while not confounding competence with performance, is a major obstacle to the development of valid and reliable PI measures. Recently, a PI measure developed based on The Model of Personal Competence presented a problem-solving based approach to the measurement of PI (Yalon-Chamovitz, and Greenspan, 2005). The solution provided in this study is to measure a participant's ability to analyze and comprehend important aspects of everyday practical tasks, with built in errors, depicted by video. The attempt to tap an individual's ability to discern mistakes in performing everyday tasks has parallels in other areas of intellectual or academic assessment. For example, the "Syntactic Maturity" sub-test of the Test of Written Language-2 (TOWL-2), requires the subject to identify the grammatical mistakes in a written story (Hammill, and Larsen, 1988); and the "Picture Completion" sub-test of the WISC-R, requires the subject to identify the missing element in a picture of a common object (Wechsler, 1974). Use of such an approach in assessing PI would address the above-noted obstacles, (a) by using depictions of real-life practical events, one could address the ecological validity problem, and (b) by framing the assessment on understanding (rather than performance) of various practical tasks, one could ensure that the instrument is a relatively pure measure of PI operationally defined as the ability to identify, explain, and solve everyday problems (Yalon-Chamovitz, and Greenspan, 2005).

The Video-Based Measure of practical Intelligence (VMPI) was developed to assess PI among adults with intellectual disabilities (Yalon-Chamovitz, and Greenspan, 2005). The VMPI include a video-based portrayal of a series of five everyday tasks scenes, each imbedded with 3 errors that might realistically be encountered in the process of performing the task in real life.

While watching the scene, the participant is requested to (1) indicate whenever the main character encountered a problem or was erring; (2) explain what is the problem or error; and (3) recommend an appropriate solution.

Below is an example of part of an everyday task scene taken from Yalon-Chamovitz, and Greenspan (2006):

> A man enters a bathroom carrying a very full laundry basket. He starts loading the laundry into the washing machine. He keeps pushing more and more laundry into the machine and then tries unsuccessfully to shut the door. He repeats his attempts to shut the door three more times ...

Once the participant indicated a problematic situation, the screening is paused and the participant is requested to provide explanation as to the nature of the problem as well as a recommended solution. Scoring is based on actual problem identification (yes / no) as well as accuracy and appropriateness of both problem explanation and problem solving.

CONCLUSION

Intelligence tests were originally developed to screen for academic failure. With the broadening of our understanding and definition of *intelligence*, so to must testing be updated. *Practical intelligence*, as part of this broader, dynamic view of intelligence refers to the cognitive underpinning of everyday function. How close are we to being able to tap those cognitive, underlying components conceptualized as practical intelligence? In the not too distant past, PI was often dismissed on the grounds of not providing a measure that approaches the long lasting psychometric stability of traditional intelligence tests. Though still far from comparable validity and reliability, the various PI and tacit knowledge measures surveyed provide in-dismissible support for the cognitive basis of PI. These measures, though in need of additional repetition to base their validity, provide a platform for further research and study of PI as a major component of human existence.

Questions regarding the interrelationship between PI and tacit knowledge need to be further explored, as well as the interrelated effect of experience on tacit knowledge. The role of PI in the various stages of skill acquisition as well as the developmental aspects of PI among children and youth need elucidating. Future research should also emphasize further development of measurement methods, other than paper-and-pencil tests, that are more appropriate for measuring non-academic constructs such as practical intelligence.

REFERENCES

Baum, J.R., and Bird, B.J. (2005). Practical intelligence of entrepreneurs: Exploring the "know how" of opportunity exploitation. *Academy of Management Annual Meeting*, Hawaii.

Brody, N. (2000). History of theories and measurement of intelligence. In R. J. Sternberg (Ed.), *Handbook of Intelligence*. Cambridge: Cambridge University.

Campione, J. C., Brown, A. L., and Ferrara, R. A. (1982). Mental retardation and intelligence. In R. J. Sternberg (Ed.), Handbook of human intelligence. New York: Cambridge University.

Carraher, T. N., Carraher, D., and Schleimann, A. D. (1985). Mathematics in the streets and in school. *British Journal of Developmental Psychology*, *3*, 21-29.

Ceci, S. J. (1990). *On Intelligence ... More or Less: A Bio-Ecological Treatise on Intellectual Development*. Englewood Cliffs, NJ: Prentice-Hall.

Ceci, S.J., and Liker, J., (1986). Academic and nonacademic intelligence: an experimental separation. In R. J. Sternberg, and R. K. Wagner, (Eds.), *Practical Intelligence: Nature and Origins of Competence in the Everyday World*. New York: Cambridge University.

Ceci, S. J., and Liker, J. (1988). Stalking the IQ-expertise relationship: When the critics go fishing. *Journal of Experimental Psychology: General, 117*, 96-100.

Chang, K. M. (2002). *Influence of non-cognitive factors on complex dynamic decision-making using computer-based simulations*. Unpublished doctoral dissertation, University of Minnesota, Minnesota.

Davidson, J. E., and Downing, C. L. (2000). Contemporary models of intelligence. In R. J. Sternberg (Ed.), *Handbook of Intelligence*. Cambridge: Cambridge University.

Denney, N. W., and Palmer, A. M. (1981). Adult age differences on traditional and practical problem-solving measures. *Journal of Gerontology, 36*, 323-328.

Gardner, H. (1993). *Multiple intelligences: The theory in practice*. New York: Harper Collins.

Goodnow, J. J. (1986). Some lifelong everyday forms of intelligent behavior: organizing and reorganizing. In R. J. Sternberg and R. K. Wagner (Eds.), *Practical intelligence: Nature and origins of competence in the everyday world*. (pp. 143-162). New York: Cambridge University.

Gottfredson, L. S. (2003). Dissecting practical intelligence theory: Its claims and evidence. *Intelligence, 31*, 343-397.

Greenspan, S. (1981). Defining childhood social competence: A proposed working model. In B. Keogh (Ed.), *Socialization influences on exceptionality*. (pp. 1-41). Greenwich, CT: JAI.

Greenspan, S., and Driscoll, J. (1997). The role of intelligence in a broad model of personal competence. In D. P. Flanagan, J. Genshaft and P. L. Harrison (Eds.), *Contemporary intellectual assessment: theories, tests, and issues*. (pp. 131-150). New York: Guilford.

Grigorenko, E. L., and Sternberg, R. J. (2001). Analytical, creative, and practical intelligence as predictors of self-reported adaptive functioning: a case study in Russia. *Intelligence*, *29*, 57-73.

Grigorenko, E. L., Meier, E., Lipka, J., Mohatt, G. Yanez, E., and Sternberg· R. J. (2004). Academic and practical intelligence: A case study of the Yup'ik in Alaska. *Learning and Individua Differencesl*, *14*, 183-207.

Hammill, D., and Larsen, S. (1988). *Test of Written Language (TOWL-2)*(2nd ed.). Austin, TX: Pro-Ed.

Hedlund, J., Forsythe, G. B., Horvath, J. A., Williams, W. M., Snook, S., and Sternberg, R. J. (2003). Identifying and assessing tacit knowledge: understanding the practical intelligence of military leaders. *The Leadership Quarterly*, *14*, 117-140.

Hedlund, J., Wilt, J. M., Nebel, K. L., Ashford, S. J., and Sternberg, R. J. (2006). Assessing practical intelligence in business school admissions: A supplement to the graduate management admissions test. *Learning and Individual Differences*, *16*, 101-127.

Hofstadter, D. R. (1999). Consistency, competence and geometry. In D. R. Hofstadter (Ed.), *Godel, Escher, Bach: An Eternal Golden Brain* (pp. 82-88). New York: Random house.

Intelligence and achievement testing: Is the Half Full Glass Getting Fuller? (2006) Retrieved July 23rd, 2006, from http://www.psychologymatters.org/iqtesting.html..

Kyllonen, P. C., (2003). Practical intelligence: Factors, methods, issues, directions. *International Symposium on Emotional and Practical Intelligence, Berlin, July 2003.*

Lave, J., Murtaugh, M., and de la Roche, O. (1984). The dialectic of arithmetic in grocery shopping. In B. Rogoff and J. Lace (Eds.), *Everyday cognition: Its development in social context* (pp. 67-94). Cambridge, MA: Harvard University.

Luckasson, R., Coulter, D. L., Polloway, E. A., Reiss, S., Schalock, R. L., Snell, M. E., et al. (1992). *Mental retardation: Definition, Classification, and systems of support.* (9th ed.). Washington, D.C.: American Association on Mental Retardation.

Mathias, J. L., and Nettelbeck, T. (1992). Validity of Greenspan's model of adaptive and social intelligence. *Research in Developmental Disabilities*, *13*, 113-129.

McDaniel, M. A., (2003). Practical intelligence: The emperor's new cloths. *International Symposium on Emotional and Practical Intelligence, Berlin, July 2003.*

McDaniel, M. L., and Whetzel, D. A. (2005). Situational judgment test research: Informing the debate on practical intelligence theory. *Intelligence*, *33*, 515-525.

McGrew, K. S., and Bruininks, R. H. (1989). The factor structure of adaptive behavior. *School Psychology Review*, *18*, 64-81.

McGrew, K. S., Bruininks, R. H., and Johnson, D. R. (1996). A confirmatory Factor-Analysis investigation of Greenspan's model of personal competence. *American Journal on Mental Retardation*, *100*, 353-545.

Murtaugh, M., (1985). The practice of arithmetic by American grocery shoppers. *Anthropology and Education Quarterly*, *16*, 186–192.

Scribner, S., (1984). Studying working intelligence. In: B. Rogoff, and J. Lave, (Eds.), *Everyday cognition: its development in social context.* Cambridge, MA: Harvard University. Pp. 9-40.

Scribner, S. (1986). Thinking in action: some characteristics of practical thought. In R. J. Sternberg, and R. K. Wagner, (Eds.), *Practical intelligence: nature and origins of competence in the everyday world.* (pp. 13–30). New York: Cambridge University.

Smith, L. B. (2005). Cognition as a dynamic system: Principles from embodiment. *Developmental Review, 25,* 278-298.

Stemler, S. E. and Sternberg, R. J. (2006). Using Situational Judgment Tests to Measure Practical Intelligence. In J. A. Weekley, R. E. Ployhart, E. Robert E (Eds). *Situational judgment tests: Theory, measurement, and application.* (. 107-131). Mahwah, NJ: Lawrence Erlbaum.

Sternberg, R. J., Grigorenko, E. G., and Bundy, D. A. (2001).The Predictive Value of IQ. *Merrill-Palmer Quarterly, 47,* 1-41.

Sternberg, R.J., (1985). Beyond IQ: a triarchic theory of human intelligence. , Cambridge Univ. Press, New York.

Sternberg, R. J. (1986). A frame work for understanding conceptions of intelligence. In R. J. Sternberg and D. K. Detterman (Eds.), *What is intelligence? contemporary viewpoints on its nature and definition.* (pp. 3;19). Norwood, NJ: Ablex.

Sternberg, R.J. (1997). Successful intelligence. New York: Plume.

Sternberg, R.J. (1999). Intelligence as developing expertise. *Contemporary Educational Psychology, 24,* 359-375.

Sternberg, R. J. (2003). Our research program validating the triarchic theory of successful intelligence: reply to Gottfredson. *Inelligence, 31,* 399-413.

Sternberg, R. J., and Wagner, R. K. (1993). The g-ocentric view of intelligence and job performance is wrong. *Current Directions in Psychological Science, 2,* 1-5.

Sternberg, R. J., Wagner, R. K., Williams, W. M., and Horvath, J. A., (1995). Testing common sense. *American Psychologist, 50,* 912-927.

Sternberg, R. J., Forsythe, G. B., Hedlund, J., Horvath, J. A., Wagner, R. K., Williams, W. M., et al. (2000). *Practical intelligence in everyday life.* New-York: Cambridge University.

Sternberg, R. J., Nokes, C., Geissler, P. W., Prince, R., Okatcha, F., Bundy, D. A., and Grigorenko, E. L. (2001). The relationship between academic and practical intelligence: A case study in Kenya. *Intelligence, 29,* 401-418.

Thorndike, R. M. (1997). The early history of intelligence testing. In D. P. Flanagan, J. L. Genshaft., and P. L. Harrison (Eds.) Contemporary Intellectual Assessment: Theories, Trends and Issues. New York: Guilford.

Wagner, R. K. (1987). Tacit knowledge in everyday intelligent behavior. *Journal of Personality and Social Psychology, 52,* 1236-1247.

Wagner, R. K. (2000). Practical Intelligence. In R. J. Sternberg (Ed.), *Handbook of Intelligence.* (pp. 380-395). New-York: Cambridge University.

Wagner, R. K., and Kistner, J. A. (1990). Implication of the distinction between academic and practical intelligence for LD children. In H. L. Swanson and B. Keogh (Eds.), *Learning disabilities: Theoretical and research issues.* (pp. 75-93). Hillsdale, NJ: Lawrence Erlbaum.

Wagner, R. K., and Sternberg, R. J. (1991). *Tacit Knowledge Inventory for Managers: User Manual.* San Antonio, TX: The Psychological Corporation.

Wechsler, D. (1974). *Manual for the Wechsler Intelligence Scale for Children-Revised (WISC-R).* Cleaveland, OH: The Psychological Corporation.

Widaman, K. F., and McGrew, K. S. (1996). The structure of adaptive behavior. In J. W. Jacobson and J. A. Mulick (Eds.), *Manual of Diagnosis and Professional Practice in Mental Retardation.* (pp. 97-110). Washington DC: American Psychological Association.

Yalon-Chamovitz, S. (2000). *Everyday wisdom in people with mental retardation: Role of experience and practical intelligence.* Unpublished doctoral dissertation, University of Connecticut, Connecticut.

Yalon-Chamovitz, S., and Greenspan, S. (2005). Ability to identify, explain and solve problems in everyday tasks: Preliminary validation of a direct measure of practical intelligence. *Research in Developmental Disabilities, 26,* 219-230.

In: Leading-Edge Psychological Tests and Testing Research   ISBN: 978-1-60021-571-1
Editor: Marta A. Lange, pp. 159-171   © 2007 Nova Science Publishers, Inc.

Chapter 9

KASAHARA'S SCALE OF MELANCHOLIC TYPE PERSONALITY AS A SHORT PSYCHOLOGICAL TEST EVALUATING A PERSONALITY TRAIT OF DEPRESSIVES

Hirofumi Veki
Gifu University
Japan

ABSTRACT

Typus melancholicus (TM) as described by Tellenbach in Germany is one of the concepts of pre- and intra-morbid personality traits of depressive subjects. The core features of TM are a compulsive desire for orderliness, and conscientiousness in interpersonal relationships. Based on the descriptive and anthropological TM concept, one brief TM-questionnaire has been developed in Japan: Kasahara's Inventory for the Melancholic Type Personality (KIMTP). Sufficient reliability and validity of this psychological test evaluating MT were shown in a German sample population. And factor analysis of KIMTP revealed 2 distinct clusters of items, which represented "harmony in personal relationships" (Factor 1) and "social norms" (Factor 2).

As a next step for exploring the validity of KIMTP, we studied the correlation between KIMTP and the NEO-Five Factor Inventory (NEO-FFI), which is used worldwide as one of the standard psychological tests evaluating personality. We found that TM evaluating with KIMTP was characterized by high Conscientiousness($r=0.29$, $p=0.036$) and high Agreeableness($r=0.45$, $p=0.001$). These results indicate that TM is not a personality trait, but rather a constellation of personality traits, and consists of multiple dimensions. In conclusion, KIMTP as a short psychological test evaluating a personality trait of depressives may discriminate the TM personality with some degree of universality despite cultural differences and be useful in cross-cultural comparisons of TM.

INTRODUCTION

Personality traits typical of depressive subjects have been described [1-9]. Recently, there has been a considerable amount of studies concerning the effect of personality on the etiology and treatment outcome of depression. Typus melancholicus (TM) as described by Tellenbach [10] is one of these concepts of pre- and intra-morbid personality traits of depressive subjects. The core features of TM are a compulsive desire for orderliness, and conscientiousness in interpersonal relationships. Kraus [11], Tellenbach's protégé and coworker in Heidelberg, reformulated the concept of TM in terms of social role performance and intolerance of ambiguity.

On the other hand, TM has been noted by very few Anglo-American investigators. Review articles have defined it as a variation of obsessive type personality. Wttrenborn and Maurer [12], concluded that the tendency toward obsessional brooding and moodiness is state dependent in soma patients and may temporarily persist as an interepisodic manifestation of depressive illness. They speculated that at the onset of a depressive episode, the combination of intensified obsessions and suppressed anger serves as a defense in a person overwhelmed by stress and preoccupied with fear of losing control.

Based on these descriptive and anthropological studies of TM according to the Heidelberg school of psychopathology, von Zerssen [13,14] developed Zerssen's F-List (F-List) and the Biographical Personality Interview (BPI) [15]. In Japan, two brief TM-questionnaires have been developed: Kasahara's Inventory for the Melancholic Type Personality (KIMTP) [16] (see Appendix) and the Depression Related Personality Scale (DRP) [17]. To the best of our knowledge, almost all studies with F-List or KIMTP found that depressive subjects display higher TM scores in comparison with control subjects, except for the two studies by Furukawa et al. [18] and Matussek and Feil [19]. The uni-dimensionality of the concept of TM and TM-questionnaires has been assumed, a priori. However, Matussek and Feil [19] extracted four factors from the F-List. These four F-List subscales were termed "feelings of guilt and inferiority, fears of loss", "subordination to order and authority", "contact avoidance and contact inability", and "lack of self-assertiveness and responsibility". This categorization suggests that TM comprises heterogeneous personality traits. Furukawa et al. [20] studied the correlation between two measures of TM, F-List and KIMTP, and the NEO-Five Factor Inventory (NEO-FFI) [21]. They found that TM was characterized by high Conscientiousness, high Agreeableness and, to a lesser degree, high Extraversion [20]. They questioned the uni-dimensionality of the TM concept and concluded that TM is not a personality trait, but rather a constellation of personality traits. Based on these findings, we can suppose that the TM concept consists of multiple dimensions.

The aim of this present study was to examine the reliability and validity of TM on KIMTP and then the dimensions of TM on KIMTP using factor analytic procedures. Finally we explored the correlation between KIMTP and NEO-FFI to strengthen the validity of KIMTP measuring TM.

SUBJECTS AND METHODS

Subjects

Subjects comprised 58 patients diagnosed with F32 or F33 unipolar affective disorder according to the ICD-10 DCR [22] who were in- or outpatients treated in the period from September 1997 to January 1998 at Münster University Hospital, and 81 control subjects.

Patients were given an ICD-10 diagnosis after examination by more than one experienced senior psychiatrist who performed a non-structured clinical interview and was blind to each patient's individual KIMTP scores. Depressive patients with any organic mental disorder or drug and/or alcohol abuse were excluded from the study. Depressive patients with a personality disorder (F6 according to the ICD-10 DCR) were also excluded from the study. The mean (SD) age of patients was 49.5 (14.1) years. Of the 58 patients, 38 were men (mean age ± SD; 52.7 ± 13.1 years), and 20 were women, (mean age ± SD; 43.4 ± 14.2 years). All depressive subjects received some kind of antidepressant medication. Depression at the initial examination was mild in 5 patients, moderate in 21, and severe in 32. Thirty-eight of the 58 (65.5%) patients were diagnosed with endogenous depression by more than one experienced senior psychiatrist on the basis of somatic symptoms described in the ICD-10 DCR (F32 or F33 with somatic symptoms according to the ICD-10 DCR) (22). The remaining 20 subjects were diagnosed with non-endogenous depression. Of the 38 endogenous depressive patients, 13 were men (mean age ± SD; 51.1 ± 11.6 years), and 25 were women (mean age ± SD; 53.8 ± 13.9 years). Of the 20 non-endogenous depressive patients, 11 were men (mean age ± SD; 47.7 ± 14.3 years), and 9 were women (mean age ± SD; 38.1 ± 13.0 years).

Control data were obtained from staff members of the hospital and university students. Control subjects were investigated using the Inventory to Diagnose Depression (IDD) [23]. All those whom the IDD diagnosed as suffering from major depression and those with a past history of any mental disorder or psychiatric treatment were excluded from the study. The mean age of controls was 35.7 (12.0) years. Of the 81 controls, 45 were men (mean age ± SD; 36.7 ± 12.9 years), and 36 were women (mean age ± SD; 34.3 ± 10.8 years). Informed consent was obtained from all subjects prior to participation.

QUESTIONNAIRES

Kasahara's Inventory for Melancholic Type Personality (KIMTP) (See Appendix)

Kasahara [16] developed the 15-item KIMTP questionnaire in 1984 to evaluate TM in depressed patients in Japan. The KIMTP was developed on the basis of clinical experience and without empirical study. KIMTP is coded on a four-point scale (0 = not true, 1 = somewhat true, 2 = mostly true, and 3 = completely true), and no reversed items are present. The final score can range between 0 and 45. Kasahara did not intend his checklist as a psychometric test, but within 10 years research flourished and established this as a standard instrument for studying TM in Japan. Sato et al. [24,25,26] established both the reliability and validity of KIMTP for determining TM in the Japanese. Administering F-List and KIMTP,

Sato et al. [27] found that the KIMTP was significantly more specific than the F-List in distinguishing depressed patients from normal controls, although both scales exhibited similar sensitivity. For our first cross-cultural exploration of TM, we translated it into German using the back-translation procedure.

Von Zerssen's F-List (F-List) [13, 14]

The original F-List consisted of 104 items, 66 of which measured Tellenbach's TM and 53 of which measured Kretschmer's cyclothymic temperament [28]. The F-List items are rated on a four-point scale ("completely true," "mostly true," "somewhat true," and "not true" are scored as 3, 2, 1, and 0 points, respectively), with 34 reversed items and 8 items weighted two-fold to reflect their importance in delineating TM.

NEO-Five Factor Inventory (NEO-FFI) [21]

Adding three new factors (openness, agreeableness and conscientiousness) to Eysenck's Big Two [29], the original dimensional model of personality (neuroticism and introversion-extraversion), MacCrae and Costa developed a personality questionnaire with five factors model. It consists of 60 items selected from the 240 of its parent inventory, the Revised NEO Personality Inventory (NEO PI-R) [30]. Each item is answered on a five-point Likert scale ("Strongly disagree," "Disagree," "Neutral," "Agree," "Strongly agree"); 12 items each are prepared for the five dimensions of Neuroticism (N), Extraversion (E), Openness (O), Agreeableness (A), and Conscientiousness (C), so that each dimension is given a score between 0 and 48. There are two versions of the NEO-PI-R: Form S for self-reports and Form R for relatives' ratings. The Form R of the NEO-FFI corresponds to that of the NEO PI-R.

Completion of the Questionnaires

To control for the effects of depression, we administered the questionnaire to patients during a period of remission, when they scored less than 7 points on Hamilton's 17-item depression scale (HDS) [31,32]. The mean (SD) HDS score of patients was then 3.4 (1.5).

Statistical Analysis

To assess reliability of the KIMTP, we calculated the Cronbach'S alpha coefficient and the item-total correlation. In addition, we made two personality assessments with the KIMTP, during remission and again at 1-month follow up. Fifty-two of the 66 patients completed both questionnaires. We studied the correlation between scores using this test-retest procedure.

To evaluate the construct validity of the KIMTP, we compared scores between patients and control subjects. To evaluate the concurrent validity of the KIMPT, we compared KIMTP scores with F-List scores. We studied the partial correlation coefficients between KIMTP and F-List score for the patient and control groups, controlling for the effects of sex and age.

The scores of the two groups were compared with Student's t-test or Student's paired t-test for continuous variables. Pearson's correlation coefficient was used to explore the relationship between continuous variables. A P value ≤ 0.05 (two-tailed) indicated a statistically significant difference.

In order to clarify the dimensionality of the TM scores, factor analyses of the TM scores were conducted using principal factor analysis followed by varimax rotation. The optimum number of factors was determined by inspection of the scree plot. For each subject, the score for each factor was determined by adding the scores for all items with a loading greater than 0.4 in that factor. Reliability for each factor was assessed by Cronbach's alpha. Intercorrelation between the scores of the two factors and their correlation with the total KIMTP score were tested with Pearson's correlation coefficient.

Comparisons were made between endogenous depressive patients, non-endogenous depressive patients, and healthy volunteers for total KIMTP score and factor scores using analysis of covariance (ANCOVA), adjusting for sex and age. To assess group differences, we applied a Bonferroni-type correction in which the level of significance was adjusted (p = 0.05/3). A p-value less than 0.05/3 (two-tailed) indicated a statistically significant difference.

Statistical calculations were performed with SPSS for Windows, Version 10.0 (SPSS Japan Inc., Tokyo, Japan).

RESULTS

The Reliability and Validity of TM on KIMTP

The Cronbach's alpha coefficient for patient KMT scores was 0.65 and that of controls was 0.67. Pearson's correlation coefficients between the total KIMTP score and each test item are in the wide range of 0.260 (item 13) to 0.667 (item 5) in patients and 0.083 (item 13) to 0.608 (item 11) in controls. Only the item 13 in control subjects was statistically unrelated to KIMTP total scores in controls.

Overall total KIMTP score was 31.3 (5.2) in the first analysis and 30.4 (5.2) in the second analysis, with no statistically significant difference between them. Pearson's correlation coefficient for overall total KIMTP scores between the two tests was 0.71, with the individual items being statistically similar.

There was a statistical difference in mean KIMTP scores between patients and control subjects (31.4(5.2) vs. 27.1(5.1), $p < 0.001$), between female patients and female controls (32.2(5.0) vs. 27.5(5.0), $p < 0.001$), and between male patients and male controls (30.1(5.5) vs. 26.7(5.2), $p < 0.05$). There was a statistical difference in mean F-List scores between patients and control subjects (139.5(16.5) vs. 122.8(17.2), $p < 0.001$), between female patients and female controls (142.3(13.5) vs. 127.0(17.2), $p < 0.001$), and between male patients and male controls (134.5(20.2) vs. 119.2(16.6), $p < 0.005$).

The partial correlation coefficients between the KIMTP and F-List scores for the patient and control groups were 0.40 ($p < 0.005$) in patients and 0.53 ($p < 0.001$) in controls.

The Dimensions of TM on KIMTP Using Factor Analytic Procedures

The results of factorial analysis of the scores of the 15 KIMTP items permitted extraction of five factors with an eigenvalue above 1. These factors were responsible for 62.7% of the variance. The first two factors yielded eigenvalues greater than 2, and inspection of the scree plot suggested a two-factor solution. We therefore chose to report for further discussion a two-factor model accounting for 37.6% of the variance. In the factor analysis, we extracted individual KIMTP items that showed factor loading above 0.40. Factor 1 consists of five items: No. 6-I would rather avoid confrontation with others; No. 5-I cannot say no when someone asks me to do something; No.10-I would not do something extreme; No. 11-I do not like to be conspicuous; and No. 7-I am rather timid. The factor loading were 0.80, 0.64, 0.59, 0.59, and 0.56, respectively. Factor 2 consists of 3 items: No. 4-I give importance to my social duty; No. 3-I have a strong sense of responsibility; and No. 9-I give importance to common sense. The factor loadings were 0.87, 0.66, and 0.48, respectively.

The first factor was labeled *harmony in personal relationships* and pertained to items which seemed to be related to not only an attitude to maintain order with others but also an asthenic sensitivity to others. The second factor was labeled *social norms* and pertained to items concerning a lack of adaptability and a persistence in standard. The internal consistency of the two factors were 0.77 for harmony in personal relationships (factor 1) and 0.73 for social norms (factor 2). Chronbach's alpha values for these two factors reached the acceptable range for internal consistency (i.e. over 0.70; Cicchetti [33]). The total KIMTP score is the sum of the 15 items retained, with a possible range of 0 to 45. The factor 1 score (sum of items 5, 6, 7, 10, and 11) and factor 2 score (sum of items 3, 4, and 9) had a possible range of 0 to 15 and 0 to 9, respectively. The Pearson correlation coefficient between factors 1 and 2 was 0.16 ($p = 0.06$). The Pearson correlation coefficient for the relation between the total KIMTP score and the factor 1 score was 0.80 ($p < 0.01$); that between the total KIMTP score and the factor 2 score was 0.52 ($p < 0.01$).

We conducted then ANCOVA for total KIMTP score and 2 factor scores controlling for sex and age of subjects as covariates, three depression groups as main effects, and sex × three depression groups as an interactive effect. Total KIMTP mean scores (SD) of endogenous depressive patients (n=38), nonendogenous depressive patients (n=20), and controls (n=81) were 31.22(5.37), 31.30(5.29), and 26.41(4.51), respectively. Factor 1 mean scores (SD) of endogenous depressive patients, nonendogenous depressive patients, and controls were 9.87(4.52), 9.43(3.91), and 6.75(2.75), respectively. Factor 2 mean scores (SD) of endogenous depressive patients, nonendogenous depressive patients, and controls were 7.24(1.67), 7.65(1.09), and 6.75(1.62), respectively.

Endogenous depression and non-endogenous depression patients showed significantly higher KIMTP total scores than control subjects: ANCOVA: F $(2, 130) = 9.12$, p=0.001. Endogenous depression and non-endogenous depression patients showed significantly higher factor 1 scores than control subjects: ANCOVA: F $(2, 130) = 7.87$, p=0.001. There was, however, no significant difference in KIMTP total and 2 factor scores between endogenous depression and non-endogenous depression patients.

Correlation between the KIMTP and NEO-FFI Scores

The partial correlation coefficients between the KIMTP [16] and NEO-FFI [21] factor scores for the patients were 0.45 (p < 0.005) in the factor "agreeableness" and 0.29 (p<0.05) in the factor "conscientiousness". The partial correlation coefficients between the F-List total scores and NEO-FFI factor scores for patients were 0.45 (p < 0.001) in the factor "agreeableness".

DISCUSSION

Validity and Reliability of KIMTP

The items on Kasahara's KIMTP concern Tellenbach's Typus melancholicus [10], Kretschmer's cyclothymia [28], and Shimoda's immobilithymia [34]. Kasahara [16] developed this inventory based on clinical experience without empirical study. Sato et al . [24,25,26] established both the reliability and validity of the KMT test for determining Typus melancholicus in the Japanese.

Our study is the first to explore the reliability and validity of the KIMTP in a country other than Japan. The Cronbach's alpha coefficient we obtained demonstrated the internal consistency of the test in our sample population. Among patients every KIMTP item showed a significant item-total correlation, consistent with the findings of Sato et al. [26] Among our control subjects, however, Item 13 showed no significant item-total correlation. It could be that Item 13, "I am rather cheerful," was considered by some control subjects as to describe hyperthymia, a component of manic patients and contradictory to Typus melancholicus. Indeed, Item 13 is similar to the Item 30 of the Munich Personality Test (MPT) [35], "Other people consider me lively," which is characteristic of "Extraversion" and contradictory to "Rigidity" so far as factorial structure is concerned. "Rigidity" is considered to be equivalent to Typus melancholicus. Kasahara [16] originally intended Item 13 to identify Kretschmer's cyclothymia, syntonia, and slight optimism and to provide one item describing Typus melancholicus. The relatively homogeneous patient group of patients, as compared to the more disparate group of control subjects, might have answered Item 13 as Kasahara had originally intended. Further study is needed to investigate whether these divergent results are based upon differences between patients and controls or between the cultures of Germany and Japan. Re-evaluation is needed to make this KIMTP item significant in the German. The KIMTP was replicable in the test-retest procedure.

KIMTP and F-List scores in patients were significantly higher than those in controls. Adjusted for sex and age, significant correlation existed between the KIMTP and F-List in patients and in controls, providing evidence that the KIMTP has both constructive validity and concurrent validity. We consider the KIMTP to have sufficient reliability and validity in German populations for cross-cultural explorations of Typus melancholicus.

Given the wide use of KIMTP in different countries, it is important to explore its validity through investigations of differences in KIMTP scores between depressive patients and normal subjects sharing various culture backgrounds. There is one non-empirical study that treats this matter. Ogawa et al. [36] explored the personality of depressive patients by clinical interviews based on the KIMTP and concluded that in France, considered an "individualistic" society, there are large variations in premorbid personality traits and a high frequency of neurotic tendencies. This indicates cultural difference in the premorbid personality of depressed patients. Further study is needed to explore whether "Typus melancholicus" is associated with depression world-wide.

Factor Structure of KIMTP

In this our study, factor 1 was labeled *harmony in personal relationships*. Tellenbach [10] described one constitutive basic trait of the melancholic type as a certain relation of the melancholics to order, which may be termed orderliness. Order pervades co-human relations, above all, with at times a downright petty concern to maintain an atmosphere free of disturbances, frictions, conflicts, in particular from being in default in any manner, shape, or form. Harmony in personal relationships seems to correspond to order in co-human relations of Tellenbach's TM. Timid characteristic of this factor shows an asthenic or sensitive aspect of harmony in personal relationship. In other words, this factor could be termed dependence in relationships with others. Factor 2 was labeled *social norm*, and this factor exercises a patently prohibitive function and may cover not only social life but also work life. Tellenbach [10] described its function in work life as follows; work life is pervaded with diligence and conscientiousness, devotion to duty, and trustworthiness. At no price does one permit oneself to become indebted to others, thus maintaining the inner man in order. It is usual to hear "I've never done anything bad, anything improper."

It should be concluded from these KIMTP factor analyses that factors 1 and 2 represent the core personality dimensions of monopolar endogenous depressive patients, as described by Tellenbach. In other words, these results may indicate the conceptual validity of our factor analysis of KIMTP.

Although we extracted factors 1 and 2 according to the scree plot inspection, factor 3 represents meaningful constellations of personality that may have important clinical implications. Factor 3 might be labeled *preciseness in affairs* and pertains to items that appear to be equivalent to Tellenbach's [10] expression of dealing with everyday matters. In dealing with everyday matters, there is a conscious and diligent emphasis on cleaning up and keeping things tidy. According to Kasahara's original KIMTP concept [37], factor 4 is a trait of syntone in the sense of Kretschmer's cyclothymia [28], and factor 5 is a trait of Shimoda's immodithymia [34] which indicates perfectionism and enthusiasm in the workplace. Our discussion from here forward is limited to factors 1 and 2.

Dimensions of KIMTP

KIMTP factors 1 and 2 resemble the factors described by Matussek and Feil [19], who extracted four factors from the F-List: feelings of guilt and inferiority, fears of loss (ZF 1), subordination to order and authority (ZF 2), contact avoidance and contact inability (ZF 3), and a lack of self-assertiveness and responsibility (ZF 4). KIMTP factor 1 "harmony in personal relationships" is similar to ZF 4 and in part to ZF 1 in the attribution "feelings of inferiority and fears of loss" that was expressed clinically as timid and sensitive in personal relationships. KIMTP factor 2 "social norm" is similar to the factor ZF 2. On the other hand, KIMTP factor 1 and 2 have no similarity with the MPT rigidity factor [35], which consists in part of F-List and is considered to be an important component of TM [37,38].

It is supposed that each of the above, the TM inventory, F-List, DRP, KIMTP, and a part of MPT, contains different and/or in part common TM dimensions with one another. Recently, Kronmueller et al. [39] has conducted a systematic comparison of four TM questionnaires; F-List, DRP, KIMTP, and the 14 –item Ambiguity Tolerance Scale (AT-14) [40]. In a factor analysis of the items of these four questionnaires, four dimensions were differentiated: Dependence, Intolerance of Ambiguity, Norm-Orientation, and Perfectionism. They concluded that TM personality is not a single trait but consist of four related but separate traits. They mentioned from psychotherapeutic point of view that there is the possibility to select particular treatment techniques for particular TM characteristic and also to develop new treatment techniques.

Base on these factor analytic procedures, they developed the Typus Melancholicus Personality Inventory (TMPI), which consists of 26 items. In their study, KIMTP showed moderate to high correlation with the TMPI subscales, Dependence, Norm-orientation, and Perfectionism. The Dependence factor of TMPI corresponds to the factor 1 of KIMTP in our study, and the Norm-orientation to the factor 2. These results indicates.

Total KIMTP score and 2 factor scores tend to show higher TM scores in depressive patients than in control subjects. To be more precise, total KIMTP and factor 1 scores of endogenous and non-endogenous depressive patients were significantly higher than those of control subjects. This indicates that factor 1 "harmony in personal relationships" is an essential TM personality dimension on KIMTP for depressive patients.

On the other hand, we failed to show a significant difference of KIMTP total and 2 individual factor scores between endogenous depressive and non-endogenous depressive patients. Matussek and Feil [19] and Sato et al. [38] reported similar results. The results of our study were inconsistent with Tellenbach's original concept that TM is specific for endogenous depression in comparison with non-endogenous depression.

The endogeneity defined by Tellenbach [10] is different from the endogeneity diagnosed by the ICD-10 operational criteria [22] that we used in the present study. This conceptual discrepancy of endogeneity may have led to the present results. Another and more probable reason is that recent studies dealing with TM showed prevalence of TM between 30% and 70% in endogenous depressive patients [41], and that the TM personality trait can be recognized in neurotic depressive patients almost as frequently as in endogenous depressive patients [42]. In effect, TM is not specific for endogenous depressive patients. It follows from these findings that there was no different TM scores between endogenous and non-endogenous depression.

Comparison of KIMTP with NEO-FFI

For validating the TM concept, a comparison between TM inventories is needed. A comparison of TM inventories with standard personality assessment inventories such as NEO-FFI is also needed for further study for validation of TM concept. Furukawa et al. [20] studied the correlation between two measures of TM, F-List and KIMTP, and the NEO-Five Factor Inventory (NEO-FFI). They found that TM was characterized by high conscientiousness, high agreeableness and, to a lesser degree, high extraversion. In our study, KIMTP scores were significantly correlated with both agreeableness and conscientiousness. This result almost corresponded with that of Furukawa's study with Japanese patients except for extraversion finding, and may indicate constructive validity of TM on KIMTP from the transcultural point of view.

CONCLUSIONS

Two subscales of the KIMTP were identified; "harmony in personal relationships (factor 1)" and "social norms (factor 2)". These subscales show overlaps with Tellenbach's original concept of TM. Factor 1, "harmony in personal relationships," differentiates depressive patients from control subjects and might be considered a core dimension of TM on the KIMTP. The KIMTP is useful in clinical settings because of the small number of items. It is hardly affected by cultural differences, making cross-cultural TM studies possible. Confirming the dimensions of TM facilitates comparative study with other personality questionnaires and also exploration of the validity of TM.

This our study might contribute to distinguish depressed patients form normal controls and further form the basis for the investigation of the effect of TM personality on clinical outcome and on psychotherapeutic treatment.

APPENDIX

Kasahara's Inventory for the Melancholic Type Personality

1. I like to work.
2. When I start something, I always finish it thoroughly.
3. I have a strong sense of responsibility.
4. I give importance to my social duty.
5. I cannot say no when someone asks me to do something.
6. I would rather avoid confrontation with others.
7. I am rather timid.
8. I am nervous about what other people think of me.
9. I give importance to common sense.
10. I would not do something extreme.
11. I do not like to be conspicuous.
12. I sometimes get excited easily.
13. I am rather cheerful.
14. I like to arrange my belongings.
15. I am neat.

REFERENCES

[1] Angst, J., and Clayton, P. (1986). Premorbid personality of depressive, bipolar, and schizophrenic patients with special reference to suicidal issues. *Compr. Psychiatry*, 27, 511-532.

[2] Angst, J. (1989). Praemorbide Persoenlichkeit – Methodische Probleme. In: Janzarik W (ed.) *Persoenlichkeit und Psychose*. Enke, Stuttgart, 72-81.

[3] Boyce, P., Parker, G., Barnett, B., Cooney, M., and Smith, F. (1991). Personality as a vulnerability factor to depression. *Br. J. Psychiatry*, 159,106–114.

[4] Cadoret, R.J., Baker, M., Dorzab, J., and Winokur, G. (1971). Depressive disease: personality factors in patients and their relatives. *Biol. Psychiatry*, 3, 85–93.

[5] Hirschfeld, R.M., Klerman, G.L., Lavori, P., Keller, M.B., Griffith, P., and Coryell, W. (1989). Premorbid personality assessments of first onset of major depression. *Arch. Gen. Psychiatry*, 46, 345-351.

[6] Kendler, K.S., Kessler, R.C., Neale, M.C., Heath, A.C., and Eaves, L.L. (1993). The prediction of major depression in women: toward an integrated etiologic model. *Am. J. Psychiatry*, 150, 1139–1148.

[7] Kendell, R.E., and Discipio, W.J. (1970). Obsessional symptoms and obsessional personality traits in patients with depressive illnesses. *Psychol. Med.*, 1, 65–72.

[8] Kitamura, T., Shima, S., Sugawara, M., and Toda, M.A.(1993). Psychological and social correlates of the onset of affective disorders among pregnant women. *Psychol. Med.*, 23, 967–975.

[9] Kuwabara, H., Sakado, K., Uehara, T., Sakado, M., Sato, T., and Someya, T.(1999). The Japanese version of Interpersonal Sensitivity Measure: its reliability and validity (in Japanese). *Arch. Psychiatr. Diagn. Clin. Eval*, 10, 333–341.

[10] Tellenbach, H. (1961). *Melancholie. Problemgeschichte, Endogenität, Typologie, Pathogenese*, Klinik. Springer, Berlin.

[11] Kraus, A.(1977). *Sozialverhalten und Psychose Manisch-Depressiver*. Stuttgart, Enke.

[12] Wittenborn, R.J., and Maurer, S.H. (1977). Persisting personalities among depressed women. *Arch. Gen. Psychiatry*, 34, 968-971.

[13] v. Zerssen, D. (1969). Objektivierende Untersuchungen zur prämorbiden Persönlichkeit endogen depressiver (Methodik und vorläufige Ergebnisse) In: Hippius H, Selbach H (ed.) Das Depressive Syndrome. *Urban and Schwarzenverg*, München, 183–205.

[14] v. Zerssen, D., Koeller, D.-M., and Rey, E.-R.(1970). Die prämorbide Persönlichkeit von endogen Depressiven. Eine Kreuzvalidierung früherer Untersuchungsergebnisse. *Confin. Psychiat.*, 13, 156–179.

[15] v. Zerssen, D. (1944). Personlichkeitszuge als Vulnerabilitatsindikatioren – Probleme ihrer Erfasung. *Fortsch. Neurol. Psychiatr.*, 61, 1–13.

[16] Kasahara, Y. (1984). Depression seen in general medical clinics. *Psychosom. Med.*, 24, 6–14.

[17] Yoshimatsu, K., Miguchi, M., Miyake, Y., Ozaki, A., Minagawa, K., Takeuchi, T., and Ito, R. (1989). On the cross-generational differences of personality traits: Applying "Depression Related Personality Trait Scale (DRP)". *Jap. J. Soc. Psychiatry.*, 12, 90–97.

[18] Furukawa, T., Nakanishi, M., and Hamanaka, T.(1997). Typus melancholicus is not the premorbid personality trait of unipolar (endogenous) depression. *Psychiatry Clin. Neurosci.*, 51, 197–202.

[19] Matussek, P., and Feil,, W.B.(1983). Personality attributes of depressive patients. *Arch. Gen. Psychiatry*, 40, 783–790.

[20] Furukawa, T., Yamada, A., Tabuse, H., Kawai, K., Takahashi, K., Nakanish,i M., and Hamanaka, T. (1998). Typus melancholicus in light of the five-factor model of personality. *Eur. Arch. Psychiatry Clin. Neurosci.*, 248, 64–69.

[21] Costa, P.T. Jr., and McCrae, R.R. (1992). NEO-PI-R professional manual: Revised NEO Personality and NEO Five-Factor Inventory (NEO-FFI). Odessa, FL, *Psychological Assessment Resources.*

[22] World Health Organization (1993). The ICD-10 Classification of Mental and Behavioral Disorders: *Diagnostic Criteria for Research.* World Health Organization, Geneva.

[23] Zimmerman, M., Coryel, W., Corenthal, C., and Wilson, S.:(1986). A self-report scale to diagnose major depressive disorder. *Arch. Gen. Psychiatry*, 43, 1076–1081.

[24] Sato, T., Sakado, K., and Sato, S.(1992). Differences between two questionnaires for assessment of Typus melancholicus, Zerssen's F-list and Kasahara's scale: The validity and relationship to DSM-III-R personality disorders. *Jpn. J. Psychiatry Neurol.*, 46, 603–608.

[25] Sato, T., Sakado, K., and Kobayashi, S.(1992). The measurement of Typus melancholicus using questionnaires; reliability and validity of Zerssen's F-List (in Japanese). *Clin. Psychiatry*, 34, 139–146.

[26] Sato, T., Sakado, K., Nishioka, K., and Kasahara, Y.(1996). Reliability of Kasahara's scale for assessment of the melancholic type of personality (Typus melancholicus) . *Clin. Psychiatry*, 38, 157–162.

[27] Sato, T., Sakado, K.. Uehara, T., and Sato, S.(1994). Age distribution of the melancholic type of personality (Typus melancholicus) in outpatients with major depression: a comparison with a population without a history of depression. *Psychopathology*, 27, 43–47.

[28] Kretschmer, E. (1921). *Körperbau und Charakter.* Springer, Berlin Heidelberg New York.

[29] Eysenk, H.J.(1947). *The Maudsley Personality Inventory.* University of London Press, London.

[30] Costa, P.T. Jr., and McCrae, R.R. (1992). Revised NEO Personality Inventory (NEO PI-R) and NEO Five-Factor Inventory (NEO-FFI): professional manual. *Psychological Assessment Resources,* Inc., Odessa, Florida.

[31] Prien, R.F., Carpenter, L.L., and Kupfer, D.L. (1991). The definition and operational criteria for treatment outcome of major depressive disorder. A review of the current research literature. *Arch. Gen. Psychiatry*, 48, 796-800.

[32] Frank, E., Prien, R.F., and Jarret, .RB. (1991). Conceptualization and rationale for consensus definitions of terms in major depressive disorder. Remission, recovery, relapse, and recurrence. *Arch. Gen. Psychiatry*, 48, 851-855.

[33] Cicchetti, D.V. (1994). Guidelines, criteria, and rules of thumb for evaluating normed and standardized assessment instruments in psychology. *Psychol. Assess,* 6, 284-290.

[34] Shinfuku, N., and Ihda, S. (1969). Über den prämorbiden Charakter der endogenen Depression - Immmodithymie -(später Immobilithymie) von Shimoda. *Fortschr Neurol Psychiat Grenzgeb*, 37, 545-552.

[35] v. Zerssen, D., Pfister, H., and Koeller, D. –M. (1988). The Munich Personality Test (MPT) - a short questionnaire for self-rating and relatives' rating of personality traits: formal properties and clinical potential. *Eur. Arch. Psychiatr. Neurol. Sci.*, 238, 73–93.

[36] Ogawa, T., and Koide, H.. (1992). Cultural variations of premorbid personality of endogenous depression: A transcultural study. *Jpn. J. Psychiatry. Neurol.*, 46, 831-839.

[37] Sakado, K., Sato, T., Uehara, T., Sato, S., Sakado, M., and Kugamai, K. (1997). Evaluating the diagnostic specificity of the Munich personality test dimensions in major depression. *J. Affect. Dis.*, 43, 187–194.

[38] Mundt, C., Backenstrass, M., Kronmüller, K.-T., Fiedle,r P., Kraus, A., and Granghellini, G. (1997) Personality and endogenous/major depression: an empirical approach to Typus melancholicus. *Psychopathology*, 30, 130–139.

[39] Kronmueller, K.-T., Backenstrass, M., Kocherscheidt, K., Hunt, A., Fiedler, P., and Mundt, C. (2005). Dimensions of the typus melancholicus personality type. *Eur. Arch. Psychiatry Clin. Neurosci.*, 255, 341-349.

[40] Kischkel, K.H. (1984). Eine Skala zur Erfassung von Ambiguitaetstoleranz. *Diagnostica*, 30:144-154.

[41] Kronmüller, K.-T., Backenstrass, M., Reck, C., Kraus, A., Fiedler, P., and Mundt, C.(2002). Einfluss von Persönlichkeitsfaktoren und –struktur auf den Verlauf der Major-Depression. *Nervenarzt*, 73, 255–261.

[42] Tölle, R. (1987). Persönlichkeit und Melancholie. *Nervenarzt*, 58, 327–339.

In: Leading-Edge Psychological Tests and Testing Research
Editor: Marta A. Lange, pp. 173-182

ISBN: 978-1-60021-571-1
© 2007 Nova Science Publishers, Inc.

Chapter 10

TOWARDS ECONOMIC WECHSLER-LIKE TESTING: ADAPTIVE INTELLIGENCE DIAGNOSTICUM (AID 2)

Klaus D. Kubinger

Department of Psychology
Division for Psychological Assessment and Applied Psychometrics
University of Vienna, Liebiggasse 5
A-1010 Vienna/Austria

ABSTRACT

This paper serves to emphasize that if psychological consulting based on Wechsler-like test-batteries is to be carried out - due to their content conceptualization - then certain economic test improvements are needed. It is a matter of administering items, whose solutions are neither too easily found by the testee, nor whose solutions are obviously highly improbable. What is being asked for here is adaptive testing. Although, it is quite routine to apply a psychometric foundation of adaptive testing, the common technique of computerized so-called tailored testing is in no way a proper means in the case of (material and social) interaction which Wechsler-like test-batteries focus on. However branched testing can be applied without the online use of a computer. Such an approach has already been established in the AID 2 test-battery since 1985. This paper deals with the illustration of item generation and administration, psychometric quality checks, error of aimed-for ability parameter estimation, and last but not least it's handling by practitioners. There is evidence that adaptive testing as realized in AID 2 is superior to pertinent conventional testing, particularly with respect to administration duration and error of estimation.

Keywords: Wechsler test-battery, adaptive testing, test economy, item response theory, parallel test.

1. INTRODUCTION

There is no doubt that Wechsler's intelligence test-batteries represent a certain standard in psychological assessment. Regardless of whether the testees are pre-schoolers, children, juveniles, adults or even senile people a pertinent battery can be applied all over the world. The batteries' polarization into verbal scales and performance scales has convinced practitioners from the very beginning (Wechsler, 1939) up until this very day. Above all, the chief purpose of the Wechsler concept is of practical importance, that being to stimulate a testee's interaction with certain materials as well as with the psychologist him/herself. Consequently, it can indeed be said that millions of decisions based on Wechsler scores have been made and various treatment has been carried out as a result of these tests.

Of course, since the first issues of the Wechsler test-batteries psychometric standards have changed considerably and not all test batteries fit these standards (cf. Kubinger, 1998). However, as a certain psychometric restoration is not really considered a challenge, we shall not deal with the topic in this paper. There is however a serious problem with regard to Wechsler test-batteries' efficiency for practice. Maybe decades ago, minor efficiency of a test battery was not of any relevance; and practitioners were most likely not aware of the meaning of the relatively high standard errors of measurement, that is reliabilities that are too low. However, nowadays time is money and consulting that is based on almost unserious measurements is often very risky due to the possibility of subsequent lawsuits.

For this reason, new approaches to efficient measuring will subsequently be presented in the following. This approach also includes acceptable errors of measurement. That is to say, the paper deals with the administration of a test by means of a kind of adaptive testing. Be sure that a theoretical foundation will not be given once again (cf. Weiss, 1982), rather just an illustration of how adaptive testing actually works within a Wechsler-like test-battery which has already been widely used by practitioners for years.

2. THE HANDICAP OF CONVENTIONAL TESTING AS THE WECHSLER SUBTESTS DO

Conventional testing means that all the same items have been conceived for all testees regardless of age and achievement level, respectively. If we consider only childen and juveniles, that being for instance the WISC IV population, then it is a matter of fact that within every age-homogeneous group only very few items discriminate. Most items bear no information because almost every testee of a certain age-homogeneous group does either solve it with high probability or fails with a similar high probability. These items are either too difficult for this group or too easy. It would actually not do any harm if these items were deleted for a testee within one of these groups!

Bear in mind that the administration of items that are too easy may depress a testee's achievement motivation. However items that are too easy occur almost with every testee at the very beginning of a conventional administered test, particularly concerning Wechsler subtests. Also bear in mind that the administration of items that are too difficult may frustrate the testee. However items that are too difficult occur nevertheless most definitely for every testee towards the end of a conventional administered test, particularly concerning Wechsler subtests: Every testee finishes with a certain subtest after having failed 3 to 5 items and then starts with the next subtest.

However, even if authors of conventional tests were aware of these phenomena within conventional psychometrics there is no means of handling individual item deletion in the case that a testee's level is out of range – disregarding scoring a deleted item as either solved or not solved. The latter is not a fair strategy because solution and failure, respectively, results merely from a high probability but is not at all determined.

3. THE WAY OUT OF CONVENTIONAL TESTING'S HANDICAP

Of course, the administration of items which concentrates on testing at the individual level of a testee's ability is much preferred. This is adaptive testing. Most practitioners have in the meantime become very familiar with the principles of adaptive testing (e.g. Kubinger, 2003). The question to be considered therefore regards the condition of certain psychometric presuppositions. If pertinent models of item response theory hold, parameter estimation of a testee's ability is possible whatever sample of items of the item pool have been administered. And hence a selection of those items that best fit any individual's ability level is possible. This works at best by a stepwise selection of the items where each item depends on the testee's actual parameter estimation. Item response theory has proven then that it is quite common that only a few items suffice for relatively small standard errors of estimations.

Though, efforts towards adaptive testing are, primarily, restricted to computerized administration because of the extensive computing algorithms necessary for the indicated parameter estimation. That is to say that tailored testing needs such an estimation for every testee after every item administered, taking into account whether that item is solved or not. And, of course, computer testing is out of the discussion if, indeed, a testee's interaction with various materials as well as with the psychologist himself is the main purpose for using a Wechsler-like test-battery – at most, a computerized-online estimation of the ability parameter would be feasible but definitely not the presentation of the items or even a testee's item processing.

However, there is some modification of tailored testing that in principle offers the same advantages but does not require a computer for the test procedure. It is the idea of so-called branched testing. Instead of estimating the asked-for ability parameter after every item items are grouped in advance. These item subsets themselves are arranged into a certain branched network design so that according to a testee's score in a certain item group the psychologist may choose the next best level-adapted item group for administration.

This kind of branched testing will be sketched in the following. The test-battery under discussion will serve as an example. It is the (German-made) AID 2 (Adaptive Intelligence Diagnosticum; Kubinger and Wurst, 2000), edited first in 1985. It is actually conceptualized for six to 16 year old children und juveniles. Starting with a first subset of five items, appropriate to the age, a second and subsequently a third subset of five items is administered, both of the latter depends on the preceding score of the testee (cf. Fig. 1). If the testee solves one item at the most, a subset one level below is recommended. If at least four items are solved then a subset one level higher is advised. Only if two or three of the five items are solved is the subset at an equivalent level administered. Exactly this kind of branched testing design applies to five of the 14 subtests of AID 2, the other subtests illustrate alternative designs.

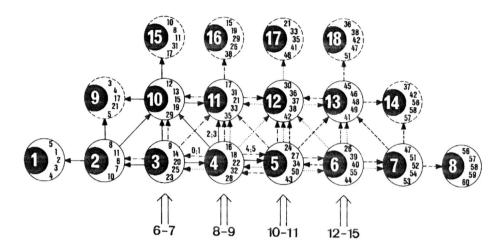

Figure 1. The branched testing design for AID 2. Circles represent different subsets up-leveled from left to right. Each subset contains five items, the number of each corresponding to the level of difficulty. The age of the testee determines the starting point. Because branched testing terminates after the third subset, dashed-line subsets consist of items of solid-line subsets.

Such a design guarantees that every testee is tested with almost optimal items. In the long run, it is not likely that the items administered will be too easy or too difficult, it is rather the case that many items that conform to the appropriate level are used instead. In other words, the standard error of estimation comes close to the ideal minimum that would be achieved by using tailored testing.

4. PSYCHOMETERIC QUALITY OF AID 2

All the respective subtests of AID 2 are based on the well-known Rasch model or 1-PL model (cf. for instance Hambleton, Swaminathan and Rogers, 1991). As a matter of fact, if this model holds it is possible to estimate the asked-for ability parameter (which allows for fair comparisons of all testees), even if they performed on completely different items. Bear in mind that there are model check techniques in order to prove whether the Rasch model holds with respect to a given test (cf. Glas and Verhelst, 1995, as well as Kubinger, 2005). As an illustration see in Figure 2 the graphical model check referring to subtest Applied Computing: For example, item parameter estimation based on male testees and item parameter estimations based on female testees do not differ in any relevant way – this implies that the data fit the model – this because of the fact that an essential requirement for the Rasch model to be valid for a test is that any partition of the sample of testees leads statistically to the same item parameter estimations.

At the end, eleven subtests from AID 2 stood the test. These were the subtests *Everyday Knowledge, Competence in Realism, Applied Computing, Social and Material Sequencing, Producing Synonyms, Abstracting* (the common functionalisms of things), *Analyzing and Synthesizing* (abstract figures), *Social Understanding and Material Reflection, Immediate*

Reproducing (of figural stimuli), *Learning and Remembering, Recognition of (figural) Structures.* The subtests *Immediate Reproducing* (of numerical stimuli), *Coding and Associating* and *Anticipating and Combining* (Puzzles) refer either to physics measurements ([the longest remembered] number [of digits]; [the used] time) or have stood an analogous model check according to some multi-categorical generalization of the Rasch model.

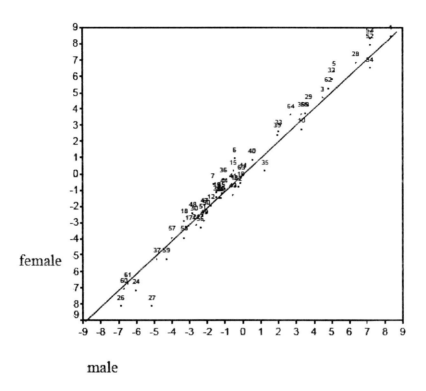

Figure 2. Graphical model check of 57 items of subtest *Applied Computing* – item parameter estimations according to the Rasch model as opposed for male and female testees (altogether 920 testees). The item numbers are arbitrarily chosen.

Whether the enormous effort of item calibration does indeed prove worthwhile can be checked as follows – take into account that according to Figure 1 60 Rasch model fitting items are needed, while the respective Wechsler-subtests very seldom exceed 30 items! Figure 3 illustrates the (expectation of the) standard error of estimation which is dependent on the aimed-for ability parameter – the standard error of estimation must be computed according to the Rasch model theory (cf. again for details for instance Hambleton, Swaminathan and Rogers, 1991). While in two thirds of the population these (estimated) ability parameters ranged between –5.5 and 5.0 (for instance in the subtest *Everyday Knowledge*), the range used in Figure 3 amounts to 20. Five cases will be illustrated: Firstly, for the branched testing design with 15 items according to Figure 1, that being four different curves, one for each of the four age-homogeneous groups – bear in mind that only the lowest wrapping curve of the standard error of estimation is of practical interest. Then the standard error estimation is presented if all 60 items would be administered (conventionally), which is not really of any practical use for practitioners however does offer a good impression of the superiority of adaptive testing. Thirdly, the respective curve if 30 items with rather medium item difficulty were to be administered (conventionally) – this case is almost in accordance with the use of any Wechsler subtest, regardless of the fact that 30 out of 60 items are not at disposal but their difficulties are nevertheless rather moderate. And finally, there are two lines; the first of them at the intercept of 0.2582 that refer to 60 theoretically ideal items – these are not really but rather hypothetically existent and endure probabilities of .50 to be solved –, the second at the intercept of 0.5164 that refers to 15 theoretically ideal items.

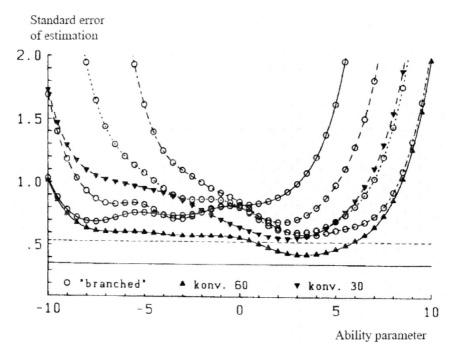

Figure 3. Standard error of estimation of the ability parameters of three different item administration procedures for AID 2 items (subtest *Everyday Knowledge*): Branched testing with 15 items for every testee according to Fig. 1 . There are four age-specific starting points and therefore four curves of estimation errors; conventional testing of all 60 items on the one hand and of 30 out of 60 items - these with rather medium item difficulty.

If we consider the lowest wrapping curve of branched testing more closely then we see that 15 items do not prove to have an essentially higher error of measurement in comparison to the use of all 60 items; this is particularly true for the case of out-ranged ability parameters which are primarily of interest for consulting. Additional errors of estimation up to 0.2 units occur only with medium ability parameters which means by a type-I-risk of 5% a maximal deviation of 2 *T*-scores. On the other hand, branched testing with 15 items endures an essentially lower error of measurement in comparison to conventional testing with 30 items if we consider the relevant out-ranged ability parameters – for 30 items in conventional testing the additional error very often amounts up to 0.35 units, that is 3 *T*-scores. And evidently there is a wide-spread almost equal error of estimation for branched testing.

5. FURTHER ADVANTAGES FROM
USING AN ADAPTIVE TESTING ITEM POOL

AID 2 also offers some additional administration procedures.

First of all, if the error of estimation of a comparable conventional test is the critical mark then branched testing might even be interrupted after the second subset of five items, that is to say administration of the subtests would cease after just 10 items. This procedure may be applied, for instance, in the case of screening whether a testee exceeds a certain minimum ability . The latter particularly in the case of the testee mastering the first subset as well as the second subset by solving two to three items; also then if two or three items are solved in the second subset – a testee's achievement level is then already almost sufficiently determined.

One should take into account that it is also possible to administer AID 2 conventionally. A psychologist may choose a certain composure of three subsets that he/she then administers to every testee irrespective the testee's age and achievement level. Even a conventional two-subset administration is imaginable. Of course, the error of estimation would become much greater in these cases.

Finally, an item pool of 60 Rasch model fitting items enables the establishment of a convincing parallel test concept for retesting a testee. While retesting is a routine affair in consulting practice where Wechsler test-batteries are being applied, AID 2 offers testing with parallel tests that consist explicitly of items not yet administered to the testee under consideration. Nevertheless, the testee's first time achievement level is thereby taken into account!

6. HANDLING OF AID 2

Practitioners may yet hesitate to use the AID 2 instead of pertinent Wechsler test-batteries because the administration of the test seems more fuzzy-like. However, they do not have to work through the branched testing design of Figure 1 all on their own . Figure 4 demonstrates that administration can be directed by a programmed instruction. After the appropriate subset of items has been administered, the psychologist is directed to the next subset according to the number of items the testee has solved. That is to say, every item should be scored immediately.

The aimed-for estimation of the ability parameter can be quoted from a table according to the path through Figure 1 design and the respective number of solved items. In other words, all such estimations have been done in advance. The (estimated) ability parameters are then easily converted into T-scores and percentile norms, respectively, by using another table. If even this amount of effort seems too much, practitioners may use the computer program AIDScore that is free of charge. Using this, all test scores, even including a test profile with confidence intervals, are available after a two to three minute input of the data. As a rule, administration requires no more than 60 minutes.

1 Name an animal that gives us milk.

cow, sheep, goat

2 What does a locomotive run on?

electricity, (electric) current, steam, coal, diesel

 3 Which rodent builds dams out of tree-trunks in the water?

Beaver

4 The orang-outang is an anthropoid ape. Name another kind of anthropoid apes.

gibbon, gorilla, chimpanzee

5 How many days are there in a week?

Seven

raw score	Age			
	6-7	8-9	10-11	12-15
0; 1	②	②	-	-
2; 3	⑩	⑩	-	-
4; 5	④	⑪	-	-

Figure 4. Extract from AID 2 manual, subtest *Everyday Knowledge*. According to a testee's age and raw score in subset ❸ the psychologist is recommended to choose the next subset.

7. ABILITIES MEASURED BY AID 2

After the psychometric quality of adaptive testing has been argued, the content quality of AID 2 shall also be sketched. As a rough description the AID 2 subtests comprise of *Everyday Knowledge, Competence in Realism, Applied Computing, Social and Material Sequencing, Immediate Reproducing* (of numerical stimuli), *Producing Synonyms, Coding and Associating, Anticipating and Combining* (Puzzles) *Abstracting* (the common functionalisms of things), *Analyzing and Synthesizing* (abstract figures), *Social Understanding and Material Reflection*, and resemble – as concerns item contents – the Wechsler subtests which comprise of Information, Picture Completion, Arithmetics, Picture Arrangement, Digit Span, Vocabulary, Coding, Object Assembly, Similarities, Block Design, and Comprehension.

There are, of course, several modifications in addition to their proven Rasch model fit. For instance, *Everyday Knowledge* refers to the ability to become informed about things that are commonly present nowadays, but it does not refer to an all-round education. The missing parts of the items in *Competence in Realism* focuses on aptitudes that make the respective everyday thing function or not. *Immediate Reproducing* (of numerical stimuli) offers the test person several chances to solve an item and in particular to reproduce the digits both forwards and backwards separately whereby the scoring takes place with two test scores. *Coding and Associating* lead also to two different test scores, one of which measures a recall performance by coding from memory. The puzzles in *Anticipating and Combining* have a given anchor that all other parts border on. *Analyzing and Synthesizing* (abstract figures) uses patterns where red cubic surfaces often border with other red cubic sufaces and where white cubic surfaces border with other white cubic surfaces. There are also three optional subtests which serve as a kind of learning disorders diagnosis: *Immediate Reproducing* (of figural stimuli), *Learning and Remembering*, and *Recognition of (figural) Structures. Immediate Reproducing* (of figural stimuli) illustrates the capacity of the short term memory with respect to information presented consecutively – for example four tapped pictures out of a 7 times 7 table. *Learning and Remembering* discloses the memory's capacity after a stimulus is presented twice – nine senseless syllables are acoustically presented twice in a row but the second time in a different sequence. *Recognition of (figural) Structures* examines the ability of the decomposition of abstract figures into given units.

A factor analysis resulted in four factors: Information processing in the given social surroundings, information processing of new contents, capacity of intellectual apprehension, and ability of (re-) producing by structuralization.

Finally, it is worthwhile mentioning that for many AID 2 subtests a non verbal instruction also exists. This is for testing testees who have hearing deficiencies, who have a foreign language as their native tongue, and those with social handicaps. Recent results show that AID 2 is also applicable for testees older than 16, the norms of which do not differ enormously.

The test-battery AID 2 is currently only normed for the German-speaking population. The psychometric quality has also only been established just for this population. However, a US-English item translation and adaptation does exist, as well as a British-English version and furthermore an Italian, a Hungarian, and a Turkish version. They have already been empirically tested and are available from the author.

8. Conclusions

There is, after all, impressive evidence that for commonplace consulting adaptive testing is applicable even without the online use of a computer. In particular, it can be said that it does not just work out to be more economical in comparison to conventional testing but also offers other advantages such as adaptive and conventional short versions and above all parallel tests for retesting. According to empirical experience, the psychological benefits of adaptive testing are, on the one hand, a severe reduction of frustration due to failure and, on the other hand, one avoids deflating the achievement motivation of the testee due to the fact that no challenge is presented.

References

Glas, A.W. and Verhelst, N.D. (1995). Testing the Rasch model. In G.H. Fischer and I.W. Molenaar (Eds.), *Rasch Models* (pp. 69-95). New York: Springer.

Hambleton, R.K., Swaminathan, H. and Rogers, H. J. (1991). *Fundamentals of item response theory.* London: SAGE.

Kubinger, K.D. (1998). Psychological assessment of high ability - world-wide used Wechlers's intelligence scales and its psychomtric shortcomings. *High Ability Studies, 9,* 237-251.

Kubinger, K.D. (2003). Adaptives Testen [Adaptive testing]. In K.D. Kubinger and R.S. Jäger (Eds.), *Stichwörter der Psychologischen Diagnostik* [Key-words of Psycho-diagnostics] (pp. 1-9). Weinheim: PVU.

Kubinger, K.D. (2005). Psychological Test Calibration using the Rasch model - Some Critical Suggestions on Traditional Approaches. *International Journal of Testing, 5,* 377-394.

Kubinger, K.D. and Wurst, E.(2000). *Adaptives Intelligenz Diagnostikum (AID 2).* [Adaptive intelligence diagnosticum.] Göttingen: Beltz.

Wechsler, D. (1939). *The measurement of adult intelligence.* Baltimore: Williams and Wilkins.

Weiss, D.J. (1982). Improving measuremnt quality and efficiency with adaptive testing. *Applied Psychological Measurement, 6,* 473-492.

In: Leading-Edge Psychological Tests and Testing Research   ISBN: 978-1-60021-571-1
Editor: Marta A. Lange, pp. 183-191   © 2007 Nova Science Publishers, Inc.

Chapter 11

ASSESSING REASONS ADOLESCENTS GIVE FOR LIVING: THE REASONS FOR LIVING INVENTORY FOR ADOLESCENTS (RFL-A)

Augustine Osman, Jennifer Bailey and Beverly A. Kopper
The University of Northern Iowa
Department of Psychology
Cedar Falls, Iowa 50614-0505 USA

ABSTRACT

Osman and colleagues (1998) developed the Reasons for Living Inventory for Adolescents (RFL-A) to assess five domains of reasons adolescents give for not killing themselves. Each domain closely matches the theoretical conceptualization of the target construct of reasons for living. We conducted two studies to further research with the RFL-A. Study 1 evaluated invariance of the 5-factor oblique solution across nonclinical high school ($N = 300$) and adolescent psychiatric inpatient ($N = 320$) samples. The objectives of Study 2 were to examine estimates of internal consistency reliability, known-groups validity, and differential correlates of the total RFL-A score in the separate samples of youths with diagnoses of posttraumatic stress disorder ($N = 90$) and conduct disorder ($N = 98$). The findings of Studies 1 and 2 provided additional strong support for the structural dimensions and psychometric properties of the RFL-A when used in clinical and nonclinical settings.

Keywords: *adolescents, reasons for living, suicide, psychometric properties.*

Recent attempts to assess and manage suicide related behaviors have focused on both protective and risk factors. Research in the area of suicide suggests that suicide related behaviors may be influenced by both the presence of negative factors such as parental divorce, depressive symptoms, and hopelessness, and also the absence of positive or protective factors such as emotional support from others and belief in overcoming life obstacles (e.g., see Osman, Gutierrez, Kopper, Barrios, and Chiros, 1998; Prinstein, Boergers, Spirito, Little, and Grapentine, 2000). Thus, contemporary research and self-report measures are beginning to address specific clusters of factors that may predispose the individual to engage in self-harmful behaviors, as well as those protective factors some individuals have that prevent them from engaging in suicide related behaviors (Osman, Gutierrez, Muehlenkamp, Dix-Richardson, Barrios, and Kopper, 2004).

Osman and colleagues (1998) developed the Reasons for Living Inventory for Adolescents (RFL-A), a 32-item self-report measure, to assess specific domains of reasons that adolescents give for not committing suicide. Earlier, Linehan, Goodstein, Nielsen, and Chiles (1983) had developed a similar self-report measure, the Reasons for Living (LRFL) inventory, to tap the positive characteristics associated with adult suicidal behavior. As with the LRFL, the conceptual foundation of the RFL-A was based on the cognitive-behavioral assumption that adaptive beliefs and expectancies mediate suicidal ideation and behavior. Each reason for not committing suicide, as assessed with the RFL-A is rated on a 6-point Likert-type scale, ranging from 1 (*not at all important*) to 6 (*extremely important*).

Items on the RFL-A were generated from multiple sources including high school and inpatient adolescents, high school classroom teachers, clinical social workers, and psychologists in applied settings. Each source was asked to describe reasons adolescents give for not committing suicide. Following the content validation processes, Osman et al. (1998) conducted exploratory factor analysis (EFA) and confirmatory factor analysis (CFA) to form empirically the five factor solutions. The factor loadings in the CFA and EFA ranged from moderate to high (i.e., estimates $\geq$ .40) and were statistically significant. Next, evidence for convergent, discriminate, and construct validity estimates were examined; these were also found to be adequate. Among the validation instruments were the following: The 36-item Suicide Probability Scale (SPS; Cull and Gill, 1982), the 54-item Brief Symptoms Inventory (BSI; Derogatis, 1992), the 20-item Beck Hopelessness Scale (BHS; Beck Weissman, Lester, and Trexler, 1974), and the 4-item Suicidal Behaviors Questionnaire (SBQ; Linehan and Nielsen, 1981). In particular, the RFL-A total score was found to correlate negatively and significantly with measures of suicidal behavior such as the Suicide Probability Scale (r = .57) and the SBQ-Likelihood (r = -.62) in the validation samples (see Gutierrez, Osman, Kopper, and Barrios, 2000).

The domains of the RFL-A are as follows: *Future Optimism (FO)*: The future optimism scale is designed to assess positive expectations about future events. The FO scale is composed of 7 items; an example of the FO scale item is, "I expect many good things to happen to me in the future" (Item 13).

Suicide-Related Concerns (SRC): The SRC is designed to assess attitudes, anxieties, beliefs, and fears that an adolescent may hold regarding suicide related behaviors. The SRC scale is composed of 6-items; an example of the SRC scale item is, "I am afraid to die, so I would not consider killing myself" (Item 8).

Family Alliance (FA): Items on the FA scale are designed to evaluate family factors, which serve in buffering the risk for suicidal behaviors. These factors include open family communication and being emotionally close to family members. The FA scale contains 7 items, which include statements such as "I fell emotionally close to my family" (Item 7).

Peer Acceptance and Support (PAS): The PAS scale evaluates the belief that peers and friends provide sources of support for "them with to live." The PAS is composed of 6 items; an example of a PAS item is, "My friends care a lot about me" (Item 10).

Self-Acceptance (SA): The SA scale contains 6 items and it is designed to assess perceived self-image that buffers against thoughts of suicide ideation and suicide attempts. An example of items included in the SA scale is, "I accept myself for what I am" (Item 3).

Psychometrically, the RFL-A has demonstrated high internal consistency reliability estimates for each of its five factor scales (i.e., values $\geq$ .80) with a mean interitem correlation of .40. In particular, the alpha estimates for Factor 1 (FA) was .94, Factor 2 (SRC) was .95, Factor 3 (SA), was .93, Factor 4 (PAS) was .92, and Factor 5 (FO) was .94 in the normative samples. Furthermore, the coefficient alpha estimates for the RFL-A total and scales were satisfactory.

Although the RFL-A has met a number of psychometric standards, the invariance of the 5-factor solution has not yet been examined in separate samples of clinical and nonclinical adolescents. In Study 1, we examined invariance of the 5-factor solution in large samples of high school and psychiatric inpatient adolescents. Moreover, because the performance of the RFL-A has not yet been examined in well-defined subgroups of psychiatric inpatients, we focused the primary analyses of Study 2 on the ability of scores on the RFL-A total and scales to differentiate the responses of youths with separate Axis I psychiatric diagnoses. We also examined estimates of internal consistency reliability that included coefficient alpha (and 95% confidence interval) and mean inter-item correlations of the scales of this inventory.

STUDY 1

Participants, Measures, and Procedure

This study was designed to examine invariance of the five-factor solution reported by Osman and colleagues (1998) for the instrument development and validation samples. Data were collected from two high schools and two adolescent psychiatric inpatient settings in the Midwest. Specifically, 300 high school (*M* age = 15.32, *SD* = 1.37 years) and 320 psychiatric inpatient (*M* age = 15.49, *SD* = 0.99 years) adolescents completed a brief demographic questionnaire and the RFL-A. The high school (150 boys, 150 girls) and psychiatric inpatient (160 boys, 160 girls) participants were similar in age, *t*(618) = 1.78, *p* = .08. For the high school and psychiatric inpatients, most were Caucasian, 53.0% and 83.4%, respectively.

RESULTS AND DISCUSSION

Multi-Group Confirmatory Factor Analyses

Robust Maximum Likelihood confirmatory factor analysis (CFA) was conducted using the EQS for Windows (Bentler and Wu, 2006) statistical program. Based on previous exploratory factor analytic work with the RFL-A (see Osman et al., 1998), we initially evaluated the fit of the 5-factor oblique solution separately for the high school and psychiatric inpatient samples (see Table 1; Baseline Models M1 and M2).

Table 1. Goodness-of-Fit Estimates

Model	S-B χ^2	df	RHO	R-CFI	R-NNFI	RMSEA	RMSEA (90% CI)
Baseline Models							
M1. Clinical Sample	657.82	454	.984	.972	.969	.038	(.031, .044)
N = 300							
M2. High School Sample	598.19	454	.973	.967	.964	.033	(.025, .039)
N = 320							
Invariance Models							
M3. No constraints	1,256.19	908	.984	.969	.966	.035	(.030, .040)
M4. Factor loadings Invariance	1,343.31	940	.985	.964	.962	.037	(.033, .042)
M5. Factor Loadings and Factor Intercorrelations	1,306.14	935	.983	.967	.965	.036	(.031, .040)

Note. S-B = Satorra-Bentler Adjusted Chi-square; RHO = Factor Reliability; R-CFI = Robust comparative fit index; R-NNFI = Robust non-normed fit index; RMSEA = root-mean-square error of approximation, CI = confidence interval.

Table 2. Descriptive Statistics and Reliability Analyses

Instrument	PTSD-Group[1]		CD-Group[2]		t(186)	Cohen's (d)	Coefficient Alpha		Mean Inter-item r	
	M	SD	M	SD			PTSD	CD	PTSD	CD
RFLA-FA	4.04	1.46	4.58	1.34	2.64**	(.39)	.94	.93	.69	.65
RFLA-SRC	3.60	1.63	4.11	1.77	2.05*	(.30)	.95	.96	.76	.80
RFLA-SA	3.94	1.43	4.62	1.23	3.50**	(.51)	.94	.92	.72	.66
RFLA-PAS	4.37	1.40	4.89	1.08	2.86**	(.42)	.93	.91	.69	.63
RFLA-FO	4.26	1.41	4.88	1.12	3.35**	(.49)	.95	.93	.73	.65
RFLA-32	4.05	1.23	4.62	1.07	3.40**	(.50)	.97	.97	.52	.50

Note. PTSD = Posttraumatic Stress Disorder; CD = Conduct Disorder; RFLA = Reasons for Living Inventory for Adolescents; FA = Family Alliance; SRC = Suicide Related Concerns; SA = Self-Acceptance; PAS = Peer Acceptance and Support; FO = Future Optimism.

* $p < .05$, ** $p < .01$.
[1] $N = 90$. [2] $N = 98$.

As shown in Table 1, results provided good fit to each sample data. In the invariance analyses, the first step involved evaluation of the baseline models with no constraints imposed on any of the parameters across the groups (see Model M3). This model was found to provide adequate fit to the sample data. In the second step (see Model M4), the factor loadings were constrained to be equal (invariant) across the groups. As shown in Table 1 (lower section), the fit estimates were also good. Finally, when both the factor loadings and factor intercorrelations were constrained to be equal across the groups, the model attained excellent fit estimates, suggesting invariance of the original 5-factor oblique solution across these groups. The factor loadings and factor intercorrelations were all statistically significant.

STUDY 2

This study examined estimates of internal consistency reliability, known-groups validity, and correlates of the RFL-A in samples of psychiatric inpatient adolescents with multidisciplinary team derived diagnoses of posttraumatic stress disorder (PTSD) and conduct disorder (CD).

Participants and Procedure

Using intake assessment information from a multidisciplinary treatment team, we formed two groups of study participants. Adolescent psychiatric inpatients meeting the *DSM-IV-TR* (American Psychiatric Association, 2000) criteria for posttraumatic stress disorder (related to sexual and physical abuse) were assigned to the PTSD-group (n = 26 boys, 64 girls). The mean age of this sample was 15.40 years (SD = 0.96). Participants meeting criteria for conduct disorder were assigned to the CD-group (n = 65 boys, 33 girls). The mean age of the sample was 15.52 years (SD = 1.00). All the diagnoses were assigned by a multidisciplinary treatment team within one week of admission to the adolescent unit. The participants were primarily Caucasian (61.5% PTSD-group; 51.6% CD-group).

Measures

In addition to the RFL-A and a brief demographic questionnaire, all the participants completed a packet of self-report instruments. For this study, the following instruments were scored for the primary validation analyses. The Suicidal Behaviors Questionnaire-Revised (SBQ-R; Osman, Bagge, Gutierrez, Konick, Kopper, and Barrios, 2000) has four items, each designed to tap suicide related behaviors including frequency and self-reported suicide likelihood. The Suicide Probability Scale (SPS; Cull and Gill, 1982) is composed of 36 items designed to assess attitudes and behaviors toward suicide. Each item is rated on a 4-point scale ranging from "none or a little of the time" to "most or all of the time." The SBQ-R frequency, SBQ-R likelihood and SPS were scored as potential suicide correlates of the RFL-A. The Minnesota Multiphasic Personality Inventory for Adolescents (MMPI-A; Butcher et al., 1992) has research related content scales including adolescent-depression and adolescent-anger. In this study, we used four internalizing (anxiety, depression, alienation, and low self-esteem) and five externalizing (anger, conduct problems, family problems, school problems, and social discomfort) scale scores of the MMPI-A as potential distress correlates of the RFL-A.

RESULTS AND DISCUSSION

Descriptive Statistics and Reliability Analyses

Table 2 presents the means, standard deviations and estimates of internal consistency reliability (coefficient alpha and mean inter-item correlation) of the RFL-A total and scales for the PTSD-group and CD-group samples. Result of the initial one-way multivariate analysis of variance (MANOVA) was statistically significant, Hotelling's $T^2 = .075$, $F(5, 182) = 2.75$, $p < .02$. Follow-up discriminant analysis was conducted to evaluate the relative contribution of the individual scale scores to the group differentiation. A single, statistically significant function was identified, Wilks' lambda = .930, $\chi^2(5, N = 188) = 13.35$, $p < .02$. In particular, group differences were observed on all the five RFL-A scale scores. Examination of the standardized function coefficients showed that the RFL-A Self-Acceptance scale score (coefficient = .60) was the most useful in differentiating the responses of the groups, followed by the Future Optimism, the Peer Acceptance and Support, the Family Alliance, and the Suicide-Related Concerns scale scores. Approximately 62.8% of the total samples were correctly classified. Moreover, as expected, the groups differed substantially on the RFL-A total score, $t(186) = 3.40$, $p < .01$, Cohen's $d = .50$.

Table 2 also shows results of the reliability analyses. Examination of these estimates show satisfactory evidence for internal consistency reliability for both the PTSD-group and the CD-Group. More specifically, the mean inter-item correlation for each scale, within each group, was large (i.e., values ≥ .30). In the PTSD-group, the Cronbach alpha estimate for the RFL-A score was high, .97 (95% CI = .96, .98; mean inter-item $r = .52$); a similar high estimate was obtained for the CD-Group, .97 (95% CI = .96, .98; mean inter-item $r = .50$).

Correlates of the Reasons for Living Inventory for Adolescents (RFL-A)

Table 3 shows correlations between the RFL-A total scores and scores on the validation self-report measures designed to tap (a) suicide related behaviors and (b) adolescent psychopathology. For the PTSD-group, the highest correlates of the RFL-A were suicide probability, adolescent-alienation, and adolescent-social discomfort. For the CD-group, the highest RFL-A correlates were suicide likelihood, adolescent-alienation, and adolescent family problems. It is important to note that the RFL-A total score for the PSTD-group (i.e., fewer reasons for living) was associated with several moderate levels (r values ≥ .40) of distress responses that included anxiety, depression, low self-esteem, and family problems as well. Independent correlation analyses showed substantive differences between the groups on the associations between the RFL-A and scores on measures of suicide probability ($z = 3.38$, $p < .01$) and adolescent-social discomfort ($z = 2.66$, $p < .01$).

Table 3. Correlation Analyses

Variables	Total Sample RFL-A	PTSD-Group RFL-A	CD-Group RFL-A
	Suicide Related Behaviors		
SBQ-R Frequency	-.62**	-.64**	-.57**
SBQ-R Likelihood	-.63**	-.58**	-.58**
Suicide Probability	-.53**	-.70**	-.35**
	Psychopathology – Internalizing		
a-anx	-.38**	-.46**	-.25*
a-dep	-.40**	-.46**	-.30**
a-aln	-.44**	-.47**	-.38**
a-lse	-.37**	-.43**	-.25*
	Psychopathology – Externalizing		
a-ang	-.19**	-.24*	-.18
a-con	-.20**	-.21*	-.24*
a-fam	-.42**	-.48**	-.38**
a-sch	-.18**	-.18	-.15
a-sod	-.39**	-.49**	-.14

Note. PTSD = Posttraumatic Stress Disorder, CD = Conduct Disorder, RFL-A = Reasons for Living Inventory for Adolescents, SBQ-R = Suicidal Behaviors Questionnaire-Revised, a-anx = Adolescent-Anxiety; a-dep = Adolescent Depression, a-aln = Adolescent Alienation; a-lse = Adolescent Low Self-Esteem. a-ang = Adolescent Anger, a-con = Adolescent Conduct Problems, a-fam = Adolescent Family Problems. a-sch = Adolescent School Problems, a-sod = Adolescent Social Discomfort.

GENERAL DISCUSSION

The current studies have presented evidence in support of (a) invariance of the 5-factor oblique structure of the RFL-A, and (b) specific psychometric properties of internal consistency reliability, known-groups validity, and differential correlates of the RFL-A in adolescent samples with team derived psychiatric diagnoses. More specifically, results of the multi-group analyses demonstrated that the RFL-A is appropriate for use in both clinical and non-clinical settings. In Study 2, results of internal consistency reliability suggested that the items within each subscale are strongly associated with each other. The results also suggest that scores on the RFL-A total and subscales are useful in differentiating the responses of adolescents with specific psychiatric diagnoses. In Study 2, the groups included youths with diagnoses of posttraumatic stress disorder and conduct disorder. Additionally, correlates of the RFL-A were identified for these groups.

Some of the limitations of both studies include our use of only self-report measures, the failure to include nonclinical youths in Study 2, and the fact that we did not cross-validate the team derived diagnoses. Future investigations could implement semi-structured interviews to validate team-derived diagnoses. Regardless, these findings add substantially to existing studies that have presented data in support of the structure and psychometric properties of the RFL-A.

REFERENCES

American Psychiatric Association. (2000). *Diagnostic and statistical manual of mental disorders* (4th ed., text rev.). Washington, DC: Author.

Beck, A. T., Weissman, A., Lester, D., and Trexler, M. (1974). The measurement of pessimism: The Hopelessness Scale. *Journal of Consulting and Clinical Psychology, 42,* 861-865.

Bentler, P. M., and Wu, E. J. C. (2006). *EQS for Windows structural equation program manual.* Encino, CA: Multivariate Software, Inc.

Butcher, J. N., Williams, C. L., Graham, J. R., Archer, R. P., Tellegen, A., Ben-Porath, Y. S., and Kaemmer, B. (1992). *Minnesota Multiphasic Personality Inventory—Adolescents MMPI-A: Manual for administration, scoring, and interpretation.* Minneapolis: University of Minnesota Press.

Cull, J. G., and Gill, W. S. (1982). *Suicide Probability Scale (SPS) Manual.* Los Angeles: Western Psychological Services.

Derogatis, L. R. (1992). *The Brief Symptom Inventory (BSI): Administration, scoring, and Procedures manual II.* Townson, MD: Clinical Psychometric Research.

Gutierrez, P. M., Osman, A., Kopper, B. A., and Barrios, F. X. (2000). Why young people do not kill themselves: The Reasons for Living Inventory for Adolescents. *Journal of Clinical Child Psychology, 29,* 177-187.

Linehan, M. M., and Nielsen, S. L. (1981). *The Suicidal Behaviors Questionnaire (SBQ).* Unpublished manuscript, University of Washington, Seattle, Washington.

Linehan, M. M., Goodstein, L. J., Nielsen, S. L., and Chiles, J. A. (1983). Reasons for staying alive when you are thinking of killing yourself: The Reasons for Living Inventory. *Journal of Consulting and Clinical Psychology, 51,* 276-286.

Osman, A., Bagge, C. L., Gutierrez, P. M., Konick, L. C., Kopper, B. A., and Barrios, F. X. (2001). The Suicidal Behaviors Questionnaire-Revised (SBQ-R): Validation with clinical and nonclinical samples. *Assessment, 8,* 443-454.

Osman, A., Downs, W. R., Kopper, B. A., Barrios, F. X., Besett, T. M., Linehan, M. M. et al. (1998). The Reasons for Living Inventory for Adolescents (RFL-A): Development and psychometric properties. *Journal of Clinical Psychology, 54,* 1063-1078.

Osman, A., Gutierrez, P. M., Kopper, B. A., Barrios, F. X., and Chiros, C. E. (1998). The Positive and Negative Suicide Ideation Inventory: Development and validation. *Psychological Report, 28,* 783-793.

Osman, A., Gutierrez, P. M., Muehlenkamp, J. J., Dix-Richardson, F., Barrios, F. X., and Kopper, B. A. (2004). Suicide resilience Inventory-25: Development and preliminary psychometric properties. *Psychological Reports, 94,* 1349-1360.

Prinstein, M. J., Boergers, J., Spirito, A., Little, T. D., and Grapentine, W. L. (2000). Peer functioning, family dysfunction, and psychological symptoms in a risk factor model for adolescent inpatients' suicidal ideation severity. *Journal of Clinical Psychology, 29,* 392-405.

In: Leading-Edge Psychological Tests and Testing Research   ISBN: 978-1-60021-571-1
Editor: Marta A. Lange, pp. 193-200   © 2007 Nova Science Publishers, Inc.

Chapter 12

INTRAINDIVIDUAL VARIABILITY IN COGNITIVE PERFORMANCE AND ITS NEURAL FOUNDATION - AN IMPORTANT APPROACH IN STUDYING THE DEVELOPING AND AGING MIND

Anders M. Fjell[*,1,2], *Ylva Østby*[2] *and Kristine B. Walhovd*[1,2]
[1] University of Oslo, Institute of Psychology
[2] Ullevaal University Hospital, Department of Neuropsychology

INTRODUCTION

In clinical neuropsychology and cognitive neuroscience, cognitive function is usually indexed by the score on a cognitive test. Often, such a score is based on a number of single trial results, and the mean of these single trials is used as the total score. The rationale behind this is that an increased number of trials will increase the reliability of the sum score. However, the intraindividual variability (IIV) in performance from one trial to the next is a very promising measure in itself, and may be of importance in the understanding of neurocognitive functioning both in research and in clinical practice. This is especially relevant to consider when it comes to reaction time tasks with repeated trials, which is one of the most common task formats in both clinical neuropsychology and experimental cognitive psychology. Reaction time has been interpreted as an index of the speed of information processing, and is usually measured as the mean or the median response time across multiple trials. This rests on an assumption that inter-trial inconsistencies can be treated as "noise", and that the mean constitutes the "signal" (Jensen, 1992). However, as we will try to show in the present paper, an accumulating body of evidence indicates that the variability of the single trial reaction times, the IIV, is in itself a measure of cognitive and central nervous system function. Thus, the purpose of the chapter is twofold: The first aim is to show that previous research has demonstrated that IIV is a viable concept, which deserves further exploration and

---

[*] Address correspondence to: Anders M. Fjell, University of Oslo, Department of Psychology, POB 1094 Blindern, 0317 Oslo, Norway; phone: +47 22 84 51 29; fax: +47 22 84 50 01; e-mail: andersmf@psykologi.uio.no

development. Based on this research, we argue that the concept of IIV in cognitive performance has the potential for being a potent predictor and marker for cognitive function in development and aging, in neurological and neuropsychological conditions, and in healthy adults. The second aim is to show that we need to understand the neural foundation for the phenomenon of IIV, an understanding that must be advanced at several levels of neuroscientific explanations. In a recent review paper, MacDonald et al. (2006, p 474), argues that *"Despite frequent reports of intra-individual variability, there is little synthesis, and no direct examination of the neural underpinnings."* Based on the view that the variability is related to cognitive and demographic variables, such knowledge will be very valuable in understanding the neurobiology of cognitive performance and mental capabilities.

THE CONCEPTS OF STABILITY VS. VARIABILITY AND CHANGE

IIV can take many forms, and be defined and measured in different ways. For instance, IIV can be calculated based on trial-to-trial variations within tasks or performance differences on a given task at several occasions. Alternatively, IIV can be calculated on the basis of a full neuropsychological or cognitive profile, as differences in normative performance from one test or cognitive domain to another. This last type of IIV may be better described as dispersion (Hultsch et al., 2004; Christensen et al., 1999), and the present chapter will deal with the first type only. Following Nesselroade (1991), IIV may be defined as more or less reversible short term changes in behavior, occurring more rapidly than relatively enduring intraindividual changes such as learning or development. In a task with repeated trials, the amount of IIV may be quantified as the standard deviation for each subject. Various methods take into account the influence of differences in the mean RT (Hultsch et al., 2004), and the temporal distribution of the variations in RT (e.g. Castellanos et al., 2005; Brewer and Smith, 1989).

COGNITIVE SIGNIFICANCE AND NEUROBIOLOGICAL FOUNDATION

Several lines of evidence link IIV in reaction time to general mental abilities, e.g. in the form of the psychometric *g* (Jensen, 1992, 1998) or measures of fluid intelligence (Li et al., 2004). Hultsch et al. (2000) found that greater IIV was associated with poorer performance on a range of cognitive tasks. Several other studies present converging evidence, and Hultsch et al. draw the general conclusion that IIV predict cognitive performance over and above the mean influence (see Hultsch et al. 2004, 2005 for reviews of previous research).

The exact neuropsychological meaning of the phenomenon of IIV is not known, however, and will depend, among other things, on the type of cognitive performance that is measured. The litterature has so far focused mainly on different kinds of choice reaction time tasks that load on attentional and executive capacities. Candidate explanations for the cognitive significance of IIV have therefore been attentional lapses (Williams et al., 2005; Hultsch et al., 2002), regulation of responses (Brewer and Smith, 1989, 1990), biological fundamental information processing or information processing noise/instability (Li et al., 2004; MacDonald et al., 2006), and physiological arousal rhythms (Castellanos et al., 2005). It is likely that a number of different neuroscientific phenomena have direct or indirect influence on the degree to which a person exhibits a large or a small amount of cognitive variability. For instance, it has been suggested that increased IIV is at least partly related to cognitive processes supported by frontal circuits, e.g. lapses in attention (Bunce et al., 1993) and reductions in executive capabilities (West et al., 2002). The frontal lobe hypothesis has received much support, and is based on studies of focal frontal injuries showing increased IIV (Stuss et al., 2003), and correlations between IIV and executive functioning (Bunce et al., 1993; West et al., 2002). Further support comes from the finding of increased variability in Stroop tasks for patients with dementia of a frontal type compared to patients with Alzheimer dementia (Murtha et al., 2002). Also, deficits in the utilization of reinforcements may cause variable performance in children with ADHD (Aase, Meyer and Sagvolden, 2006).

Related to the frontal hypothesis, there is evidence for the importance of neurotransmitter functioning in the explanation of IIV. Neural noise can be caused by dysfunctions in specific neurotransmitter systems, e.g. the catecholaminergic (including dopamine) and the acethylcholinergic systems (Bäckman et al., 2006; Cohen and Servan-Schreiber, 1992). MacDonald et al. (2006) summarize results showing that alterations in the dopamine system are documented in several populations that also show increased IIV, e.g. elderly, children with ADHD (see also Castellanos et al., 2006), schizophrenic patients, and patients with Parkinson's disease. Studies of the genetic foundations of dopamine functioning (the Val and Met alleles of the catechol O-methyltransferase gene and its importance for dopamine levels in the frontal cortex (MacDonald et al., 2006)), also point to a link between frontal lobe functioning and IVV. Val allele carriers have reduced dopamine function in the frontal lobes compared to Met allele carriers, and show a larger degree of IIV than Met allele carriers in speeded perceptual comparison tasks (Egan, 2001).

Neural noise has been implicated in age decline in cognitive performance, and is thought to be caused by information loss due to neural noise (Myerson et al., 1990), or even random breaks in neural networks (Cerella, 1990). It is a prominent candidate explanation for IIV, and may also be caused by disruptions in the efficiency of the conduction of the action potential along the axon. Thus, white matter alterations have been suggested as a possible mechanism related to IIV in e.g. reaction time (Russell et al., 2006). Correlations between white matter characteristics and information processing speed have been reported (Cardenas et al., 2005; Tuch et al., 2005). New and yet unpublished data points to a correlation between white matter volume and IIV in reaction time (Walhovd and Fjell, submitted). In line with the research showing increased IIV in ADHD (Klein et al., 2006; Castellanos at al. 2005), Russell et al. (2006) point to the possible connection between IIV and the newly discovered reductions in white matter integrity in ADHD (Ashtari et al., 2005). The connection between IIV and white matter is supported by evidence showing that white matter volume increases until middle-age, before declining (Walhovd et al., 2005ab), and that this quadratic, inverse U-form may fit with the nonlinear changes in IIV with increasing age (see below). The white matter hypothesis is intriguing, because it relates IIV directly to flow of information in the CNS. This fits nicely also with models of neuromodulatory effects on variability.

The functioning of cerebellum may also be of importance for individual differences in IIV, perhaps in controlling motor and timing functions (Castellanos et al., 2005) or in controlling higher cognitive processes as attention (Kamitani et al., 2003). The functioning of glia cells in the energy supply to neurons involved in cognitively high-loaded attentional processes, and in the indirect influence on the myelinization process in development, has also been proposed as a hypothesis, possibly integrating both cortical, white matter and neurotransmitter contributions to IIV (Russell et al., 2006).

IIV AS A MEASURE OF MATURATION AND DEGENERATION OF THE CNS

Most studies of maturation and aging have focused on mean differences between groups or between time points. However, a few studies have also looked at changes in IIV throughout the life-span (Li et al., 2004; Williams et al., 2005). There is growing consensus that the relationship between intra-individual variability in cognitive performance and age is best described by a U-formed curve, with large intra-individual variability both in children and in older adults (Li et al., 2004; Williams et al., 2005; Klein et al., 2006; MacDonald et al., 2006). As noted by MacDonald et al. (2006), this pattern parallels the inverted U-shaped changes in cognitive performance across the life-span. In studies of development, IIV analyses have been conducted both on normal children (Li et al., 2004; Williams et al., 2005; Klein et al., 2006; Brewer and Smith, 1989) and in patient groups (e.g. Brewer and Smith, 1990), especially ADHD (e.g. Klein et al., 2006; Castellanos et al., 2005). Brewer and Smith (1989, 1990) postulated that increased ability to monitor and regulate speed-accuracy trade-offs in reaction time tasks causes the reductions in reaction time that is seen during development, and that the poorer regulation in younger children causes larger IIV. The same mechanism is also used to explain the larger IIV in children with mental retardation. Klein et al. (2006) found that children with ADHD showed higher levels of IIV in reaction times than other children on a number of different tasks. The authors suggested that increased load on working memory leads to more processing variability without increasing the number of errors, and that children with ADHD may suffer from cortical under-arousal, resulting in increased IIV in this group. Castellanos et al. (2005) argues that the increased IIV in ADHD children may be caused by catecholaminergic deficiency in the ability to modulate very-low-frequency fluctuations in neuronal activity, which represents a fundamental cause of transient, but relatively frequent lapses in attention (2-4 times per minute). This may again underlie such behavioral symptoms as difficulty sustaining attention, forgetfulness, disorganization, and careless errors.

An important question is whether increased IIV has the same neuropsychological meaning and is caused by the same mechanisms at each extreme of the life-span. Executive and frontally based cognitive functions are known to mature late in development and decline fast in aging. Thus, the mechanism proposed by Brewer and Smith may well be applicable to explain both extremes of the U curve. Williams et al. (2005) and Li et al. (2004) on the other hand, have found some evidence for different processes in childhood and late life, where IIV is related to a general information processing function thoroughout the lifespan whereas aging may be characterized, additionally, by increased attentional lapses. Thus, it is likely that the large IIV in children and elderly reflects at least partly different mechanisms. This, however, needs to be more thoroughly studied in future research.

CONCLUSION AND DIRECTIONS FOR FUTURE RESEARCH

In this chapter, we have showed that the concept of IIV in cognitive tasks is related to maturation and aging, neurological and neuropsychological deficits, as well as general intellectual function in healthy adults. Through studies of patients, children and elderly, hypotheses about the neurobiological foundation for intraindividual differences can be put forth. However, we have very limited knowledge about the neural foundation for these differences as they occur in normal individuals. If this issue is addressed directly in future research, new and exciting knowledge, important for understanding the relationship between the brain and individual differences in cognitive function, will most likely be the result. Specifically, intraindividual differences in e.g. reaction time should be correlated with white matter integrity, both in children, adults, and elderly. This can be done by use of diffusion tensor imaging.

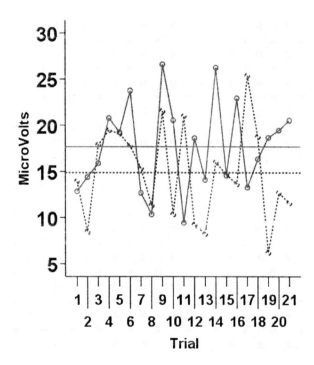

Figure 1. The figure displays the amplitude variations from trial to trial at the electrode Cz in response to deviant non-target stimuli (the so-called P3a component). The blue/ solid line represents the results for a 67 year old female with an IQ of 112, and the red/ dotted line is the results for a 76 year old man with an IQ of 99. Both participants had a standard deviation of P3a amplitude of close to 5 MicroVolts, but the mean for the oldest participant is considerably lower (14.87 vs. 17.67 MicroVolts), making the standard deviation relatively larger in comparison to the mean. Preliminary analyses indicate that larger trial-to-trial fluctuations in P3a amplitude is negatively correlated with general mental ability (WASI IQ-scores), age, and thickness of the cerebral cortex in specific regions (Fjell and Walhovd, preliminary data).

Further, variability should not only be measured at the behavioral response level, but should be addressed directly in neuroimaging studies. High field fMRI makes it possible to assess the BOLD response in single trials. Even more directly related to the neuronal activity are electrophysiological recordings. Single trial analysis of event-related electrophysiological potentials has been hampered by the large amount of background noise from EEG unrelated to stimuli presentation. However, recent techniques may overcome this problem (e.g. Jaskowsky and Verleger, 2000), making it possible to quantify variability across single trials in event-related electrophysiological potentials. This would likely yield important results of the neural basis for differences in IIV in cognitive performance. Data from our own lab indicate large IIV of the amplitude of electrophysiological responses (see figure 1), and that IIV in P3a amplitude correlates with both cognitive performance and the thickness of cerebral cortex in specific regions (Fjell and Walhovd, preliminary data).

REFERENCES

Aase, H., Meyer, A. and Sagvolden, T. (2006). Moment-to-moment dynamics of ADHD behaviour in South African children. *Behavioral and Brain Functions, 2*, 11.

Ashtari, M., Kumra, S., Bhaskar, S. L., Clarke, T., Thaden, E., Cervellione, K. L., Rhinewine, J., Kane, J. M., Adesman, A., Milanaik, R., Maytal, J., Diamond, A., Szeszko, P. and Ardekani, B. A. (2005). Attention-Deficit/Hyperactivity Disorder: A preliminary diffusion tensor imaging study. *Biological Psychiatry, 57*, 448-455.

Bäckman, L., Nyberg, L., Lindenberger, U., Li, S. C. and Farde, L. (2006). The correlative triad among aging, dopamine, and cognition: current status and future prospects. *Neuroscience and Biobehavioral Reviews, 30*, 791-807.

Bellgrove, M. A., Collinson, S., Mattingley, J. B., Pantelis, C., Fitzgerald, P B., James, A. C. and Bradshaw, J. L. (2004). The functional neuroanatomical correlates of response variability: evidence from a response inhibition task. *Neuropsychologia, 42*, 1910-1916.

Brewer, N. and Smith, G. (1989). Developmental changes in processing speed: influence of speed-accuracy regulation. *Journal of experimental psychology: General, 118*, 298-310.

Brewer, N. and Smith, G. A. (1990). Processing speed and mental retardation: deadline procedures indicate fixed and adjustable limitations. *Memory and Cognition, 18*, 443-450.

Bunce, D. J., Warr, P. B. and Cochrane, T. (1993). Blocks in choice responding as a function of age and physical fitness. *Psychology and Aging, 8*, 26-33.

Cardenas, V. A., Chao, L. L., Blumenfeld, R., Song, E., Meyerhoff, D. J., Weiner, M. W., and Studholme, C. (2005). Using automated morphometry to detect associations between ERP latency and structural brain MRI in normal adults. *Human Brain Mapping, 25*, 317-327.

Castellanos, F. X, Sonuga-Barke, E. J., Scheres, A., Di Martino, A., Hyde, C. and Walters, J. R. (2005). Varieties of attention-deficit/hyperactivity disorder-related intra-individual variability. *Biological Psychiatry, 57*, 1416-1423.

Cerella, J. (1990). Aging and information-processing rate. In J. E. Birren and K. W. Schaie (Eds): *Handbook of the psychology of aging. 3rd ed, pp. 201-221.* San Diego, CA: Academic Press.

Christensen, H., Mackinnon, A. J., Korten, A. E., Jorm, A. F., Henderson, A. S., and Jocomb, P. (1999). Dispersion in cognitive ability as a function of age: A longitudinal study of an elderly community sample. *Aging, Neuropsychology, and Cognition, 6*, 214-228.

Cohen, J. D. and Servan-Schreiber, D. (1992). Context, cortex, and dopamine: a connectionist approach to behavior and biology in schizophrenia. *Psychology review, 99*, 45-77.

Egan, M. F., et al. (2001). Effect of COMT Val Met genotype on frontal lobe function and risk for schizophrenia. *Proceedings of the National Academy of Science U.S.A., 98*, 6917-6922.

Hultsch, D. F., Hunter, M. A., MacDonald, S. W. S., and Strauss, E. (2005). Inconsistency in response time as an indicator of cognitive aging. In J. Duncan, L. Phillips, and P. McLeod (Eds.): *Measuring the mind, pp. 33-58*. Oxford, UK: Oxford University Press.

Hultsch, D. F., and MacDonald, S.W.S. (2004). Intraindividual variability in performance as a theoretical window onto cognitive aging. In R. A. Dixon, L. Bäckman, and L-G Nilsson (Eds.): *New frontiers in cognitive aging, pp.65-88*. Oxford, Great Britain: Oxford University press.

Hultsch, D. F., MacDonald, S. W. and Dixon, R. A. (2002). Variability in reaction time performance of younger and older adults. *The Journals of Gerontology. Series B, Psychological Sciences and Social Sciences, 57*, P101-115.

Hultsch, D. F., MacDonald, S. W. S., Hunter, M. A., Levy-Bencheton, J., and Strauss, E. (2000). Intraindividual variability in cognitive performance in older adults: Comparison of adults with mild dementia, adults with arthritis, and healthy adults. *Neuropsychology, 14*, 588-598.

Jaskowski, P. and Verleger, R. (2004). An evaluation of methods for single-trial estimation of P3 latency. *Psychophysiology, 37*, 153-162.

Jensen, A. R. (1992). The importance of intraindividual variation in reaction time. *Personality and individual Differences, 13*, 869-881.

Jensen, A. R. (1998). The suppressed relationship between IQ and the reaction time slope parameter of the Hick function. *Intelligence, 26*, 43-52.

Kamitani, T., Kuroiwa, Y., Li, M., Ikegami, T. and Matsubara, S. (2003). Relationship between cerebellar size and variation of reaction time during a visual cognitive task in normal subjects. *Journal of Neurology, 250*, 1001-1003.

Klein, C., Wendling, K., Heuttner, P., Ruder, H. and Peper, M. (2006). Intra-subject variability in attention-deficit hyperactivity disorder (ADHD). *Biological Psychiatry, in press*.

Li, S-C., Lindenberger, U., Hommel, B., Aschersleben, G., Prinz, W. and Baltes, P. B. (2004). Transformations in the couplings among intellectual abilities and constituent cognitive processes across the life span. *Psychological Science, 15*, 155-163.

MacDonald, S. W. S., Nyberg, L., Bäckman, L. (2006). Intra-individual variability in behavior: links to brain structure, neurotransmission and neuronal activity. *Trends in Neurosciences, 29*, 474-481.

Murtha, S., Cismaru, R., Waechter, R. and Chertkow, H. (2002). Increased variability accompanies frontal lobe damage in dementia. *Journal of the International Neuropsychological Society, 8*, 360-372.

Myerson, J., Hale, S., Wagstaff, D., Poon, L. W. and Smith, G. A. (1990). The information-loss model. A mathematical theory of age-related cognitive slowing. *Psychological Review, 97*, 475-487.

Nesselroade J. R. (1991). The warp and woof of the developmental fabric. In R. Downs, L. Liben and D. S. Parlermo (eds): *Visions of aesthetics, the environment, and development: The legacy of Joachim F. Wohlwill, pp. 213-240*. Hillsdale, NJ: Earlbaum.

Russell, V. A., Oades, R. D., Tannock, R., Killeen, P. R., Auerbach, J. G., Johansen, E. B. and Sagvolden, T. (2006). Response variability in attention-deficit/hyperactivity disorder: a neuronal and glial energetics hypothesis. *Behavioral and Brain Functions, 2,* 30.

Stuss, D. T., Murphy, K. J., Binns, M. A. and Alexander, M. P. (2003). Staying on the job: the frontal lobes control individual performance variability. *Brain, 126,* 2363-2380.

Tuch, D. S., Salat, D. H., Wisco, J. J., Zaleta, A. K., Hevelone, N. D., and Rosas, H. D. (2005). Choice reaction time performance correlates with diffusion anisotropy in white matter pathways supporting visuospatial attention. *Proceedings of the National Academy of Sciences USA, 102,* 2212-2217.

Walhovd KB, Fjell AM, Reinvang I, Lundervold A, Eilertsen DE, Quinn BT, Dale AM, Makris N, Fischl B (2005a): Effects of age on volumes of cortex, white matter and subcortical structures. *Neurobiology of Aging, 26,* 1261-1270.

Walhovd KB, Fjell AM, Reinvang I, Lundervold A, Dale AM, Quinn BT, Salat D, Makris N, Fischl B (2005b): Neuroanatomical aging: Universal but not uniform. *Neurobiology of Aging, 26,* 1279-1282.

West, R., Murphy, K. J., Armilio, M. L., Craick, F. I. M. and Stuss, D. T. (2002). Lapses of intention and performance variability reveal age-related increases in fluctuations of executive control. *Brain and Cognition, 49,* 402-419.

Williams, B. R., Hultsch, D. F., Strauss, E. H. and Hunter, M. A. (2005). Inconsistency in reaction time performance across the lifespan. *Neuropsychology, 19,* 88-96.

INDEX

F

G

H

I

W

Wales, 48
weakness, 55
Wechsler Intelligence Scale, 157
weight loss, 69
welfare, 110
well-being, 72, 73, 75, 132, 134, 142, 143
well-being therapy, 142
wellness, 136
Western countries, 63
wetting, 6
wheezing, 90
white matter, 195, 196, 197, 200

winter, 153
women, 33, 36, 42, 56, 57, 58, 59, 62, 63, 64, 65, 67, 68, 70, 121, 161, 169
workers, 119, 147
working memory, 3, 21, 196
workplace, 166
World Health Organisation, 75
worry, 17, 32, 34, 36, 46, 49, 66
writing, 9

Y

yes/no, 40
yield, 135, 136, 198